TRANSITION TIME

THE VETERAN'S GUIDE TO A THRIVING TRANSITION

"His master said to him, 'Well done, good and faithful servant! You were faithful over a few things; I will put you in charge of many things. Share your master's joy.'"
— Matthew 25:23 (CSB)

Jacob H. Cox Jr., Ph.D.
Major (USA, Retired)

Published by Grith LLC, 2021

Published by Grith LLC

ISBN 978-1-7359889-0-0 (pbk); ISBN 978-1-7359889-1-7 (ebk)

First Edition

Published in the United States of America

Published 2021

For information regarding special discounts for bulk purchases, please contact Grith LLC Special Sales at (845) 204-8863 or visit online at grith-llc.com.

grith

Grith LLC, Publishing,

P.O. Box 1084, Grovetown, GA 30813

Ordering Information:

Tel: (845) 204-8863

www.grith-llc.com

To God who blessed me, to my wife who loves and supports me, to my parents who saw me to the starting line, to my brothers and sisters in arms who helped hone me, and back again to God who is my alpha and omega, my cup overflows because of you.

CONTENTS

ACKNOWLEDGMENTS

Writing a book like this takes countless hours of research and writing, followed by grueling hours of editing. None of that would have been possible without the complete support of my wonderful and Godly wife, Laura. Thank you for your love, devotion, and flexibility throughout our twenty-two years of military service and now twenty-four years of marriage!

I must also say thank you to Scott Lathrop, COL (Retired), who helped me prepare for my transition from service. Having a mentor as you transition from service is a huge blessing, and more so when he is also a friend. Thank you for reaching out to me in the early stages of my transition, providing your feedback on my resume, and offering your encouragement all along the way.

Finally, thank you to all the United States Armed Forces men and women for your service and sacrifice. I wrote this book for you, and my prayer is it will help you reach greater heights following your transition from service!

1

TRANSITION TIME IS COMING

> *My ambition in life is not just to survive but to thrive with every bit of grit, gratitude, and faith I can muster.*

Let me guess! You saw the cover of this book, read its title, and wondered if it might be a worthwhile read. To better address that question, please let me offer a couple of my own. Are you a service member wondering about your post-military career or a veteran already in it? Does knowing you can take steps right now—no matter where you are in your current or post-military career—to secure your financial independence interest you? If so, pull up your bootstraps or slip on your loafers and keep reading as we spend these chapters investing in your future to ensure you become a thriving veteran in your post-military years!

The one certainty of military service is it will one day end. Even if you spend thirty or more years in the military, you likely have another thirty or more waiting for you after it is over. So, what comes next? Knowing our eventual transition is coming makes it no surprise that most of us ask ourselves this question. It is a genuine concern and one that grows more pressing as our departure from service approaches. Unfortunately, far too many service members delay preparation for this event until it is already upon them. Some are not ready to think about leaving the military just yet. Others believe they still have plenty of time. As a result, few reach their transition with a plan in place. Fewer still reach their transition with a plan to ensure their post-military years are thriving ones!

Nevertheless, if I have managed to hold your attention this long, then chances are you will not be a part of that statistic who just stumble through their transition into whatever comes next! Better yet, as you complete the journey that awaits you in these pages, you will lay out a plan for your next mission, thriving in your post-military life!

Speaking of a plan, do you have one in place for your transition already? If so, great. Maybe you can tweak or improve it using the content within these pages. If not, then let this book be your guide. Throughout your military service, you have learned the value of planning. Even though plans seldom survive the battlefield, we do it anyway. Why? Because, by planning, we can explore many possibilities, so even when things go awry, as they sometimes do, we continue moving toward our end state—mission completion. In that regard, your transition is just another mission to complete, and like any mission, we will plan for a successful operation.

> ***"He who fails to plan is planning to fail."***
>
> ***—Winston Churchill (attributed)***

As you progress through this book, its content will help you build your plan or help fill the gaps in your current one. It will also help you develop your goals with some critical self-reflection exercises and create a plan to reach them throughout your transition journey. For instance, read and consider the following questions.

1. Are you prepared for your transition?
2. Do you know where you will live after the military, or does that even matter?
3. Will you receive retirement pay, and is it enough to sustain your post-military life?
4. Do you know which civilian careers best align with your skills?
5. Do you have a resume, and is it right for the career you want?
6. Do you have an elevator/sales pitch for potential employers?
7. Have you built an online profile to attract potential employers?
8. Have you developed a professional network?
9. If you are thinking about starting a business, are you ready?
10. Are you aware of the veteran benefits dedicated to assisting you before, during, and after your transition?
11. Are you already building wealth?
12. Are you already wealthy?

If the answer to any of the above questions is no, then you will find plenty of valuable insights in this book. Whether you are retiring, completing your term of service, exiting the military earlier than expected, or just preparing for your eventual departure from the military, this book will offer you reliable resources to ensure your successful transition. It includes advice for developing resumes and the other products that will help you sell yourself to employers and land your ideal job while also building wealth to ensure you will not always need one. After all, this book is not just about surviving your transition; it is about thriving in the years that follow! If I have sparked your interest, then please keep reading!

Here's the deal. Hard work works—successful people prove it all the time.

The Next Adventure

Setting out on another career path after military service can challenge anyone. But you are approaching this new adventure as a veteran. That means you bring a unique set of skills (often unmatched) to any company, organization, or agency. Your life in the military has made you disciplined, confident, accustomed to hard work and adversity, assertive, and mission-oriented. These are all skills that employees need and desperately want. In fact, some companies are specifically seeking people with your skill sets, so keep that in mind as you traverse the pages of this book.

That said, just possessing these skills is often not enough to get you hired. You must be able to communicate these skills and experiences to potential employers in a way that allows them to see you as the valuable employee you will be. That requires a game plan. At the minimum, this plan will involve researching your target company, identifying your applicable skills, creating a solid resume, preparing for the interview, and then deciding what to do with the offer when it comes in. To accomplish this, you need to gain insight into what a potential employer values and how your military background aligns with those desires. You also need to effectively communicate how you address a company's needs and values to people who are unfamiliar with military jargon and acronyms.

Throughout this process, we will also work to make sure you do not sell yourself short. Our country has invested significant resources to make you the person you are today. The leadership, communication, teamwork, resource management, and critical thinking skills you developed during your years of service readily apply to academic, industry, and government positions. Likewise, the military placed great trust in you, and you have handled significant responsibilities. Regardless of where you served, many potential employers know this about you already.

Initially, as you continue reading, your transition may seem daunting as you seek to address all the requirements associated with securing the right opportunity. Likely, it will require some hard work on your part to ensure you build the right plan—one that is uniquely tailored to you. Fortunately, you are not only accustomed to planning but to hard work too! And here is the deal. Hard work works—successful people prove it all the time.

Of course, before you can fully commit to your next career path, you need an exit strategy. You also need to target what that career will be and lay down the groundwork to ensure you achieve it. Fortunately, resources are abundant and at your disposal to help ensure your successful transition. These resources come from the military, veteran affairs, other federal and state agencies, and even academic and commercial organizations. All of which we will soon cover to help formalize your game plan. Beyond that, we will establish some wealth-building techniques that you can start using now to ensure your next adventure is a thriving one. That said, let's roll up our sleeves and get to work!

Challenges That Await Veterans

When it comes time to transition, you are not just leaving the military but leaving a culture. While serving, you lived and worked in environments unique to the military lifestyle. As a veteran, you have lived on bases, posts, installations, ships, and even submarines. You've deployed to hazardous and unique locations worldwide, and you have slept on everything from beds to ammo boxes. You have dined on meals-ready-to-eat (MREs), and you've shopped in military exchanges and commissaries. Through it all, you've enjoyed a tight-knit sense of community, whether you were fighting for survival on the front lines, meeting in places of worship, or just visiting with your buddies at restaurants, fields of friendly strife, and sometimes hospitals.

If you count all the veterans in the United States, you will find that less than 7% share the privilege and honor of serving this country as you have.[1] Less than 1% are actively serving.[2] Unfortunately, this also means that very few people relate to your background and experiences. Some may even, unwittingly or subconsciously, harbor stereotypes about service members. As a result, you may occasionally need to help potential employers to see past these stereotypes to the person and employee you are. And you can overcome this challenge by learning to carefully articulate your abilities and experiences in a way that directly relates to your targeted company's needs. However, communicating your value to potential employees may be a new experience for you. For instance, rarely have you needed to apply for your next duty assignment, create and send a resume, interview, or negotiate for compensation. Yet, these are essential skills in this next leg of your life.

So, for what reason might an employer select another applicant over equally qualified you? In various articles, researchers have identified several potential challenges a veteran applicant may face. These challenges include skills translation, skills mismatch, harmful stereotypes, and acclimation. Likewise, veterans may encounter recruiters and hiring managers who are instinctively hostile or biased against veterans based on moral, cultural, or political leanings. The media's handling of reports concerning Post Traumatic Stress and Traumatic Brain Injury has also left some people nervous about working with veterans. Of course, many other organizations and recruiters have tremendous respect for your service. They realize what you have given up serving your country, and those organizations may be more inclined to take a chance on you. Either way, you can overcome these previously mentioned barriers by leveraging your interpersonal skills to put their concerns to rest. Still, should you find one of the rare few who refuse to consider a veteran candidate, then your best move is simply to move on. If they cannot recognize veteran talent and value your experience, they are not worthy of your services, anyway. However, that is your choice. Just remember this, if you remain an active job seeker, then you will ultimately encounter many more employers who value veteran employees, and working for those employers can make for a more rewarding career.

Another challenging aspect of your transition is your salary expectation. Many veterans believe that salaries awaiting them outside the military will pay them far more than their current military pay. Sometimes, this is true, provided you have the training and certifications that immediately translate into higher-paying employment. However, this is often not the case. Hence, as you prepare for your transition, you need to determine the value associated with your qualifications and provide yourself some room to use this knowledge during negations with hiring managers.

Employers may also feel that veterans lack a sense of profit and loss. Let's be honest here. The government, and by default, the military, is set up to spend money. There are no rewards offered for saving money. Sometimes, when we failed to spend our allocated funds (saving money), we got rewarded with fewer funds the following year. Therefore, the government did not incentivize us to save money. That is a concern for a company that relies on profits to keep their lights on—and pay you! Unlike the government, they cannot just print more money or raise taxes. Yet, while profit and loss may not be your strength, efficiency is! Be sure to express it!

These are all challenges. Yet, challenges or obstacles are things that military members understand entirely. You already know how to adapt, improvise, and overcome. Your transition is no different. Hence, we will leverage some of your inherent military training to seize this next objective. Note that I did not say your last objective. I make this distinction because your next career may not be your final one, either. We will soon discuss that.

Finally, keep in mind that searching for jobs and changing careers is hard for everyone. Your civilian counterparts probably do not want to go through the experience any more than you do. Do not get discouraged, and do not let your veteran status become why you struggle to find job opportunities. Instead, like most of your life's achievements, your career success will probably come because of your hard work, education, hard and soft skills, communication, and even a bit of luck—a phenomenon where preparation meets opportunity. As you read this book, continue to think about how you can prepare for opportunities that suit your prior preparation as they arise. To do that, we will take a few pages to contrast military life with the civilian sector.

In the Military

In the military, there is no need to explain your skill set. Your military occupational specialty (branch designation) and rank tell everyone where you fit in the military system. Likewise, your evaluation reports suggest to everyone how well you have performed in your career designation. Your relocations, while stressful, are still predictable and structured. For instance, because everyone in the military understands the burden of frequent military moves, units are exceptionally adapted to welcome and integrate new members and their families into the organization.

Another benefit of your military life is that you frequently have much in common with your fellow service members. You train and work in some of the same places and with some of the same people. You share similar experiences. You even share a common jargon, and there are clear rules for interacting with higher and lower organizational positions and ranks. For example, giving and receiving respect is expected, especially if you are in a leadership position.

Resultantly, teamwork and collaboration form a core attribute of your workplace. These attributes also mean that mentors who are willing and qualified are frequently available to you. Your work environment allows you opportunities for sick-call or other personal matters. There is even a clear path to promotion with relatively frequent promotions and pay raises. Military pay and benefits can also be generous. For instance, the pay rate of an E-3 may equate to roughly $11.00 per hour. However, when you add the tax-free benefits of housing, substance, etc., that sal-ary approaches $20.00 an hour. You also have a wide range of services available at your fingertips. Many of them are free for you and your family, such as health care, counseling, education assistance, legal advice, and others. If it sounds like l am biased for the military, well, let's just say I've enjoyed and valued my service, and I came to appreciate the benefits of military service long ago. It has its costs and sacrifices, but it still has some substantial advantages compared to civilian occupations.

In the Civilian Sector

As a civilian, you need to understand the concerns of employers. You must also be capable of translating your military background into civilian speak, so hiring managers can better understand your value to their business. You may even have to overcome stereotypes that employers hold concerning veterans. Some concerns include whether you can fit into an informal work culture and whether you are too rigid. They also want to know if you can show creativity, lead without order-ing, avoid emotional outbursts, and make sound decisions. A failure in any of those areas could make you a potential liability for their organization.

These concerns can be alleviated if you develop stories you can share during your interviews, meetings, and chance encounters that express your ability to quickly integrate into new organizations and build strong working relationships with your co-workers. Likewise, you need to say how you have handled unpredictable challenges in innovative new ways. Come on! You know you have! Further still, have you not provided mentorship to junior members of your organization? The military runs on leadership, so you have had opportunities to motivate, coach, and guide subordinates while collaborating with your peers regularly. Be prepared to tell that story.

Looking for a civilian job is often full of uncertainty. You seldom know at the outset just how long it will take you to find a job. You may wonder if you will even find a job—let alone determine the compensation you can get. For this reason, do not discount temporary employment opportunities. Those opportunities can provide you with much-needed income and the experience and steppingstone you need to secure your next job.

Once you are inside the civilian workforce, it may take some time to understand how you fit into the organization's culture or develop informal relationships with co-workers with whom you may have little in common. Understanding when to exercise your initiative may also be a challenge as you begin your new career. Likewise, companies may expect you to follow various rules (formal and unwritten) when interacting with supervisors and subordinates. You may also find yourself in an organization where respect is not immediately given based on your position. You and your co-workers may even have to compete for limited promotion opportunities, which can discourage cooperation and the open exchange of information and resources. In such scenarios, consider your long-term impact on the organization. Such environments may require you to first model the behavior you hope to engender in others, but do this long enough, and your supervisors will notice.

Another aspect missing from the civilian sector is mentorship and personal development opportunities. Unlike the military, finding a mentor in your organization may not be possible, and you may have to take your professional development into your own hands. Still, let your supervisor know that you are looking for formal training opportunities. Sometimes you can work this in as part of your compensation package.

Civilian employers may also require you to take paid or unpaid time off for health care needs during regular working hours. Moreover, you may have to work for a set period before accruing any vacation or sick days. As a result, you may need to find health care providers and other service providers who can offer appointments outside of work hours. This policy is in steep contrast to the military's 30 days of leave per year. I will grant that leave is doled out at a rate of 2.5 days per month, but the military is good about giving day(s) with no scheduled activities and federal holidays. The result is many military members are often required to take mandatory leave-days because they accrued too many days to carry forward. Of course, you can always apply for advanced leave if needed.

Perhaps one of the most discouraging aspects of joining the civilian community is finding yourself having to start over or catch up with your civilian counterparts. You have a lot of experience, but you do not have their experience. As a result, you may have to enter employment at a lower level until you have mastered the skills employers expect from their employees. Discuss advancement, both lateral and vertical, with your supervisor. This advice assumes your supervisor will conduct an evaluation session with you. If not, you may have to take the initiative. Because you may have to take an entry-level position, you may also have to accept lower compensation. Also, keep in mind that your new salary will not usually include untaxed benefits, like housing and sustenance pay.

Even if your new salary is the same as your military salary, it will be a pay cut. With that in mind, try to alleviate your debts and scale back your discretionary spending before leaving the military. Hopefully, you have already begun living off less than you earn and contributing your excess to a savings or investment account. Having savings can help keep you going as you complete your transition, primarily if an emergency arises.

Speaking of emergencies, many employers do not automatically provide healthcare services, like health, vision, and dental. As a result, you may have to work with your employer to negotiate for these services, pay for them through the organization, or find your own. These benefits are a conversation worth having with your organization's Human Resources department. They may offer recommendations or provide a list of service providers. Reaching out to your co-workers may also land you some reliable recommendations.

Despite all these discouraging contrasts, the civilian sector is not without its positives either. For instance, you may find that you have much greater freedom of choice in the civilian sector than ever before. Don't like your job. Hey, you can quit! I do not recommend you abuse that, but it's an option. Industry has a lot more freedom to fire employees as well. You may also enjoy more time off overall. I do. During my military tenure, it was not uncommon for me to rise at 0430 only to crawl back into bed at Midnight. Those made for long weeks, and my health sometimes suffered for it. Now I average better than six and a half hours on weekdays, but I am still experimenting with what hours work best. I have tried eight-hours, but it leaves me feeling tired when I wake. To each their own, I suppose.

Another freedom you may enjoy is dressing how you want, embracing some fads, and relaxing the constant lookout for that lieutenant colonel who calls you out for not noticing them in passing. Instead, you can meet your fellow employees on your terms and base your interactions on merit rather than rank. You also have freedom and time to pursue your passions. Finally, you may enjoy less structure and less stress that comes with working outside of the military. While your colleagues are losing their minds about some late report, you are like, 'well, no one is going to die today.'

What to expect

The principles for securing a job are pretty straightforward. However, to master them, you must learn to think like employers and understand what makes their organizations successful. When you identify these factors, you will begin to see which skills you can offer employers that directly contribute to their success. Once you recognize these skills, you can research, find, and attract employment opportunities that need them. Of course, attracting these employers requires self-marketing on your part for them to see how your skills will help their bottom-line.

While these principles may be simple, they are not necessarily well known or practiced. Hence, we will learn to use tactics and techniques that you may be unaccustomed to from your military service. Fortunately, your military experience has provided you with skills we can leverage to ensure your successful transition. Case in point, your military experience has provided you with an extensive array of traits, soft skills, and technical skills that will contribute to any civilian workplace's success. For that reason, we will soon commit some time to identify your transferable skills—some of which you may not have even realized you have. We will then investigate hiring trends across industry, academia, and government. We will also discuss how to analyze job postings and develop a targeted resume to secure your interview and bring your job hunt closer to its eventual end. Afterward, we will explore networking and interviewing for jobs and how to brag about yourself and evaluate job offers when they come in.

In each chapter that follows, I will begin with an introductory summary. When needed, I will provide a list of documents and items to complete that chapter's objectives. I have included some helpful resources in Appendix A as well. As you work through this book, you will develop several products, and you should gather some resources (e.g., award writeups, evaluations, certificates, and counseling statements) to complete them. So, start putting together a binder (aka an "I Love Me Book") of information that will help you convey your experience to potential employers during your transition.

My Experience

It was 2016, and I was a Major (O-4) working to complete my Ph.D. at the Georgia Institute of Technology (Georgia Tech) in electrical and computer engineering. I was previously selected to be a returning faculty at the Department of Electrical Engineering & Computer Science (EECS), United States Military Academy, West Point, NY. I was also one of the first selects to join the Army's new Cyber Branch as a 17A Cyber Operations Officer. My career was set, or so I thought. That year I was passed over for promotion to Lieutenant Colonel (O-5), and in the Army, you either move up or move out. I still had one chance for advancement the following year, but it was common knowledge that a mere fraction of those who get passed over for their first look get picked up on their second.

What's worse, I knew nothing would change in my promotion packet between 2016's promotion board and 2017's promotion board other than I would have my degree requirements completed without having received my degree. My Ph.D. program had gone exceptionally well. Not only did I finish all my requirements to earn it in less than three years, but I had also published in three journals and multiple conferences. I even had one of my papers adapted as a chapter in a book. It was a great experience, but not one that would improve my chances of promotion.

Now, lest you think I am complaining, let me add that my career was a blessed one. I entered the military as a private first class (E-3) with some college and an old truck that my parents gifted me. In the years that followed, I received opportunities I would never have found outside the military. I repelled from helicopters and enjoyed the esprit de corps of men and women who share a legacy with forces that filled the skies of Normandy. I achieved sergeant (E-5) before gaining my commission as a lieutenant (O-1), eventually reaching major (O-4). On three separate occasions, I was honored to complete degrees at excellent universities (all in the ACC). Those opportunities led to my teaching information technology to America's sons and daughters at the United States Military Academy at West Point, NY. While there, my wife and I were even able to lead remarkable young cadets on mission

Know your objective before your start. Your objective must drive your actions, or your actions will drive you somewhere else.

trips to Ukraine for three consecutive years. For all the opportunities the military provided me, I am forever grateful. Yet, transition time comes for everyone.

So, with my career path facing a sharp divergence, I needed an exit strategy for my contingency plan. Still, I was also fortunate and blessed to have a few of my old mentors reach out and help me prepare for the final board's eventual results. As fortune would have it, I had been preparing for my eventual departure for years already, so I had a resume developed and some ideas of what type of work I would pursue when I left the Army. However, there was still much I did not know about the actual transition process. But that is where it pays to be a veteran. My years in the Army had taught me much about planning, and it begins with knowing your objective. Your objective must drive your actions, or your actions will drive you somewhere else. So, I started preparing for my transition. During that preparation, the idea for this book developed.

Your story likely has some significant deviations from my own. For instance, maybe it is just your time, and you are exiting the military on your terms through retirement, Expiration of Term of Service (ETS), or resignation. Perhaps you are facing a medical board or a chapter. Or maybe you are just a forward-thinking individual who wants to nail down an exit strategy for when your transition day finally arrives. Do not worry; this book contains success building formulas for you regardless of the terms of your separation. After all, my transition and many others have gone exceptionally well, and yours can too!

Naturally, what I share in this book represents my preparations and research and other veterans' experiences for entering the job market. Having already transitioned, I have since expanded my original research to consider others following a similar path to my own. As a result, this book explores military benefits and the lessons learned by other job hunters and human resource specialists to aid your transition. I will also cover insights from various employers on what makes a job applicant appealing. As a result, I will present you with multiple opportunities to learn from others, which is a technique I prefer to *reinventing the wheel*—a task that nearly all veterans bemoan!

As for my own story and where I am today, well, I will share some of that too as we progress through these chapters. So just keep reading. Use these chapters to determine your exit plan and the new end state for your post-military life. In doing so, you will gain the tools necessary to ensure you move from a transitioned veteran to a thriving veteran over the years that follow. And if I can sprinkle a little encouragement along the way, then so be it! Now, let's dig into your considerations as you prepare for your post-military career!

2

WHAT MATTERS MOST? DO YOU KNOW?

> *There are three things extremely hard, steel, a diamond, and to know one's self. —Benjamin Franklin*

What is important to you? What are your dreams, and what are your goals? Is there a specific geographic location where you want to live? The military only covers one move for you as you transition, and employers may not cover moving expenses. That makes it important to know where you want to live. What about the career aspirations of your spouse? If you are in a committed relationship with someone already in a stable career or school, you need to consider their needs as you move forward. If your spouse is still in the military, you may have to look for more flexible career options. Do you have children in school? How might your transition affect their chances for scholarships or awards as their graduation approaches? These are but a handful of important quality of life factors that will affect you and your family's future.

One thing I have always enjoyed about military service is the feeling I could somehow put off the question, "What do you want to be when you grow up?" For over twenty years, I was a soldier who performed all the tasks required of me. Give me a mission, and let me go! When I realized my military time was ending, I quickly had to consider my goals for the next phase of my career. Did I have dreams? Before 2017, whatever plans I may have had seemed unimportant. Yet, my looming transition served as a forcing function that pushed me to narrow my career ambitions and to consider just how I wanted to spend the next ten to twenty years of my life.

I had to investigate what opportunities my skill sets allowed me to consider. I also had to consider my motivations, such as learning, improving, and doing things I find interesting. You may have other considerations, personal drivers, or ambitions. Identifying these considerations early can help guide you through creating your professional online presence, constructing your resume, identifying potential job openings, and eventually embarking on a new adventure after military service.

If you still have six or more months before you exit military service, then you may not need to apply for jobs just yet. However, it is always wise to identify what career opportunities interest you, their location, and how long the interview and hiring process may take to get an idea of when you might start working.

First Job Blues

Anyone can find a job. Jobs are everywhere. However, choosing the right career is your more significant challenge. Choose wrong, and you will most likely be looking for another job before your first anniversary. Studies seem to indicate as much. In a 2014 survey by VetAdvisor and the Institute for Veterans and Military Families (IVMF) at Syracuse University, investigators found that nearly half of all veterans leave their first post-military position in less than a year.[1] Between 60% and 80% of veterans depart their first civilian job before their second anniversary with that company. The reasons for these departures are many, with some including downsizing, performance issues, and natural employee attrition; however, these represent only a small fraction of reasons for veteran departures.[2]

Identified a New Employment Opportunity

As I previously mentioned, employers are actively seeking veterans. If employers can find you, you may continue to receive offers even after joining a new company. These offers can entice, especially if you find out later that you are underpaid compared to others working in your position. In many occupations, the talent pool is still limited, and it is common for recruiters to reach out to potential employees to see if they are considering other opportunities. With the social media tools available today, it is not uncommon for motivated recruiters and headhunters to contact employees and pull them away.

Accepted the Wrong Offer

Many veterans accept the first job offer they receive. Doing so may initially offer some stability as you depart the service; however, you may soon discover the new job/culture/team is the wrong fit. You may also realize quickly after starting the job that career advancement opportunities are limited, compensation is inadequate, or company layoffs are frequent. Finding yourself in this situation, you may soon grow disenfranchised with the company and seek employment elsewhere.

Skills or Education are not Suitable for the Position

There is always the possibility that your employer's expectations for your skills may be beyond your actual capabilities. Many companies want you to jump in and start contributing right away, and they may not have a program in place to train you adequately for the job. If you feel uncomfortable asking for help, the job can quickly become overwhelming and disappointing. In such cases, you or your employer may decide that you are not the right fit for the company.

Lack of leadership or Support

From the moment you entered military service, you were indoctrinated with the importance of leadership as a skill to be valued. You learned to lead, why leadership matters, and the importance of caring for your subordinates while staying on task to complete the mission. However, when you enter the civilian workforce, this level of attention to leadership may not exist. As a result, you may not see the level of accountability and responsibility you knew while in the military, which might lead to disillusionment—feeling you can find more meaningful work elsewhere.

Similarly, most veterans are used to bringing solutions instead of problems, going around, over, or through obstacles to accomplish their mission. If that is you, joining the civilian sector may leave you feeling stuck when you cannot find the resources or support you need. If you are uncomfortable asking your colleagues and co-workers for help, you may grow disenfranchised and start looking for work elsewhere.

Examine Your Motivations

If we have learned anything from the previous section, it is this. Most of us do not do a great job of picking our first employment opportunity. Part of that reason could be desperation to make sure we have something lined up for our post-military career. We also may not do enough to ensure our motivations and career aspirations align with the opportunity. These factors warrant consideration.

What motivated you to join the military in the first place? Was it for the money? Doubtful. How about travel and seeing the world? Maybe. However, more than likely, you volunteered because you wanted to be part of something worthwhile and honorable while also improving your station in life. In doing so, you became a part of something larger than yourself. And while that may not have contributed to your decision to join initially, it probably gave you a reason to stay. Whatever the source of your motivation, remember it when considering your next occupation and goals beyond military service. Should you deviate from what motivates you, then even a high salary—while significant—will not ensure your happiness or your fulfillment. However, knowing your motivations will serve as your azimuth as you transition, ensuring your new career is financially and personally rewarding. As you examine your reasons, the following considerations will help you prioritize them.

Financial Considerations

One of the first considerations you may have as you evaluate career opportunities beyond the military is pay. It was certainly one of mine. Not only did I want to ensure my wife and I continued to enjoy our way of life, but I also wanted to ensure my salary would allow me to continue building wealth. I also realized that the years immediately following the Army could well be my most prosperous. So, I hoped to take full advantage of the opportunity.

Even so, there are many other factors to consider. For instance, you may have to consider an initial salary less than your previous take-home pay. When you are on active duty, you enjoy an array of allowances beyond your base pay. These include a generous tax-free housing allowance, cost-of-living adjustments, and a basic allowance for sustenance.

Other income may come from flight pay, hazard pay, and additional incentive pay.

In contrast, civilian employment often lacks these types of compensation. Even if a potential employer matches your previous total compensation—because of taxes—your take-home pay will still be less. In Chapter 13, I will cover my own experiences with taxes following my transition from the military. News flash—I did not love it!

Beyond compensation, you have access to no-cost medical care, prescriptions, and other health benefits. As a retiree, you still have access to TRICARE and V.A. services; however, you must pay out of pocket for dental, vision, and disability insurance. As of January 2021, even TRICARE Select requires retirees to pay a small monthly allotment in addition to a larger catastrophic cap. This cap is the maximum you and your family pay for covered TRICARE health care services each year. If you did not retire, then your medical care is even more limited.

The cost of life insurance premiums may also be much more expensive for the same coverage you previously received. These expenses can place a significant dent in your pay. Perhaps not initially, but insurance rates—particularly term-life (discussed in Chapter 10)—continue to climb as you grow older. Be sure to consider these benefits as you ponder your offers from potential employers. As we will cover later, many offers are negotiable.

Your military transition can also be financially taxing. For instance, your last check may be delayed. Mine was. If you are retiring, your retirement pay may not begin right when you expect it, or it may be less than you expect. In my case, an assumption made by a financial clerk resulted in my retirement orders having incorrect information. Instead of receiving the retirement pay that I thought I would receive, this assumption placed me in the Redux Retirement program[3] instead of the Top Three.[4] Even after correcting my orders, incorrect ones were still somehow sent to the Defense Finance and Accounting Service (DFAS), again!

The result was my first check was less than I expected, and I had to go through having my corrected orders resubmitted. After that, DFAS gives themselves 30 days to respond to adjustments, so another pay period passed before the issue was corrected. The chances are that your transition will be much smoother, but these situations frequently arise. When they do, be patient and make sure you put enough money away to cover you while you wait. Because I had savings, the above issues were merely an inconvenience rather than significant emotional events.

Now, if you are lucky (or prepared), you will enjoy a hail and farewell on Friday and walk into your new occupation the following Monday. If that is what you are hoping for, then that scenario is possible; however, it is also far from guaranteed. Therefore, your job hunt should start well before you depart the service. It is also prudent to have nine to twelve months of living expenses saved to hold you over as you navigate your transition.

Medical Considerations

One of your first steps in the military transition process will be to contact your medical office. You want to go over any medical conditions you have developed throughout your service and set up appointments to evaluate your medical history for any qualifying disabilities. During the final six to twelve months leading to your transition, ensure you have any emerging medical issues fully documented. Doing so could prove critically essential for you later in life, especially if those conditions grow worse. If you wait until after your transition, it may be too late. There is a reason so many veterans recommend you not put off having your injuries treated and documented. Even if you get a 0% rating for a medical illness or injury when leaving the military, you can still use this rating to get treatment from the V.A. for that disability at no cost to you. You can eventually receive a higher rating should your condition worsen.

Similarly, take time to evaluate your medical conditions and consider how potential disabilities may affect your viability for various employment opportunities. For instance, veterans who have post-traumatic stress disorder (PTSD) may have a more challenging time working in loud and physically demanding jobs without treatment. In other cases, veterans with PTSD may have to undergo additional screenings to ensure their condition does not put others at risk. Case in point, the Federal Aviation Administration (FAA) requires pilots to undergo a detailed medical evaluation, which has driven some pilots to seek other employment.[5]

Please keep in mind that the above paragraph is not intended to discourage you from seeking the care you deserve or from obtaining a disability rating. Instead, by considering your disabilities, you can eliminate potential opportunities that might exacerbate your disabilities or be a non-starter for you, given your condition. For instance, if you have bad knees, steer away from a position requiring you to spend a lot of time on your feet. If you have any respiratory issues, then you may be more sensitive to specific environments than others. Whatever your disability, keep in mind that there are plenty of opportunities that will play to your strengths and help you thrive.

Family Considerations

Perhaps one of the most important considerations for your transition is family. While the transition process can challenge you, it can be equally daunting for your family. It is a time of great uncertainty for all of you. While in the military, families, more or less, accept that they will move every 2-3 years. You and they can also rely on various lifelines during drills, annual training, change of stations, and deployments. Likewise, when you transition, the military offers similar support for your family to include them in the process. It is their transition too!

For instance, if you are retiring, you will need new I.D. cards for your spouse and children. You also want to evaluate your spouse's financial requirements, should something unfortunate beset you. Will your spouse have enough funds to cover their mortgage or rent, bills, and other expenses? Should you sign up for the survivor's benefit plan (SBP)? If you are eligible, you might sign up for VGLI (Veterans' Group Life Insurance) and update all your beneficiary information. We will cover these options in greater depth in Chapters 12 and 13.

Do not put off preparing a will or designating a guardian for the will. As you put your plan together, keep your family informed about their financial standing and where to find the information they will need. If anything should happen to you, make sure your family avoids further hardship by having a plan to access needed funds and services. While you are at it, look into making arrangements for continued childcare, education, and medical care for your family.

Does your spouse already have a career? The decisions you make during your transition can have a significant impact on your spouse's employment. Just because you are getting ready to start over does not mean they are. In all likelihood, your career has probably already forced them to start over on multiple occasions.

My wife's career proved a significant consideration for my transition choices. She already worked as a nurse practitioner, and she wanted to continue working in her current position. She had previously worked with her employer as a burn nurse, so she had a history with the company. That job was her first as a nurse, and she enjoyed it. However, one of my earlier assignments forced her to leave it behind. It was a sad departure, but my wife went on to complete her nurse practitioner's degree, and years later, as I finished my Ph.D., she once again joined their ranks as a nurse practitioner providing burn care.

Her job gave her a sense of purpose, and she would commute the two-and-a-half hours from Marietta, GA, to Augusta, GA, to work seven-day schedules. When it came time for my transition, I found I could do my job anywhere and even work remotely, so it made sense for us to move to Augusta for my retirement. Doing so also provided our family with a little more stability since it ensured one of us would have full-time employment as I completed my transition. Honestly, though, it just felt right to follow her for a change!

Lastly, depending on your spouse's or children's education goals (and yours), you may need to discuss which locations will best move them closer to their goals. Would moving hurt your children's chances of obtaining a scholarship or take them away from an activity that could have long-term benefits? Will they establish residency in time to apply for in-state tuition rates? These are all discussions worth having with your family.

Security Clearance

Many military occupations require service members to carry a security clearance to perform their duties. If that is you, you are in a small pool of candidates that employers in industry, academia, and government are actively seeking. This is because many organizations beyond the military require access to U.S. Government information at various security classification levels: confidential, secret, top-secret, etc. As a result, many employment opportunities require personnel with a security clearance or the ability to get one. The job descriptions for these positions will often specify whether an active (or inactive) security clearance is required.

If you have a current clearance, then you should make it known to recruiters and potential employers. This alone can be a significant advantage for you. You should also ask about their policies for transferring or renewing your security clearance. The chances are that if your prospective employer requires you to have a security clearance, then they also have a process for validating it. Some job boards or career sites are even dedicated to individuals with security clearance. Visit ClearanceJobs.com and check out some opportunities there. This site allows U.S. citizens with an active federal clearance to connect directly with the most extensive online career network of cleared professionals and employers.

Career Interest and Values

Career interests and values may seem an odd consideration for you—especially if you think you will pursue a civilian career like your military one. The military provides excellent training, which has provided you some unique skill sets. It would be natural to want to continue using them. Still, I must ask. Are you looking for more of the same, or are you looking for a challenging new career in a completely different field?

After all the time you have given the military, you are no longer the same person who first joined. You have had many experiences; you have discovered new talents; you have conquered challenges, and you have likely been humbled a time or two. Along the way, you may also have found some new hobbies and interests. For these reasons, you owe it to yourself to cast your net a little wider than your current military occupation—at least initially, until you see if a better career path awaits you. We will soon make sure we thoroughly assess your career interests.

You also want to identify and prioritize what values are most important to you—especially in the early stages of a job search. Specifically, what work-related factors are essential to you? This is an important question since the Department of Labor acknowledges that veterans are more likely to suffer in terms of work-life balance and frequent job changes when their values misalign with their occupation.[6] So, take the time to determine where your work values lie and explore your motivations. Likewise, if you consider the work you will enjoy before starting your career search, you will have a better idea of what jobs to pursue. This knowledge will better prepare you to build your resume, complete applications, and take part in job interviews where your passions will surface. Ultimately, we will use these values with your skill sets and experiences to target the jobs where you will thrive.

Now it is time to complete a short assignment. Consider the following categories and circle or write all the sub-categories that apply to you.

After you do that, use a value of 1 (highly disagree) to 7 (highly agree) to help you rank and prioritize them.

- You enjoy working with:
  - Animals
  - Data
  - People
  - Technology
  - Things
- You prefer working:
  - Indoors
  - Outdoors
  - A little of both
- You want to work for a company with:
  - < 100 employees (small company)
  - 100 to 500 employees (mid-sized company)
  - > 500 employees (large company)
  - Not work for a company
- Your idea place to work is in a:
  - Small town or rural area
  - Town or suburban area
  - Medium-Sized City
  - Large City
- Do you want to travel?
  - A lot (over 50% of the time)
  - Moderately (between 25% and 50% of the time)
  - Some travel (greater than 10%, but less than 25% of the time)
  - A little (10% or less of the time)
  - Never
- You are someone who thrives when:
  - In the spotlight

  - o Working behind the scenes
  - o Allowed a bit of both
- Your ideal commute is:
  - o Work from home
  - o Across the street
  - o Within 15-20 minutes from home
  - o No more than 45 minutes from home
  - o Over 45 minutes
- You prefer a:
  - o Highly Structured Environment
  - o Loosely Structured Environment
  - o Unstructured Environment
- Your expected work hours are:
  - o Less than 40 hours per week
  - o Precisely 40 hours per week
  - o 40-50 hours per week
  - o 50-60 hours per week
  - o Over 60 hours per week
- The field of work you prefer is:
  - o Manufacturing
  - o Repair and service
  - o Retail
  - o Administrative
  - o Technical (Computer, Networking, Programming, etc.)
  - o Medical
  - o Academic (Education or Research)
  - o Human Resources
  - o Other
- You are willing to relocate (note that moving expenses can run around $10,000 - $12,000 for out-of-state moves):
  - o Anywhere in the world
  - o Anywhere in the U.S.

- o Specific regions of the country
- o To a specific state
- o Nowhere

Are there any other values you should consider? Do a quick search on the Internet for potential values we may have missed and add them to your list. Once you have identified and prioritized your list of values, use them as an azimuth when evaluating employment opportunities. For instance, military service consists of a highly structured environment with a well-understood chain of command and standard operating procedures. Those characteristics apply no matter where you are in the world. If that is important to you, you need to make sure the company or organization you pursue has similar characteristics.

Location Preferences

With job hunting, you will undoubtedly fall into one of three categories. Knowing where you fit will help you prioritize job opportunities.

1. You will go anywhere there is work.
2. You will consider a few locations for the right opportunity.
3. You will only consider one location, and that is it.

Skill Sets

We will identify your skill sets in later chapters but take some time to think about them now. What have you been uniquely trained to do that employers may value? Have you completed any degrees or certifications? Consider the courses listed in your military records, the credentials you received from completing military courses, other civilian certifications, and work experience. Many programs and associations are dedicated to assisting veterans with obtaining certifications, accommodations, and additional skills. In later sections, we will discuss some of these organizations and certifications in greater depth.

Education Considerations

Many of us joined the military because of the promise of education. Maybe you acquired a few degrees during your career, or maybe your priorities changed over the years. Life in the military can require a lot from you, so perhaps you never had the opportunity to take a few semesters of college, let alone complete your degree. Either way, your education will play a key role in meeting prerequisites for some careers. However, learn about the career outlook you are considering before deciding to invest in training or education needlessly. Also, set aside time to gather up your transcripts, those you earned from an academic institution or military training, as you prepare for your transition. If you do not know where to get those, we will discuss that later in this book.

What Kind of Job Seeker are You?

As your transition day approaches, you will inevitably find yourself in one (or a hybrid) of five job seeker categories.[7] Those categories include transitioning specialists, transitioning generalists, career switchers, undecided, and multi-tracker. The type(s) you fall into will play a considerable role in how you approach your transition strategy since different job seekers will approach their career options differently. By identifying what kind of job seeker you will be in the early stages of your transition, you will be better able to efficiently focus your efforts while also managing your expectations for the period following your departure from the military.

1. **Transitioning Specialist.** As a specialist, you possess expert knowledge and skills in a specific job or occupation. Rather than

working in a field, you are sought after for your subject expertise. A service member who has held a technical military career and wants to continue in that occupational area in the civilian workforce would qualify as a transitioning specialist. For example, military professionals, like Air Traffic Controllers, Network Operators, and Helicopter Technicians, may seek to continue into similar civilian workforce roles.

2. **Transitioning Generalist.** A transitioning generalist looks for a job based on soft skills, like communication skills, teamwork, flexibility, and leadership, to name a few. This job seeker wants to use their soft skills acquired through military service in the civilian workforce. For instance, a senior NCO or officer with a combat arms background may consider entering the workforce as a corporate trainer, loan specialist, sales consultant, or general manager.
3. **Career Switcher.** Much as the name suggests, this job seeker is looking for a completely different career from their current military occupation or experiences. Sometimes, these transitioning service members discovered that they were not cut out for their chosen profession later in their military career. As a result, they want to get it right the next time around. However, they have probably not received training for their alternative career choice, so they may have to pursue that training during their transition or even after they depart military service. This job seeker typically has the most significant learning curve and preparation ahead of them. Likewise, financial stability can be a little more tenuous as a steady income may not be possible while seeking a career move. For instance, a linguist may decide they want to become a software programmer; however, that may also require them to get a four-year degree. As a result, they enroll as a full-time student following their departure from the military.
4. **Undecided.** This job seeker has not yet decided on a specific

career path after military service. They may also have a particular geographic location prioritized with no defined career goals. Many transitioning veterans may find themselves in this category, if only briefly. Some retiring service members may even wonder if they even want a career and are holding off on deciding. If that is you, then there is a great book titled "What Color is Your Parachute" by the late Richard Boles that I highly recommend reading (or listening to). Dr. Boles' book is one of the most popular job-hunting books since the 1970s, and it can help you substantially define the right career and niche for you.

5. **Multi-tracker**. A variety of career options may appeal to this job seeker. These options may include a combination of employment opportunities, like education, technical training, entrepreneurship, or volunteerism. For example, a medic may attend college to become a physician's assistant while working part-time as an emergency medical technician. If you are born to hustle, this is not a terrible job seeker to be, and your outlook for a thriving transition is not looking too shabby either! Just make sure you plan some breaks for yourself from time to time.

Your Employer's Considerations

In exploring all the above considerations, I would be remiss not to discuss the one consideration that will ultimately decide if you become employed. That would be the employer. After all, you have your concerns. They have theirs too! Employers want to know what value you will bring to their organizations. You also cannot assume that your potential employer will be familiar with the military. As a result, you must express your military skills, accomplishments, and experiences in terms that someone who lacks military familiarity can quickly understand. By doing this, you can translate your experiences in a way that shows potential employers that you are the right employee for them.

For instance, most organizations care about attracting customers. Can you do that? Without customers, their businesses will probably fail, and they are acutely aware of that. Most organizations also need to make money if they are going to stay in business. Can you help them there? Consider for a moment that many employers also need people who can improve operational expenses, reduce inventory, and improve the organization's throughput. If you can contribute to any of these areas and articulate that, then you are well on your way to making a convincing argument for the value you will bring to an employer's organization.

Different companies may organize differently to address various organizational needs, cultures, and other requirements. Some may resemble the military's hierarchical structure, while others will be much flatter.

Organizational Structure Preference

A company's organizational structure determines how it organizes to perform specific activities and achieve its goals. These activities include rules, roles, and responsibilities. An organization's structure also dictates how the flow of information is passed between its organizational levels. In some structures, decisions flow from the highest levels to the bottom in a centralized manner, while in others, authority for decisions is shared across multiple echelons of the company. The organizations you consider will align with one of five structures, each having different relationships and management styles in the company—those include hierarchical structures, functional structures, divisional structures, matrix structures, and flat structures. Knowing these will give you an idea of how you will fit into these organizations, what authority you will have, and your autonomy level. Consider the structures that follow.

1. **Hierarchical Structures.** As a service member, you are already

familiar with this organizational structure; however, the government and many large companies also organize this way. A clear chain of command in these structures helps determine an employee's position, responsibility, and authority within the organization. In these organizations, departments like human resources, finance, and marketing may exist; however, every entity in the organization is subordinate to a single entity. Because of their multiple administrative layers, these organizations can suffer from bureaucracy. Just think of how long it takes or took to get your leave forms approved. The bureaucracy within these organizations can also make it challenging to support cross-functional teams, and information can pass through several filters before reaching decision-makers. Still, employees may appreciate having well-established policies and procedures, and org charts make it easy to identify where to find resources and people when you need them.

2. **Functional Structures.** As the most common organizational structure, available structures organize employees with comparable education and skills into specialized or functionalized departments with similar roles or tasks. Departments include information technology, research and development, human resources, and many others. One benefit of a functional structure includes quick decision making since members of the group can quickly reach consensus. Members can also learn from others having similar skill sets. However, members in these groups can become disconnected from other departments since they may operate as silos within the organization. While the path to promotion may be well-defined in these organizations, members stay in their department their entire career and may find promotions limited outside their department.
3. **Divisional Structures.** Divisional structures assign employees to departments set up to support certain products, services, or

regions. For instance, an artificial intelligence company may organize one department to specialize in autonomous vehicles, while others organize to provide machine learning applications for anomaly detection on networks. This organization allows companies to achieve greater efficiencies when creating products or offering services. They also tend to be self-oriented and operate as distinct revenue or business centers to attain specific, strategic goals. Members can also work with and learn from other members with different specialties, and a generalist—as opposed to a specialist—may be better suited for promotion in this structure.

4. **Matrix Structures.** Matrix Structures are considerably more complicated—combining functional and divisional models in roles and duties. In these companies, employees are bound by function and project. Groups in these organizations are repeatedly formed and reformed, allowing them to capitalize on their strengths to accomplish their tasks while maneuvering around organizational weaknesses. In a matrix structure, employees have more autonomy; however, they are expected to take on more responsibility for their work. Companies using this structure may see increased productivity from their teams and more significant innovation and creativity levels. However, employees may also serve two bosses, which can create conflicts. As a result, these organizations require a substantial planning and effort level requiring significant management resources.
5. **Flat Structures.** The flat structure attempts to do away with the supervisor by taking a bottom-up approach to leadership. In this organization, everyone is essentially their boss, which makes the organization highly decentralized. As a result, these organizations may suffer from less bureaucracy, but communication in these organizations is paramount. When companies adopt this structure for day-to-day operations, they may organize a more organized top-down management style for short-term or temporary projects.

Your Considerations Matter

As we close out this chapter, remember that your goals and motivations matter. Let them serve as your azimuth as you explore job opportunities and all the considerations that come with them. If you can determine your work preferences and values now, that effort will ensure you find the right job that will allow you to thrive beyond your transition. With that in mind, it is time to think about what careers best align with your skills and values.

3

TARGETING YOUR NEXT CAREER (OR MAYBE JUST BRACKETING)

> ***Choose a job you love, and you will never have to work a day in your life. —Confucius***

Throughout my military career, one of the wonderful benefits I enjoyed was never really having to answer the question that plagues so many high school and college graduates—that being, *"What do you want to be when you grow up?"* Since the military primarily provided my career goals and expectations, I avoided answering this question for over 20 years. Unfortunately, as my transition date approached, I realized my deferment was rapidly ending. You might say it was "danger close." Perhaps you have enjoyed putting off your career decision, or maybe you already have an idea in mind. In either case, you owe it to yourself to use the time before your transition to explore the career opportunities available to you. You may find that you already made the right choice, or the effort may push you to branch out into a career you previously have not considered.

In the last chapter, I challenged you to consider your considerations and preferences. Keep those foremost in your mind as you progress through this one. After all, it should go without saying that if you find a job that aligns with your work preferences, transferable skills, ambitions, and financial needs, then that job will ultimately be more rewarding for you. The right career may even serve as a source of fulfillment beyond your financial needs.

Still, you are uniquely you, so this chapter will not set out to target a specific career. Instead, it will seek to guide you through identifying a range of occupations and professions for which you may qualify. From there, we will begin bracketing these career options. If you are unfamiliar, bracketing is a military technique used to adjust fire by spotting impacts, both over and short of a target, to establish a bracket (or boundary) and then successively splitting that bracket in half until the target is hit or the desired boundary is obtained. Using your experiences, considerations, skills, and education along with the resources discussed in this book, we will apply the above concept to help determine which of your career options are best suited to your capabilities and interests. So, keep an open mind as we spend this chapter highlighting the possibilities and resources you can use to research and identify your next career. Through this process, you will hopefully come to realize that your military occupation is more of an azimuth than a destination.

> ***"Far and away the best prize that life offers is the chance to work hard at work worth doing."***
>
> ***—Theodore Roosevelt***

Your Military Occupation is an Azimuth, Not a Destination

Undoubtedly, as you transition from the military, you will complete some mandatory career planning classes. These classes are provided by programs, like the Transition Assistance Program (TAP), Army Career and Alumni Program (ACAP), and or Transition Goals, Plans, Success (GPS). All of which attempt to provide transitioning service members with the skills, outlook, contacts, and networking skills needed to conduct a successful job search, pursue higher-level education, or even start a business.

In these courses, instructors will often summarize best practices used by many other veterans who have already transitioned to find a job. These classes are great resources, and you should make the most of the opportunity. For instance, these courses provide instruction on writing resumes, searching for jobs, developing your elevator pitch, completing interviews, and much more. These programs also help you identify resources for finding career opportunities. You can find the TAP Virtual Curriculum course online at https://webdm.dmdc.osd.mil/dodtap/virtual_curriculum.html.

However, these courses are also highly condensed, only lasting a couple of weeks. As a result, it can be challenging to produce polished products (e.g., your resume, elevator pitch, etc.), let alone make a career choice that will affect the rest of your life before the course's completion. But that is okay because you are reading this book, and while this book will cover how to develop the above products later, we will begin addressing your career options now! Perhaps the greatest bit of misinformation that a transitioning military member can leave one of these courses with is your military occupation somehow limits your employment options to a handful of possibilities.

While it is true that your military training has provided you with specific skill sets that may transition well to certain occupations, these options might not be the be-all and end-all here. If they are, that is great. I left the Army as a cyber operations officer, and I did not want to travel too far from my base skills in networking and information systems. Yet, the military has a history of pointing out that doing a thing one way is often just "a way" and not necessarily "the way." So, identifying career opportunities based on your military occupation is a way. It just may not be the best one for you.

A much more comprehensive range of occupations may be open to you beyond the ones provided by a military occupational crosswalk (MOC). However, they are still an excellent place to start. MOC resources allow service members and veterans to enter their military occupation into a web-based search application that renders a translation of the veteran's work experience and associated job titles. Of course, the results can often be rather obvious, such as recommending that a military truck driver become a civilian truck driver or that someone with a combat arms background become a security guard. In such cases, veterans may feel their career options are limited after completing a crosswalk. But again, that is okay because a crosswalk provides an initial azimuth. Nothing is stopping you from taking a new azimuth as you embark on your career finding journey. For that reason, we will use multiple career translation tools to identify career opportunities. We will then expand that list using other methods before applying our bracketing techniques to choose the best options for you.

Impact of Experience on Career Translation

Having accumulated substantial leadership experience and skills over their time in the military, many transitioning veterans wonder how that experience translates to the civilian sector. For instance, does your background qualify you for an entry or senior-level position? The answer to that question is it depends. However, knowing what those dependencies are will help you better bracket the jobs that most align with your background and experience.

Remember that you will probably want to target specific job titles commensurate with your years of military experience and knowledge. Still, your military experience may have gaps when compared to the experiences of your civilian counterparts. As a result, you may have to consider positions beneath the one you initially targeted if you want to get your foot in the door. From there, you just have to hustle!

If you apply to positions for which you are underqualified, your applications will probably get tossed aside. Likewise, recruiters may see you as overqualified and unwilling to accept the pay rate offered if you apply for positions that fall below your qualifications. As a result, you need to bracket just where your experience, education, and skill set place in the market before applying. There are also some general guidelines to consider while determining your experience-level when entering the market (see Table 1 - Determining Position Level by Experience.). For instance, if you worked as a warrant officer in information systems for over 12 years, employers may consider you for mid- to senior-level positions in information systems management. However, suppose you apply for a job that provides on-site support for databases. In that case, you may be considered for a junior-level position because of your actual years of experience working directly with databases.

Table 1 - Determining Position Level by Experience.

Position	Years
Jr. Level	0-5 years
Mid-Level	6-13
Sr Level	14+ years
Project/ Program 1	14+ years w/ some industry program management experience
PM 2	PM 1 plus 5+ years of industry PM experience

Regardless of where your experience lies, remember there is still time to gain the qualifications needed to expand your bracket—both before and after you are hired. Identifying where your experiences fit does not prevent you from shooting for the stars. Instead, doing so will introduce you to a range of jobs you qualify for now and others you could be eligible for with a little extra work. If, throughout this process, you discover your dream job, then apply!

Plans will carry you farther than your dreams ever could!

Even if that dream job proves unobtainable, nothing is stopping you from applying to the same company at a lower level to gain the experience and qualifications needed to get that job, eventually. It comes down to how flexible and willing you are to put plans in place to achieve your dreams. Once you do, you may realize that your plans will carry you farther than your dreams ever could!

Educational Impact on Career Translation

Education is another factor that can augment how your experience translates to a potential career. For instance, many jobs may set an entry requirement of four years of experience; however, a bachelor's degree in that occupational area may be enough for the company to wave the experience requirement. Hence, degrees in technical fields are highly sought after. Likewise, an advanced degree can often supplant work experience requirements for various positions.

Other factors that can help augment your career translation results are skills. Sought-after skills include logistics, system/software architecture, and cyber experience, to name just a few. Many newer opportunities may require technical certificates and background experience instead of a four-year degree. For instance, project management and program management positions often require specialized expertise to manage complex initiatives and require specialized certificates.

Impact of Security Clearance on Career Translation

Whether you have a security clearance will also help determine which occupations your unique experience will qualify you to pursue. As I mentioned in chapter two, a security clearance alone may cause employers to seek you out—potentially for jobs you are not even considering. You can find out about those opportunities by just making it known on the right job boards and on sites like LinkedIn.com that you have a clearance. As you can see, multiple factors contribute to career opportunities and finding the one that is uniquely suited to you can be challenging. Fortunately, many organizations exist to assist veterans with advice, guidance, and tips for translating their military experience, education, and skills into successful career opportunities.

Career Translation and Transition Resources

When it comes to establishing an initial list of potential careers, various organizations (both for-profit and non-profit) have developed tools to help you get the process started. In this section, we cover some of these and explore how to use them. Many of these sites allow you to enter your Military Occupational Code (MOC), Military Occupational Specialty (MOS), or other Rating as a launch point. The purpose of your crosswalk is to map your military occupation to civilian career opportunities. Your crosswalk also includes translating your military skills, training, and experience into civilian skills, education, and credentialing appropriate for civilian opportunities.

Military Occupation Codes (MOC) Crosswalk

The Military Occupation Codes (MOC) Crosswalk is used by My Next Move for Veterans and O*NET and helps users find a civilian career comparable to their military occupation. It translates military skills, training, and experience into civilian skills, education, and credentialing appropriate for civilian jobs.

My Next Move for Veterans

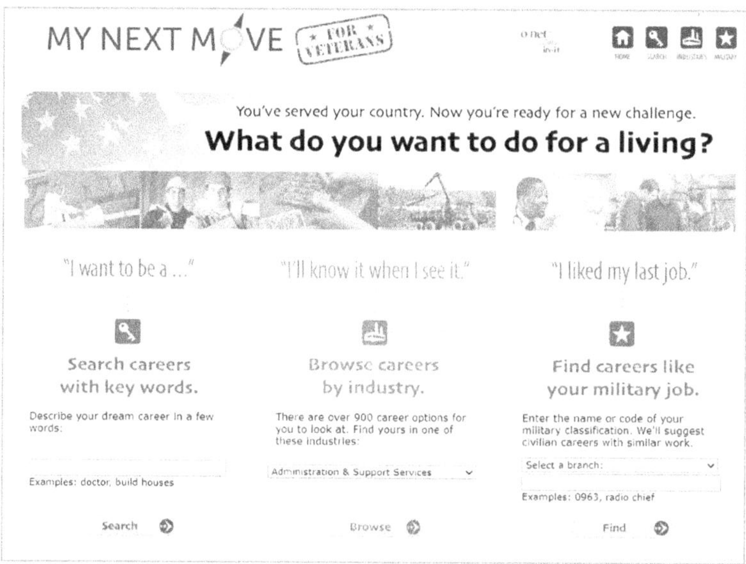

Figure 1 - My Next Move Website - https://www.mynextmove.org/vets/

Whether you are looking to search for potential careers by keywords, industry, or military terms, My Next Move for Veterans offers an interactive tool for job seekers to explore careers. See their landing page in Figure 1 - My Next Move Website - https://www.mynextmove.org/vets/.

My Next Move for Veterans is sponsored by the U.S. Department of Labor and developed by the National Center for O*NET Development. By visiting mynextmove.org/vets, you can explore over 900 different career options spread across 21 industries. You will also learn about the skills, tasks, salaries, and employment outlook for each career via their easy-to-read career reports. These career reports contain an abundance of information, like descriptions of people in this career field and the technology they use. It also includes knowledge, skills, abilities, and personalities they tend to have, along with education requirements, salary, job outlook (such as growing, holding steady, or declining), and links to other career information sources.

Figure 2 - Results from My Next Move for Veterans

Suppose you are interested in a career field but lack the qualifications or want to identify comparable careers. In that case, another nice feature about this site is that you can get a list of similar jobs from its generated career reports. All you need to do is 'click' and explore other options you may not have previously considered. This career report also provides links to help you find training, certifications, apprenticeships, job boards, and local salary information. See Figure 2 - Results from My Next Move for Veterans for one such career report.

My Next Move for Veterans also uses a web-based version of the O*Net Interest Profiler, a web-based tool for assessing an individual's vocational interests. We will discuss this tool in a subsequent section; however, the web-based version of this tool uses 60 items and user information (e.g., work experience and education) to point you toward careers you might enjoy.

Work through this site yourself and identify some career opportunities.

Job Opportunities	**Job Opportunities**

Occupational Information Network (O*NET)

The O*NET program, also sponsored by the U.S. Department of Labor/ Deployment and Training Administration (USDOL/ ETA), is a comprehensive resource of occupational descriptions and data for job seekers, workforce development offices, human resources professionals, students, researchers, and others. It is also the nation's primary source of occupational information. One goal of the site is to help its users understand the rapidly changing nature of work and its effects on the workforce and the U.S. economy.

The O*NET database contains hundreds of standardized and occupation-specific descriptors for almost 1,000 occupations spanning the entire U.S. economy. It is also freely available to the public and continuously updated by a broad range of workers in each discipline. Besides being used by My Next Move, as we discussed previously, O*NET information is used by millions of individuals each year. Given so many people and applications rely on this database, be sure to visit it and explore your career options frequently.

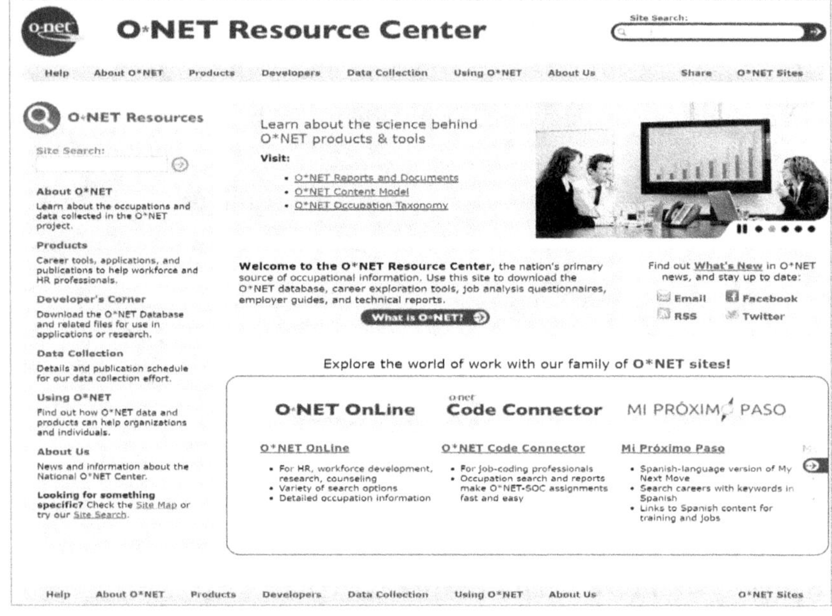

Figure 3 - https://www.onetcenter.org/

Since My Next Move For Veterans relies on O*NET for much of its information, it should be no surprise that O*NET provides a mix of knowledge, skills, abilities, tasks, and activities associated with each of its occupations. These descriptors serve as a measurable set of standardized variables that define key occupational features. The day-to-day aspects of these occupations and the qualifications and interests of a typical worker span hundreds of descriptors collected by O*NET and other federal agencies, like the Bureau of Labor Statistics. The content on O*NET can be an excellent resource for:

1. first-time job seekers
2. new job explorers

3. career changers
4. students
5. career counselors
6. school counselors
7. vocational rehabilitation counselors
8. State Occupational Information Coordinating Committees (SOICCs)

Using O*NET Online, you can explore multiple capabilities. Some of which include:

1. exploring occupations
2. performing skill-based searches for occupations
3. finding and comparing similar/related occupations
4. reading summary reports that include essential worker requirements and characteristics
5. viewing detailed reports or custom reports with filtering options for the type and level of the displayed information
6. using the crosswalk tool to find similar occupations in other classification systems
7. connecting to other online resources for career information

Below are some examples of options, by category, offered by O*NET online:

1. Skills
2. Necessary Skills (Mathematics, Writing, Reading Comprehension, etc.)
3. Cross-Functional Skills (Equipment Selection, Quality Control Analysis, etc.)
4. Generalized Work Activities (41 general types of job behaviors that occur at multiple jobs)

5. Interests (six occupational types that align with a worker's interests to derive which occupations might be most fulfilling)
6. Work Styles — 16 work style characteristics connect a worker's priorities with occupations that mirror or develop those values, such as persistence, initiative, cooperation, etc.
7. Work Context — 57 physical and social factors affect work's nature, such as physical and structural work characteristics.
8. Experience and Training — five "Job Zones" that highlight education and training levels associated with occupations.

Now that you have seen the site take a moment to explore it. When I began preparing for my retirement, I visited this site several times to evaluate the options I got from my occupation's translation. I recommend you do the same. While I will cover some useful tools on these sites, I will not cover them all. You can access the site at https://www.onetonline.org/.

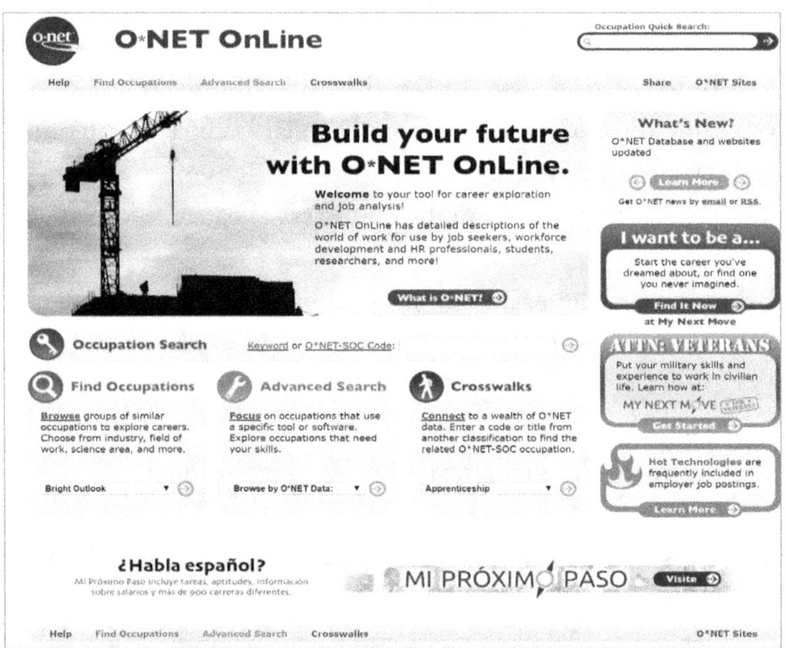

Figure 4 - O-NET Landing Page

Some aspects of this website may change over time, but you should find a "Crosswalk" link somewhere on this page. As of this publication, there are two links on the page. Depending on the 'Crosswalks' link you choose (Figure 4 - O-NET Landing Page), you will land on one of the pages shown below. For the first page, utilize the Military section and provide your Branch and Occupational Specialty. In my case, it is Army and 17A for Cyber Operations. If you land on the other page, just enter your Branch and Occupational Specialty, and click 'Go.'

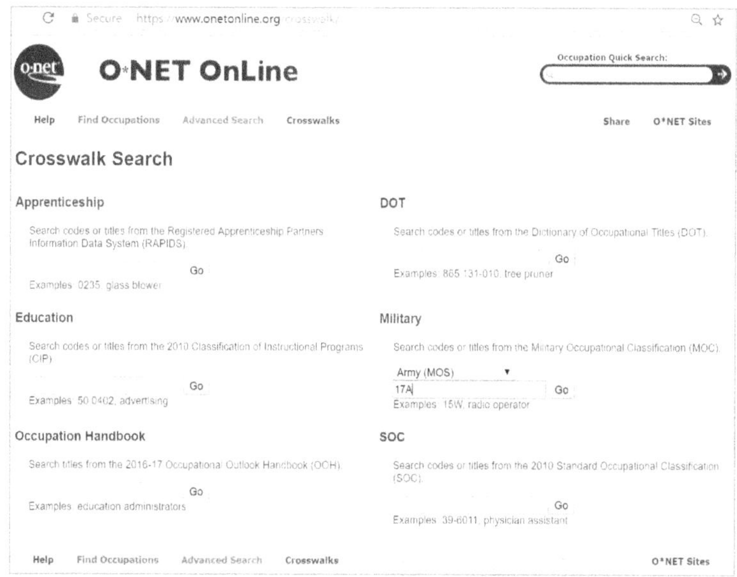

Figure 5 - O*Net Crosswalk Search

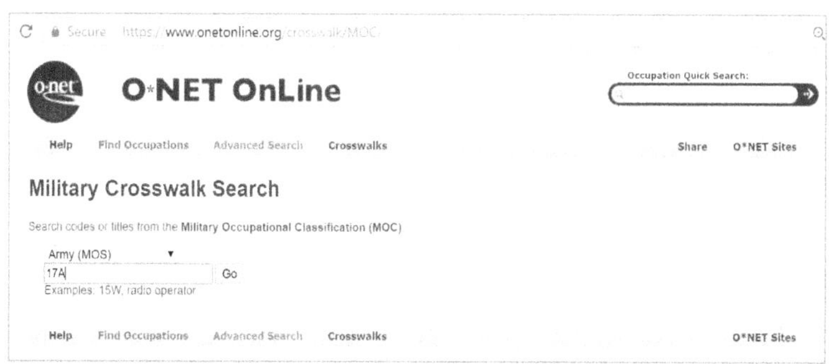

Figure 6 - O*NET Military Crosswalk Search

The provided web page should give you the results of your Military Crosswalk Search. In my case, the results yielded two options: Cyber Operations Officer and Combat Surveillance and Target Acquisition Crewman. I immediately discounted the second option since that has nothing to do with my military occupation. However, the first option fits my military background, and I can see that it aligns with Computer and Information Systems Managers. Notice it also shows that this profession has a Bright Outlook, and there is an index number of 11-3021 00 assigned to this occupation.

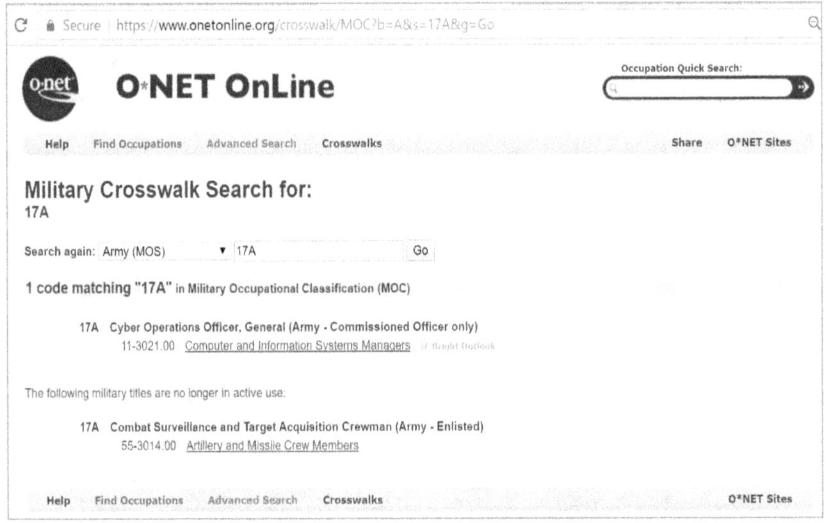

Figure 7 - Military Crosswalk Results

Let us click on the offered link and look at the generated report. The sections break down as follows:

1. Summary Report for: [Job index–Occupation Name]
2. Tasks
3. Technology Skills
4. Tools Used
5. Knowledge

6. Skills
7. Abilities
8. Work Activities
9. Detailed Work Activities
10. Work Context
11. Job Zone
12. Education
13. Credentials
14. Interests
15. Work Styles
16. Work Values
17. Related Occupations
18. Work & Employment Trends
19. Job Opening on the Web
20. Sources of Additional Information

Because of the provided report's length, I will only show some sections and ask you to follow the website itself. Figure 8 - Summary Report shows the beginning of this report. It begins with a summary report for Computer and Information Systems Managers and a sample of reported job titles. These can be helpful when you are completing job searches on other sites. If you do not find the occupation you are looking for, then try some of these other titles. Also, note that the career field's job outlook appears in this section.

Figure 8 - Summary Report

The report next displays a listing of tasks associated with this occupation. We see that directing daily operations, reviewing project plans, and meeting with department heads are routine tasks that people in this field frequently perform.

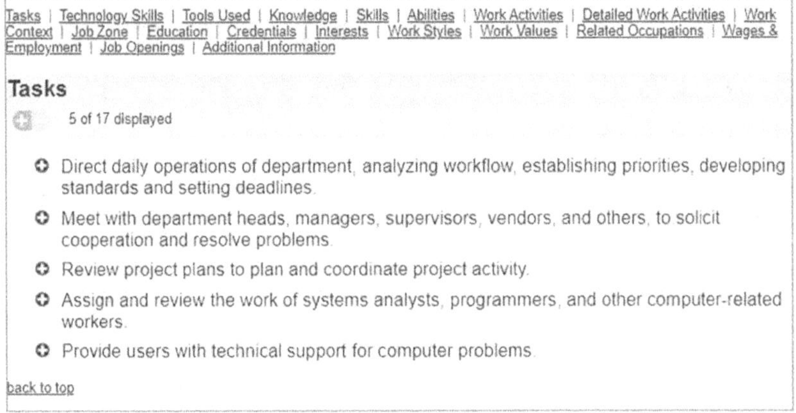

Figure 9 - Tasks

After providing a list of everyday tasks, the report moves on to other occupation requirements, like Technology, Skills, and Knowledge. Hence, knowledge of circuit boards, processes, software, practical applications, and business management, including excellent communication skills, all form an appropriate knowledge base for this job. We also see several Technology Skills, such as database management, web platform development, etc. Additionally, O*NET shows which sub-skills are hot (desirable) for the market. If you see that one of your skills appears as a popular item (e.g., C/C++, Python, Ruby on Rails, etc.), make sure those skills appear on your resume and social media profiles. Doing so will help ensure you draw the attention of recruiters looking to fill these skill-based positions.

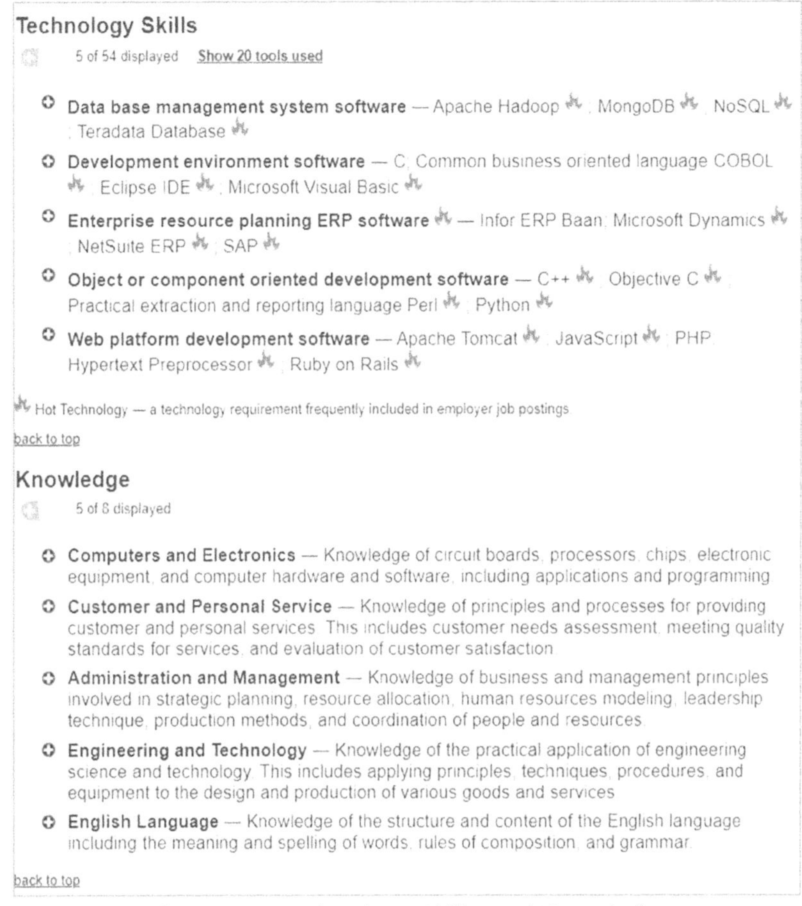
Technology Skills

5 of 54 displayed Show 20 tools used

- Data base management system software — Apache Hadoop ; MongoDB ; NoSQL ; Teradata Database
- Development environment software — C; Common business oriented language COBOL ; Eclipse IDE ; Microsoft Visual Basic
- Enterprise resource planning ERP software — Infor ERP Baan; Microsoft Dynamics ; NetSuite ERP ; SAP
- Object or component oriented development software — C++ ; Objective C ; Practical extraction and reporting language Perl ; Python
- Web platform development software — Apache Tomcat ; JavaScript ; PHP Hypertext Preprocessor ; Ruby on Rails

Hot Technology — a technology requirement frequently included in employer job postings

back to top

Knowledge

5 of 8 displayed

- Computers and Electronics — Knowledge of circuit boards, processors, chips, electronic equipment, and computer hardware and software, including applications and programming.
- Customer and Personal Service — Knowledge of principles and processes for providing customer and personal services. This includes customer needs assessment, meeting quality standards for services, and evaluation of customer satisfaction.
- Administration and Management — Knowledge of business and management principles involved in strategic planning, resource allocation, human resources modeling, leadership technique, production methods, and coordination of people and resources.
- Engineering and Technology — Knowledge of the practical application of engineering science and technology. This includes applying principles, techniques, procedures, and equipment to the design and production of various goods and services.
- English Language — Knowledge of the structure and content of the English language including the meaning and spelling of words, rules of composition, and grammar.

back to top

Figure 10 - Technology Skills and Knowledge

The next sections cover Skills and Abilities. As represented here, skills are more in line with the soft skills we previously discussed, while Technology Skills align with hard-skills. So, skills that pertain to Computer and Information Systems Managers include critical thinking, reading comprehension, monitoring, etc. Notice that this section shows that there are 54 skills I should be prepared to address in my interviews and social media. We also see a list of expected skills that range from deductive reasoning to problem sensitivity (the ability to detect something is amiss with a product, project, or system).

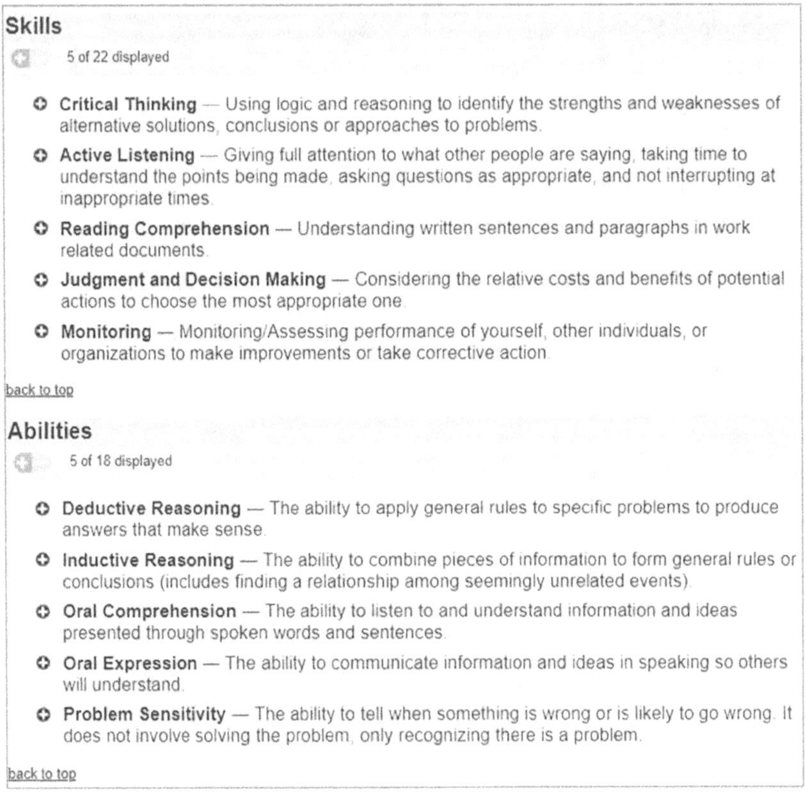

Skills

5 of 22 displayed

- **Critical Thinking** — Using logic and reasoning to identify the strengths and weaknesses of alternative solutions, conclusions or approaches to problems.
- **Active Listening** — Giving full attention to what other people are saying, taking time to understand the points being made, asking questions as appropriate, and not interrupting at inappropriate times.
- **Reading Comprehension** — Understanding written sentences and paragraphs in work related documents.
- **Judgment and Decision Making** — Considering the relative costs and benefits of potential actions to choose the most appropriate one.
- **Monitoring** — Monitoring/Assessing performance of yourself, other individuals, or organizations to make improvements or take corrective action.

back to top

Abilities

5 of 18 displayed

- **Deductive Reasoning** — The ability to apply general rules to specific problems to produce answers that make sense.
- **Inductive Reasoning** — The ability to combine pieces of information to form general rules or conclusions (includes finding a relationship among seemingly unrelated events).
- **Oral Comprehension** — The ability to listen to and understand information and ideas presented through spoken words and sentences.
- **Oral Expression** — The ability to communicate information and ideas in speaking so others will understand.
- **Problem Sensitivity** — The ability to tell when something is wrong or is likely to go wrong. It does not involve solving the problem, only recognizing there is a problem.

back to top

Figure 11 - Soft Skills and Abilities

General work activities and detailed work activities are next covered. The work activities section offers a high-level view of the duties usually associated with the occupation. Here, we can see that this career's typical work activities include interacting with computers, collecting information, and identifying objects, actions, and events. The subsequent section, "Detailed Work Activities," provides more specific activities tailored to the occupation.

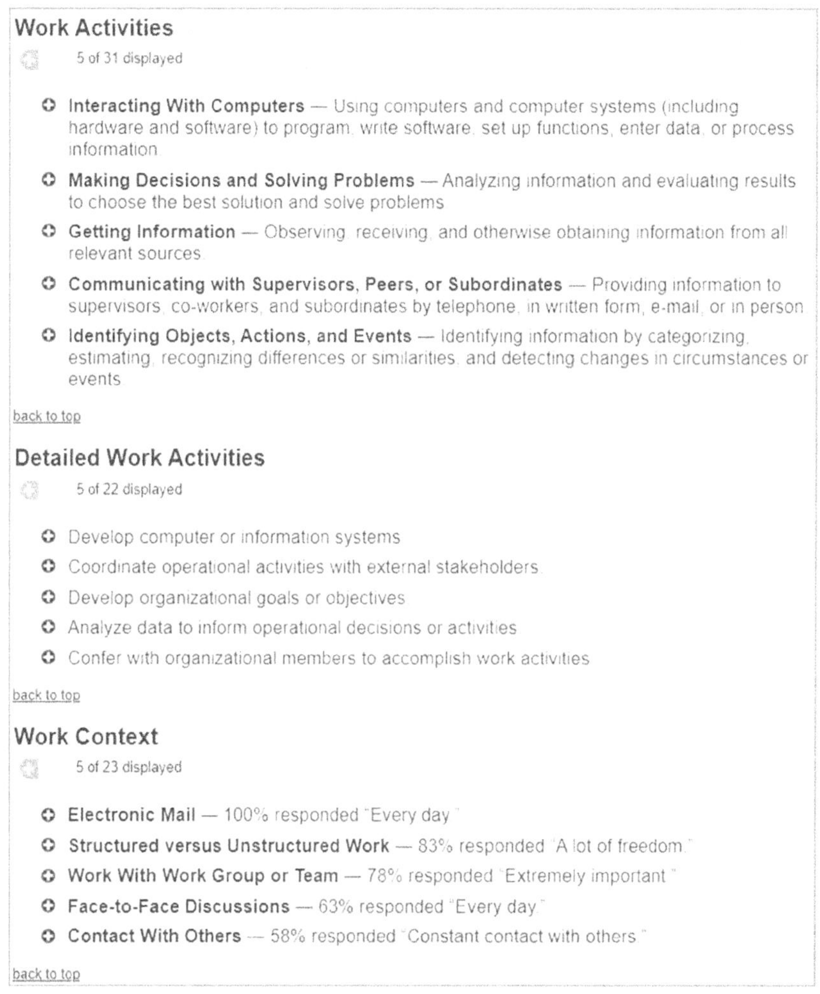
Work Activities

5 of 31 displayed

- **Interacting With Computers** — Using computers and computer systems (including hardware and software) to program, write software, set up functions, enter data, or process information.
- **Making Decisions and Solving Problems** — Analyzing information and evaluating results to choose the best solution and solve problems.
- **Getting Information** — Observing, receiving, and otherwise obtaining information from all relevant sources.
- **Communicating with Supervisors, Peers, or Subordinates** — Providing information to supervisors, co-workers, and subordinates by telephone, in written form, e-mail, or in person.
- **Identifying Objects, Actions, and Events** — Identifying information by categorizing, estimating, recognizing differences or similarities, and detecting changes in circumstances or events.

back to top

Detailed Work Activities

5 of 22 displayed

- Develop computer or information systems.
- Coordinate operational activities with external stakeholders.
- Develop organizational goals or objectives.
- Analyze data to inform operational decisions or activities.
- Confer with organizational members to accomplish work activities.

back to top

Work Context

5 of 23 displayed

- **Electronic Mail** — 100% responded "Every day."
- **Structured versus Unstructured Work** — 83% responded "A lot of freedom."
- **Work With Work Group or Team** — 78% responded "Extremely important."
- **Face-to-Face Discussions** — 63% responded "Every day."
- **Contact With Others** — 58% responded "Constant contact with others."

back to top

Figure 12 - Work Activities and Context

Beyond the activities associated with the occupation, the report will also provide you with context (or situational information) for the job. For instance, this report shows that Computer and Information Systems Managers can expect to deal with e-mail and regularly handle structured and unstructured work. Face-to-face discussions, teamwork, and overall responsibility for various projects are other aspects of this career.

Another useful aspect of this report is its Job Zone section, which shows just how your background and experience stack up with the competition. According to the job zone for Computer and Information Systems Managers, this career carries a Job Zone Four classification, which means this field requires considerable preparation. Such positions require at least a bachelor's degree, while some do not. Likewise, hiring managers expect you to have a significant amount of work-related experience (several years) in this field.

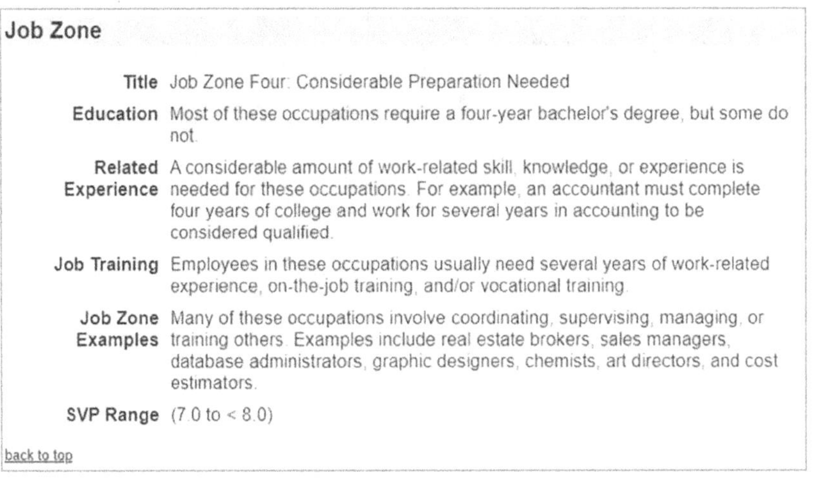

Job Zone

Title	Job Zone Four: Considerable Preparation Needed
Education	Most of these occupations require a four-year bachelor's degree, but some do not.
Related Experience	A considerable amount of work-related skill, knowledge, or experience is needed for these occupations. For example, an accountant must complete four years of college and work for several years in accounting to be considered qualified.
Job Training	Employees in these occupations usually need several years of work-related experience, on-the-job training, and/or vocational training.
Job Zone Examples	Many of these occupations involve coordinating, supervising, managing, or training others. Examples include real estate brokers, sales managers, database administrators, graphic designers, chemists, art directors, and cost estimators.
SVP Range	(7.0 to < 8.0)

back to top

Figure 13 - Job Zone 4

In this section, two items that may not be immediately familiar to you (they were not to me) are the Job Zone levels and the SVP Range. For O*NET, Job Zones are broken into five categories, ranging from one (unskilled—no preparation) to five (highly skilled—extensive preparation). All the zones are listed below.

Job Zones

- Job Zone One: Little or No Preparation Needed
- Job Zone Two: Some Preparation Needed
- Job Zone Three: Medium Preparation Needed
- Job Zone Four: Considerable Preparation Needed

- Job Zone Five: Extensive Preparation Needed

SVP or Specific Vocational Preparation is defined in Appendix C of the Dictionary of Occupational Titles as follows.

> ***Specific Vocational Preparation (SVP): The amount of elapsed time required by a typical worker to learn the techniques, acquire the information, and develop the facility needed for average performance in a specific job-worker situation.***

Keep in mind that the SVP represents the acquired training from school, work, military, institutional, or vocational environments, not just the orientation time needed to integrate a new employee into a job's unique conditions. Vocational training includes any of the following.

- Vocational education (high school, shop or commercial training, technical school, art school, and college courses having specific vocational objective)
- Apprenticeship training (for jobs requiring apprenticeships only)
- In-plant training (organized classroom study provided by an employer)
- On-the-job training (serving as a trainee on the job under the instruction of a qualified worker)
- Essential experience in other jobs (holding lesser positions that lead to higher-level employment or serving in different positions that qualify)

Under the above guidelines, the following explains the SVP or Specific Vocational Preparation values shown in the O*NET Online Occupational Summary Report's Job Zone section.

1. Short demonstration only
2. Anything beyond a short demonstration up to and including one month
3. Over one month up to and including three months
4. Over three months up to and including six months
5. Over six months up to and including one year
6. Over one year up to and including two years
7. Over two decades up to and including four years
8. Over four decades up to and including ten years
9. Over ten years

One last note about the Job Zone section is that Job Zones on these reports are generic. For instance, the above figure mentions accountants, not Computer and Information Systems Managers, so job zone results may only loosely fit the occupation you are pursuing. The four other categories of Job Zones are listed below for completeness.

Job Zone One: Little or No Preparation Needed

Education	Some of these occupations may require a high school diploma or GED certificate.
Related Experience	Little or no previous work-related skill, knowledge, or experience is needed for these occupations. For example, a person can become a waiter or waitress even if he/she has never worked before.
Job Training	Employees in these occupations need anywhere from a few days to a few months of training. Usually, an experienced worker could show you how to do the job.
Job Zone Examples	These occupations involve following instructions and helping others. Examples include food preparation workers, dishwashers, sewing machine operators, landscaping and groundskeeping workers, logging equipment operators, and baristas.
SVP Range	(Below 4.0)

Figure 14 - Job Zone 1

Job Zone Two: Some Preparation Needed

Education These occupations usually require a high school diploma.

Related Experience Some previous work-related skill, knowledge, or experience is usually needed. For example, a teller would benefit from experience working directly with the public.

Job Training Employees in these occupations need anywhere from a few months to one year of working with experienced employees. A recognized apprenticeship program may be associated with these occupations.

Job Zone Examples These occupations often involve using your knowledge and skills to help others. Examples include orderlies, counter and rental clerks, customer service representatives, security guards, upholsterers, and tellers.

SVP Range (4.0 to < 6.0)

Figure 15 - Job Zone 2

Job Zone Three: Medium Preparation Needed

Education Most occupations in this zone require training in vocational schools, related on-the-job experience, or an associate's degree.

Related Experience Previous work-related skill, knowledge, or experience is required for these occupations. For example, an electrician must have completed three or four years of apprenticeship or several years of vocational training, and often must have passed a licensing exam, in order to perform the job.

Job Training Employees in these occupations usually need one or two years of training involving both on-the-job experience and informal training with experienced workers. A recognized apprenticeship program may be associated with these occupations.

Job Zone Examples These occupations usually involve using communication and organizational skills to coordinate, supervise, manage, or train others to accomplish goals. Examples include hydroelectric production managers, travel guides, electricians, agricultural technicians, barbers, court reporters, and medical assistants.

SVP Range (6.0 to < 7.0)

Figure 16 - Job Zone 3

Job Zone Five: Extensive Preparation Needed

Education Most of these occupations require graduate school. For example, they may require a master's degree, and some require a Ph.D., M.D., or J.D. (law degree).

Related Experience Extensive skill, knowledge, and experience are needed for these occupations. Many require more than five years of experience. For example, surgeons must complete four years of college and an additional five to seven years of specialized medical training to be able to do their job.

Job Training Employees may need some on-the-job training, but most of these occupations assume that the person will already have the required skills, knowledge, work-related experience, and/or training.

Job Zone Examples These occupations often involve coordinating, training, supervising, or managing the activities of others to accomplish goals. Very advanced communication and organizational skills are required. Examples include pharmacists, lawyers, astronomers, biologists, clergy, neurologists, and veterinarians.

SVP Range (8.0 and above)

Figure 17 - Job Zone 5

The Education section of this report is straightforward. It provides percentages of people in this career field who have higher-level degrees. For this occupation, we can see that 62% of folks working in this career field have a bachelor's or master's degree, while 26% lack a degree. It also provides links you can use to seek additional information to get training, certifications, licenses, and apprenticeships. These links can be helpful if you do not have all the qualifications you need for this occupation and still have time to prepare. You can most times use your G.I. Bill and other education benefits to have the government cover your training costs. That can be helpful if you are in the job seeker category of Career Switcher or Undecided.

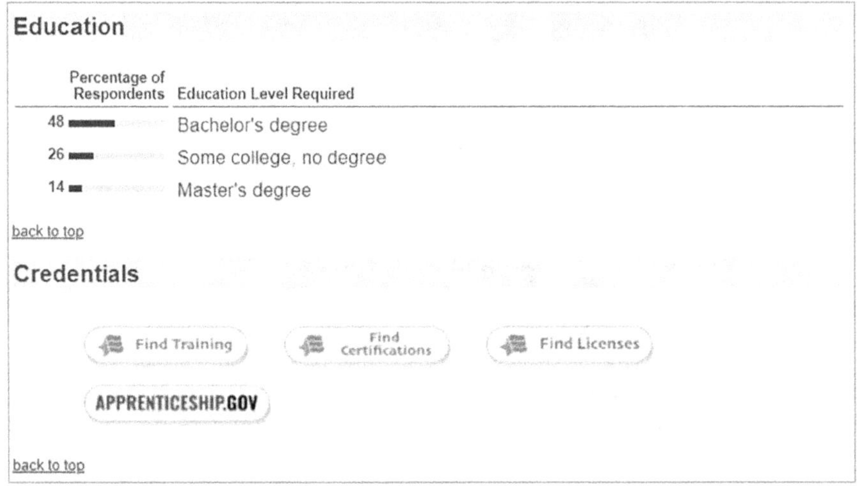

Figure 18 - Education Statistics

The O*NET occupation report also delivers an Interest code based on the top-three leading attributes associated with the occupation. It represents user preferences for work environments and outcomes. For Computer and Information Systems Managers, that code is ECI (Enterprising, Conventional, and Investigative). The below list provides the attributes seen on O*NET's, and Figure 19 - Interests shows the Interests section for the report.

- **Realistic** — Realistic occupations frequently involve work activities that include practical, hands-on problems, and solutions. They often deal with plants, animals, and real-world materials like wood, tools, and machinery. Many occupations require working outside and do not involve a lot of paperwork or working closely with others.
- **Investigative** — Investigative occupations frequently involve working with ideas and require an extensive amount of thinking. These occupations can involve searching for facts and figuring out problems mentally.
- **Artistic** — Artistic occupations frequently involve working with forms, designs, and patterns. They often require self-expression, and the work can be done without following a clear set of rules.
- **Social** — Social occupations frequently involve working with, communicating with, and teaching people. These occupations often involve helping or providing service to others.
- **Enterprising** — Enterprising occupations frequently involve starting up and carrying out projects. These occupations can involve leading people, making decisions, taking risks, and entering business ventures.
- **Conventional** — Conventional occupations frequently involve following set procedures and routines. These occupations can include working with data and details more than with ideas. Usually, there is a clear line of authority to pursue.

The Work Styles section provides personal characteristics that can affect someone's job performance. For example, Computer and Information Systems Managers place high importance on Attention to Detail, Integrity, Dependability, Initiative, and Cooperation. Some other work styles that O*NET might use for different occupations include Achievement/Effort, Adaptability/Flexibility, Leadership, Persistence, Self Orientation, etc.

Interests

All 4 displayed

Interest code: **ECI** Want to discover your interests? Take the O*NET Interest Profiler at My Next Move.

- **Enterprising** — Enterprising occupations frequently involve starting up and carrying out projects. These occupations can involve leading people and making many decisions. Sometimes they require risk taking and often deal with business.
- **Conventional** — Conventional occupations frequently involve following set procedures and routines. These occupations can include working with data and details more than with ideas. Usually there is a clear line of authority to follow.
- **Investigative** — Investigative occupations frequently involve working with ideas, and require an extensive amount of thinking. These occupations can involve searching for facts and figuring out problems mentally.
- **Realistic** — Realistic occupations frequently involve work activities that include practical, hands-on problems and solutions. They often deal with plants, animals, and real-world materials like wood, tools, and machinery. Many of the occupations require working outside, and do not involve a lot of paperwork or working closely with others.

back to top

Figure 19 - Interests

Work Styles

5 of 16 displayed

- **Attention to Detail** — Job requires being careful about detail and thorough in completing work tasks.
- **Integrity** — Job requires being honest and ethical.
- **Dependability** — Job requires being reliable, responsible, and dependable, and fulfilling obligations.
- **Initiative** — Job requires a willingness to take on responsibilities and challenges.
- **Cooperation** — Job requires being pleasant with others on the job and displaying a good-natured, cooperative attitude.

back to top

Work Values

All 3 displayed

- **Working Conditions** — Occupations that satisfy this work value offer job security and good working conditions. Corresponding needs are Activity, Compensation, Independence, Security, Variety and Working Conditions.
- **Support** — Occupations that satisfy this work value offer supportive management that stands behind employees. Corresponding needs are Company Policies, Supervision: Human Relations and Supervision: Technical.
- **Achievement** — Occupations that satisfy this work value are results oriented and allow employees to use their strongest abilities, giving them a feeling of accomplishment. Corresponding needs are Ability Utilization and Achievement.

back to top

Figure 20 - Work Styles

Of course, since you are researching potential career options, O*NET also provides you with a list of related occupations to expand your bracket. The chances are that one or two exist that you have not considered in the Related Occupations section.

Related Occupations

5 of 9 displayed

13-1081 01	Logistics Engineers
15-1211 00	Computer Systems Analysts
15-1241 00	Computer Network Architects
15-1299 08	Computer Systems Engineers/Architects
27-2012 05	Media Technical Directors/Managers

back to top

Figure 21 - Related Occupations

Yet another great aspect of this report is its Wages & Employment Trends section. In this section, you can learn about the median wage—keep in mind that this is not an average. All it means is that if you lined up 100 jobs in order of their salary, the first 50 would have a wage of the median value or less. Figure 22 - Employment Trends shows the wages for Computer and Information Systems Managers. However, we also need to consider that the median salary is based on national values. So, think about what salaries look like in the areas you are considering employment.

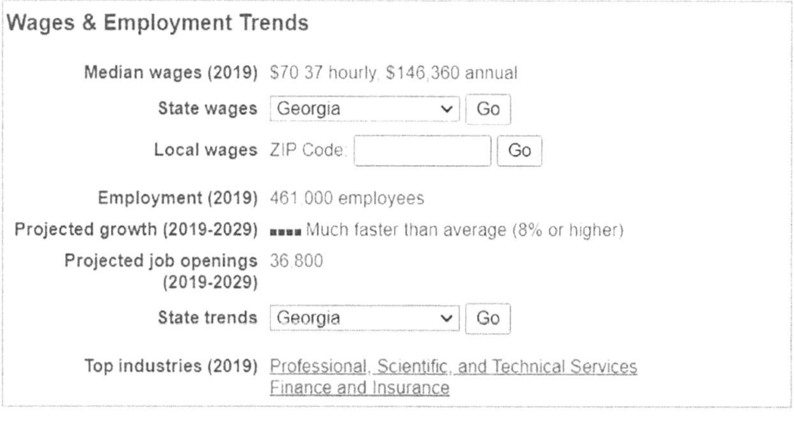

Wages & Employment Trends

Median wages (2019)	$70 37 hourly, $146,360 annual
State wages	Georgia Go
Local wages	ZIP Code: Go
Employment (2019)	461 000 employees
Projected growth (2019-2029)	Much faster than average (8% or higher)
Projected job openings (2019-2029)	36 800
State trends	Georgia Go
Top industries (2019)	Professional, Scientific, and Technical Services Finance and Insurance

Figure 22 - Employment Trends

Here, I clicked on the Local Salary Info button. When the window looks like the one below, select your state and click on Go. In my case, I chose Georgia.

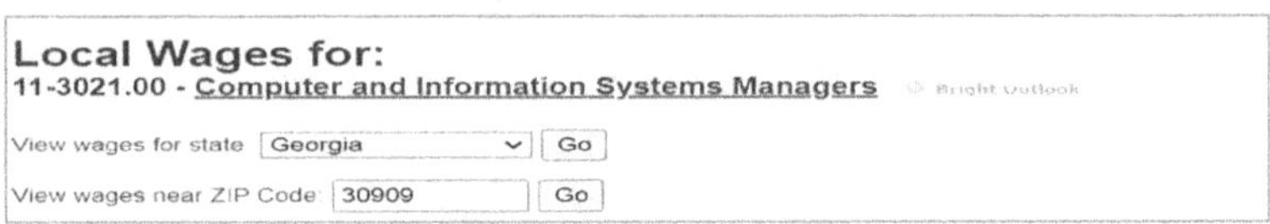

Figure 23 - State Salary Information

As might be expected, in the below figure, the median wage for Computer and Information Systems Managers in Georgia falls a little short of the national median. Many areas in Georgia have a lower cost of living than those of other states. Still, look at what else the diagram offers. We get a good idea of what an entry-level position might offer and what salaries the elite in this field are commanding.

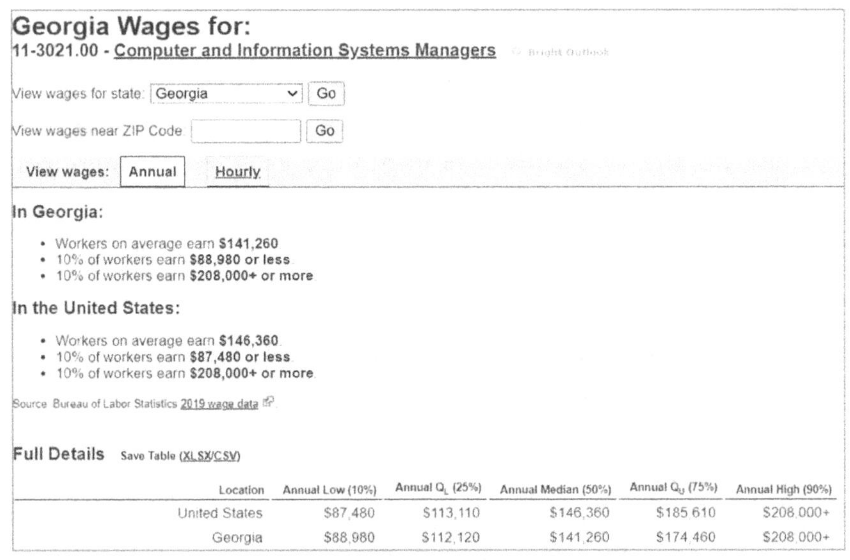

Location	Annual Low (10%)	Annual Q_L (25%)	Annual Median (50%)	Annual Q_U (75%)	Annual High (90%)
United States	$87,480	$113,110	$146,360	$185,610	$208,000+
Georgia	$88,980	$112,120	$141,260	$174,460	$208,000+

Figure 24 - Median Salaries for Computer and Information System Managers

The report also offers a section for the occupation's projected growth and job openings. In Computer and Information Systems Managers, we observe that projected growth is much faster than average (14% or higher). This holds well for folks with the right qualifications. Now, if you are interested in checking out jobs, you can even use the O*NET report as a launch point for your job hunt by clicking on the Find Jobs button.

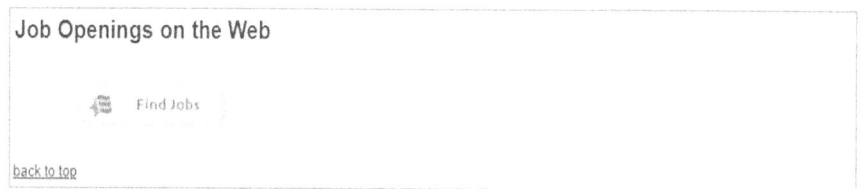

Figure 25 - Job Openings

After clicking on the Find Jobs link, a new form is provided, see Figure 26 - Job Search by State and Source. In my case, I entered Georgia in the State text box and clicked on Go. You can also search from three sources: National Labor Exchange, Career Builder, and America's Job Exchange.

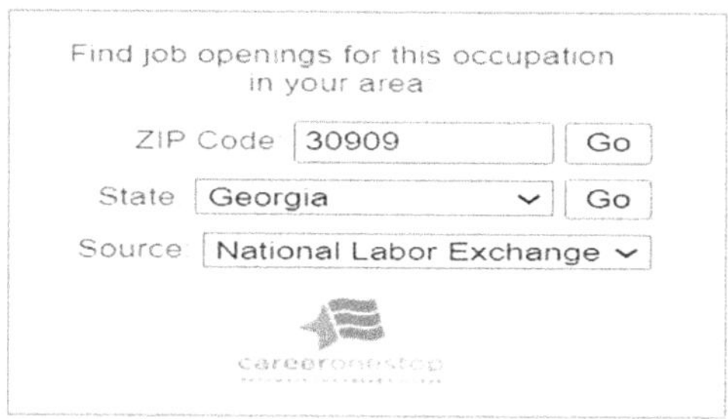

Figure 26 - Job Search by State and Source

Now that we have covered some of what this site has to offer, work through the sources yourself, and identify career opportunities. The below figure represents the next landing page you will arrive at after selecting Go. Then you need only select See Jobs.

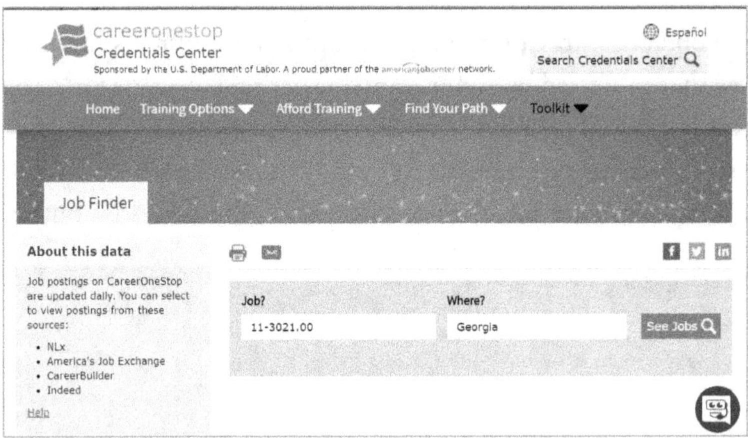

Figure 27 - Job Finder

Finally, like any useful resource, the report includes a list of references (not shown). At this point, our walkthrough of the O*NET report is complete, and you should have a list of potential career options.

Now, take some time to explore the job finder from Figure 26 - Job Search by State and Source. Work through each of the sources for your occupation and identify some additional career opportunities. We will revisit these later when we discuss job hunting.

Department of Labor

Another resource that can help you with a successful transition to civilian life is The U.S. Department of Labor (DOL). Below are some free and easy to use resources from DOL's Veterans' Employment and Training Service.

- Start at www.dol.gov/veterans. You will find employment resources and other information.
- Download the free Career One Stop mobile app or the DOL Employment Workshop eBook on Amazon. They will provide you access to valuable employment resources.
- Visit an American Job Center (or AJC) at one of over 2400 locations across the country. They will connect you with personalized career assistance available to veterans and their families. AJCs provide services ranging from in-person resume help to interviews, networking skills, and specialized training. As a veteran, you will receive priority at any American Job Center, so let them know that you have served. Your spouse can find training and employment assistance there too.

Hire Purpose

Hire Purpose, https://taskandpurpose.com/career, is a website created to assist veterans with free resume templates, samples, formatting, and resume builders. The company behind the site is Grid North Group, and they offer solutions for connecting service members, spouses, and military family members with the companies that want to reach them. Work through this website and see what other career opportunities fit your skills.

Other Career Research Tools

While the previous tools will help you identify careers that align with your military experience, that should not end your search. Take some time to explore these other job information sites, use some initial keywords from your career translation work, and see what it returns. As you discover more job titles, record them, and perform other searches on those job titles for comparable jobs or positions. Your goal here is to cast your net wide and expand your list.

As you identify the positions you are qualified for, start engaging job search websites to further assist you with the job search process. What jobs are comparable to those you find? Do some of these occupations go under different names?

- CareerBuilder.com (try, https://www.careerbuilder.com/browse)
- LinkedIn.com (try, https://www.linkedin.com/jobs/)
- Glassdoor.com (select jobs)
- Google Search
- SimplyHired.com
- Indeed.com

Other Career Finding Methods

For learning about the vast number of potential careers out there, many options exist. Some of these options include:

- Stalking your old colleagues on LinkedIn to see what opportunities they found
- Asking relatives and friends about their careers
- Apprenticeship Programs and Job Shadowing
- Small Business Administration (SBA)
- Volunteer work

- Fact-finding calls
- Employment Counseling
- Business Sections of Newspapers (Magazines)
- Job Fairs and Job Placement Services
- Attending Training Courses and Using Resources at Colleges and Universities
- Temporary Agencies
- Social Networking

What other career opportunities did you identify for yourself? List them now.

____

____

____

____

____

Tightening the Bracket

Having created a list of potential jobs, let us narrow the list and tighten the bracket. With your list in hand, revisit those LinkedIn profiles. Try to get a sense of what your contacts do on the job, identify salary ranges, and determine if they enjoy what they do. You may even consider reaching out to some of these contacts, relatives, and friends. In doing so, you can further narrow your choices. Beyond letting them know you are searching for potential opportunities, they may provide information you can use to prioritize your list. They may even recommend a job you are not considering.

For instance, I initially considered opportunities as a project manager or some other management or teaching position in information technology, cybersecurity, or engineering discipline. However, after speaking with some of my prior colleagues and friends, I learned about various research scientist positions. After they described it, I thought I had found my dream job. Let me tell you. I am grateful for those conversations because I vastly enjoy the work I now do over a pure management position.

Beyond speaking with people, perform some due diligence on the jobs you have on your list. Go back and review the considerations and values you listed earlier. How well do your listed occupations align with your values and the things that matter to you? Use these answers to prioritize your list of professions further.

As you tighten your bracket, your top choices will become more apparent. It is almost time to fire for effect; however, you need to choose your ammunition before you do. After all, you have an idea of what career you want, but how do you know the gatekeepers to those careers will grant you entry? In other words, when hiring managers look at your job application, what are you selling? We'll discuss that next.

4

WHAT ARE YOU SELLING?

> *If you have built castles in the air, your work need not be lost; that is where they should be. Now put the foundations under them. —Henry David Thoreau*

By now, you have likely identified a few potential career opportunities. Better yet, you may have found a career you are already dreaming about. Congratulations! You have built your castle in the air, and that is an excellent start to your transition. This chapter will combine your skills, education, experiences, and other qualifications to build up a foundation that supports your career ambitions. The eventual result of this work will be your resume.

If you have not identified your dream job yet, then that is okay too! Plenty of transitioning service members start jobs as steppingstones to their next career opportunity. In fact, according to a survey of transitioned military veterans conducted by Syracuse University, only 14.89% of veteran respondents stated that they were presently working in their first job.[1] With that in mind, this chapter will not only help you identify the skills, education, and experiences that make you employable, it will help you to further zero in on the jobs that best fit your capabilities. So, if this is you, you are in good company.

Henry David Thoreau, the author of the quote I used at the head of this chapter, was an American essayist, poet, philosopher, abolitionist, naturalist, tax resister, development critic, tutor, surveyor, yogi,[2] and historian. By the way, a yogi is someone who does yoga, so Mr. Thoreau may have been ahead of his time. I am sure there is a joke about hot yogi somewhere in this, but I will leave that nugget to those craftier than I.

As for the here and now, we will consider which knowledge, skills, and abilities (KSAs) you can use to build your resume and grow your network to entice potential employers to seek you out. As a result, this chapter will help you identify the skills you have developed over the years that will also benefit your future employer. With that in mind, we will delve into your past assignments and experiences, identifying some transferable skills that will serve you in various occupations and endeavors.

Knowledge

Some sources for identifying your knowledge and experience include your VMET, DD Form 214, performance and evaluation reports, training certificates, military and civilian transcripts, diplomas, certifications, and other available documentation. If you have not done so already, start gathering these documents now—if you have them.

Verification of Military Experience and Training (VMET)

Before assessing all your skills, you may find it useful to look at your Verification of Military Experience and Training (VMET), DD Form 2586 form. This "all-services" integrated form provides an overview of your military experience and training. In your VMET, you will find demographic information, descriptive summaries of military work experience, training history, and language proficiencies. Your VMET—along with your evaluation records, training certificates, awards, transcripts, and other documentation—will provide a great start towards completing your resume.

Beyond describing your work experience, the VMET document also provides recommendations for college credit associated with your military experience and training. These recommendations come from the American Council on Education (ACE) and other related or comparable job titles when available. As a result, the VMET document provides a history of your completed formal training and work experience dating back to 1985, or even earlier if recorded. The data on this document includes:

- Military occupations, titles, and pertinent dates
- Occupation description
- Additional skill codes with title and description
- Training course title, date of completion, length, and description
- Any associated ACE recommended credits
- Any off-duty education and foreign language proficiencies, as given by your Branch of Service

While a handy tool, keep in mind that your VMET is no substitute for a resume. However, it can come in handy if you need to prove that you meet specific qualifications or possess sufficient technical expertise. You can get your VMET DD Form 2586 by going to the following link:

https://milconnect.dmdc.osd.mil/milconnect/public/faq/Training-VMET.

With your DoD CAC, you can download your VMET as a PDF file. If you have any trouble accessing your VMET, this website also explains how to get a copy of your VMET through other means.

Once you log in, you can navigate to VMET using the tabs at the top of the page. Select the VMET document (DD-2586) and click the Submit button. This will allow you to download a current copy of your VMET. Throughout your career, I recommend you download this document periodically and compare it to previous downloads. In my case, I saw substantial changes in this document from four months earlier when I first downloaded it. The second one contained much less information and had an inaccurate value for my years of service. We will call it growing pains....wink....cough.

Since we are looking at this page, note that it is also the home of your DoD Transition Assistance Program (DoDTAP) for service members and veterans. If you are transitioning from the military or preparing, you may already be familiar with this site. Hence, you may already have a username and password set up. If not, then just know you may visit this site in the future to complete various modules in the Transition Assistance Program. This site tracks your completion status for VA Benefits, Financial Planning, MOC Crosswalk, and DOL Employment Workshop training sessions, among others.

FAQ / Training / VMET

Verification of Military Experience and Training (VMET)

Your Verification of Military Experience and Training (VMET) document helps you prepare resumes and job applications quickly when you separate from Service. The VMET document:

- Gathers all reported demographic, training, and experience records in one place.
- Describes your Service occupations in civilian terms.

Automated systems at each Branch of Service report occupation information to the VMET database. These systems vary, so information might not match your expectations.

That's why you use your VMET along with evaluation reports, training certificates, awards, transcripts, and similar documents to assemble a complete account of how you qualify for civilian occupations, certificates, licenses, or programs of study.

Open All FAQs | Close All FAQs

Figure 28 - DoDTAP Web Page

Earlier in chapter three, we discussed some military crosswalk tools designed to help you map your military occupation to its civilian equivalent. To prepare yourself for that venture, pay attention to the following areas of your VMET.

- All titled occupation codes
- Occupation descriptions from service file information
- Related civilian occupation titles
- Course descriptions from the American Council on Education for career exploration and educational and certification requirements
- Additional qualification (s) for skill sets you may have acquired

Service Transcripts

Another document you may find useful for identifying or validating your subject matter expertise is your service transcripts. Formerly called the Sailor-Marine American Council on Education Registry Transcript (SMART), this document was replaced by the Joint Service Transcript (JST) for Army, Navy, Marines, and Coast Guard personnel. The JST describes military schooling and work history in civilian terms, and academic institutions use it to award credit for military occupational experience and training. Your education transcripts are obtainable online or through your post-education office. To receive your JST, you can register via the JST website and have a transcript generated on-line. You can also have an official copy sent directly to the college or university you designate, and there is no limit to the number of JSTs you can request—it is also free to do so.

This document may overlap with your VMET (discussed in the previous section); however, it can also provide additional insights not shown on your VMET. These transcripts provide all your available education courses and training, even if you did not complete them while on duty. Additionally, they can help identify your competencies and strengths and their relevance to various non-military career paths. As a result, your service transcripts can help determine which career fields align with your expertise or help you discover where your training falls short. So, if you require additional education, then these transcripts can help you develop a plan to achieve your educational goals. Some things it can provide you include:

- upper and lower level credit recommendations
- course hours and descriptions
- military experience related to college credit Army American Council on Education Registry Transcript (AART) or Community College of the Air Force (CCAF)

Credentials

Credentialing involves meeting specified standards and earning official recognition of your expertise. Generally, credentialing boards—consisting of private and government organizations—set the standards for credentialing and licensing standards, including educational or apprenticeship requirements. And many occupations require credentials to meet specific professional and technical standards inherent in the tasks expected for that job.

For instance, some Project Management positions may require you to have a Project Management Professional (PMP) certification, and a Mid-Level Computer Systems Manager might be required to have a Certified Information Systems Security Professional (CISSP) certificate. Likewise, some engineering positions may require you to hold an EIT (Engineer-in-Training) or PE (Professional Engineer) license before you can work for them. In a similar vein, plumbers, carpenters, electricians, and locksmiths may have to undergo an apprenticeship and get a license to gain employment in these fields.

There is, however, a downside to credentials. They often require continued education and annual dues to maintain. Acquiring a large number of them can be unduly expensive both in terms of time and money, so make sure you consider their return on investment when contemplating which ones to obtain—if any. After all, you want to pursue the credentials that will give you the greatest bang for your buck when job hunting.

Why Is Credentialing Important

Many military specialties require certification or licensure to perform the same job as their civilian counterparts. If you are looking to transition to a career with similar requirements, then coming from one of these occupations can help ease your transition into that career. However, you still want to check with the local credentialing organizations for certification and licensure requirements before committing to relocate. For instance, federal, state, or local laws may require specific credentials to work in some occupations. Nursing and teaching represent occupations with state-specific licensing requirements, so what works for one state may not work in another.

Even if you have credentials from a field you do not wish to pursue, those credentials can still grant you access to other related careers, so do not discount their usefulness until you conduct thorough research. There are also many reasons job seekers should consider credentialing. While not all-inclusive, some reasons to pursue credentialing follow.

1. Credentials may be required by law or by an employer to qualify for employment
2. Credentials may lead to higher pay or improved prospects for promotion
3. Credentials demonstrate to civilian employers that training and skills attained in the military are on par with those gained through traditional civilian pathways

4. Credentials and experience can substitute for higher education requirements
5. Credentials demonstrate your willingness to remain relevant in your chosen field

Types of Credentials

There are three main types of credentials you are likely to come across or may already possess.

1. **Licensure**–A license is granted by governmental agencies—federal, state, or local—to individuals to practice a specific occupation. One example is a medical license for doctors. Licenses are typically mandatory; however, state and federal laws or regulations define the standards individuals must meet to become licensed.
2. **Certification**–Certifications are granted by non-governmental agencies, associations, and even private sector companies to individuals who meet predetermined qualifications. These qualifications are often set by professional associations (for example, the National Commission for Certification of Crane Operators) or industry and product-related organizations (such as Novell Certified Engineer). While certification is typically optional to conduct business, many state licensure boards and some employers require certification. For many career fields, multiple organizations may offer equivalent certifications.
3. **Apprenticeship**–A registered apprenticeship program is an industry-based approach to training that combines paid on-the-job learning with job-related education. It moves an employed apprentice from low or no skill level to the full-performance level needed for the career. Apprenticeships must also meet specific program parameters established by the National Apprenticeship Act. As a result, the U.S. Department of Labor or a State

Apprenticeship Agency must validate the standards of registered apprenticeship programs (RAP).

Of the credentials, licenses are typically mandatory. So, if you intend to pursue a civilian career with an associated license, you will need to get that license to perform the job. Certifications are typically voluntary, meaning you can get a job without them. However, more and more certifications are being required. Many Department of Defense (DoD) and contract positions already require certifications. For example, the DoD 8570 Information Assurance Workforce Improvement Program website provides a useful FAQ section that answers many certification questions.[3] For an example of some certifications commonly required for information assurance positions in the DOD, see Table 2 – Some Certifications that Meet Department of Defense (DoD) 8570.01-M Requirements.

Table 2 – Some Certifications that Meet Department of Defense (DoD) 8570.01-M Requirements

A+	CEH	CASP
Network+	GICSP	CCNP Security
CCNA-Security	GSEC	CISA
Security +	SSCP	CISM

Determining if you should pursue these certifications will depend on multiple considerations. Some of which follow.

1. Does an employer require the certification? Consider the careers you bracketed in chapter three and look at a sample of job advertisements to see whether employers require specific certifications. If so, it may be prudent to establish a plan to get them.
2. Will the certification make you more competitive? Even if the certificate is not required, having it can make your application more competitive. For instance, if you lack the experience, training, or education needed to qualify for a job, certification can make you a stronger candidate.

3. What requirements do these certifications impose on the holder? Many certifications require continued education and annual fees to maintain. For instance, some certificates require holders to complete 40 hours of continued education and pay a yearly maintenance fee. Make sure you target the certifications you need and can maintain.
4. Are you curious, and do you have the time? Some certifications may be worth it just for the sake of learning something new. Carrying proof, you completed the certification provides validation that you achieved the requisite skills needed if an opportunity arises.

For some, obtaining these certifications may seem daunting, so take advantage of military programs that can help you best prepare and get them. Sometimes, you may gain authorization to attend a government-sponsored, boot-camp style course to help you achieve the knowledge you need to pass these certification exams. If you complete these courses independently, they can run between $1500 - $5000+ for a week-long course. However, beware of certificate mills! Check to make sure your program leads to quality certifications that are accepted where you plan to work.

Degrees

Degrees offer many new and rewarding opportunities for those who get them. For instance, various studies show degree holders receive increased job opportunities and develop backgrounds more suitable for specialized careers. They also enjoy increased marketability and economic stability because of often greater earning potential. Likewise, pathways to advancement are usually limited to degree holders, and degree holders are more likely to express higher levels of job satisfaction than non-degree holders.

Why Consider a Degree

For degree holders, not only are there more jobs available than high school graduates, but existing jobs are also more accessible. According to one research study, nearly two million new jobs are posted online each quarter that require at least a bachelor's degree.[4] It is also easier for degree holders to find jobs online. Other studies report that roughly 80% of jobs requiring at least a bachelor's degree are posted online, while only 50% of non-degree jobs are posted online. These results show that degree holders have a better pool of opportunities than do non-degree holders.

Degrees also prepare job seekers for specialized careers in technology, education, and medicine. The demand for these is significant because these career fields evolve so often that only the most accomplished individuals can do the work. Because of obtaining these kinds of degrees, recipients develop the habits needed to continue working in these areas. A degree also improves your marketability. Over 80% of jobs in four of the quickest-growing occupations—healthcare, STEM, education, and government services require postsecondary education.[5]

Another point shared by the Bureau of Labor Statistics is the greater your level of education, the higher the salary you can expect. Studies show that those without a high school diploma earn an average of $27,000 per year, while those with a high school diploma average $37,000 annually. Workers with associate degrees earn an average of $43K, and bachelor's degree holders earn around $61,000. These are substantial differences. Those with higher-level degrees also enjoy a greater level of economic stability. A sad fact is that those who do not complete a degree are three times more likely to live in poverty.

There are also some high-paying career options that are only available to those with degrees. Examples include almost all medical professionals, head librarians, lawyers, accountants, veterinarians, educators, and many more. These specialized careers are also considered rewarding. For instance, 60% of bachelor's degree holders state that they are highly satisfied. I am fortunate to include myself among this number. Much of what I do for work in my occupation, I would do even if I did not get paid. However, I am blessed to have employment that allows me to get paid for doing it, anyway.

Types of Degrees

Universities and community colleges award degrees at varying levels ranging from associate degrees to doctoral degrees. However, your career goals and academic interests will best determine the degree-type and degree-category you choose. Time can also be a significant factor.

After high school, four categories of degrees are available to you. Those being the associate, bachelor's, master's, and doctoral degrees. An associate degree is typically a 2-year program that may provide training for entry-level nursing, engineering technology, and other vocational areas. A bachelor's degree is an undergraduate program that takes approximately four years to complete. It requires a student to choose a major field of study, such as engineering, math, nursing, computer science, biology, etc. The list is quite long![6] A bachelor's degree is also your key to getting accepted into a graduate program or jump-starting your career in an entry- or management-level position.

Master's degrees take one to two years to complete and will allow you to specialize in an area of study. You may have to complete a thesis or capstone project as well, but achieving this degree can qualify you for advanced- or executive-level positions. The last level is a doctoral degree. These are the most advanced degrees requiring students to complete comprehensive exams, publish research papers, and complete a dissertation involving a significant research project. Medical-related doctoral programs may require the student to complete hands-on clinical hours with actual patients. This endeavor may take several years to complete, yet doing so will qualify you to work as an expert in your field.

Your total time pursuing higher education can vary significantly depending on the degree and field of study. Time to complete them can be much longer for part-time students who work, support a family, or both. Attrition can be an issue as well. For doctoral degrees, just over 55% of students complete them, even ten years after beginning the program. When I worked as a faculty recruiter at the United States Military Academy (USMA), West Point, we selected highly qualified officers to complete doctoral degrees; yet, only 50% of those did it in three years. That is the time allotted by the Army's Advanced Civil Schooling (ACS) program. Of those, maybe 50% eventually completed their Ph.D.

Degree Requirements

Depending on the school and program you choose, you may have to meet specific prerequisites before attending. For example, many bachelor's degree-granting universities will require you to take an ACT (American College Testing) or SAT (Scholastic Assessment Test)[7] exam, covering four academic skill areas. Those areas are English, mathematics, reading, and science reasoning. You may also be required to complete a writing test. By the way, if you have children in high school, this applies to them too!

Scoring well on these exams will not only go a long way toward securing your position at a competitive university but also help you land scholarships that can further decrease your education costs. Another item you must provide is proof of high school graduation or college transcripts. Other education levels will probably require you to provide evidence of your previous education and provide results from other exams. For instance, schools may require the GRE (Graduate Record Exam) to enter a general master's program. Admission to law school may require the LSAT (Law School Admission Test). Similarly, medical school and business school may require the MCAT (Medical College Admission Test) and GMAT (Graduate Management Admission Test), respectively.

Graduate-level and or post-graduate degrees also require students to have completed an undergraduate before enrollment. Some universities may permit you to bypass a master's degree en route to your doctorate once you have completed your undergraduate degree. Mostly, however, each level of education contributes to the next level of education.

Deciding Whether to Pursue a Degree

There are sound arguments for obtaining a degree. Still, before you decide you must have one, you need to consider a few things. For instance, you probably have a career in mind for the degree you are seeking. What is the outlook for that field? For example, your study of Latin may not be a worthwhile endeavor if job prospects for people speaking a dead language are bleak. I am reasonably sure opportunities are not great for that degree unless you are a historian, theologian, or educator.

Degrees also represent a substantial undertaking, both in time and money. You could easily spend four or five years and $60,000 to $120,000, earning a bachelor's degree. In fact, after two years at Duke University, my wife racked up almost $100,000 in student loans while pursuing her nurse practitioner degree. With those numbers in mind, you need to consider your return on investment (ROI). If your targeted career choice has a high enough salary attached to it, then these numbers may work out well. If you fail to complete that degree, there is no ROI, just lost money. Fortunately, your GI Bill can help offset these costs.

You should also include your aptitude for education. How bad would it be to complete a degree only to learn you dislike using it? While I believe everyone can benefit from education, a degree may not always be necessary for your career. After all, other career paths, such as plumbers, electricians, HVAC specialists, and aircraft repairers, to name just a few, command a great wage without the degree. I frequently get quotes from plumbers and electricians who charge hourly rates of $75 to $125 per hour. So, before jumping into the degree seeker pool, make sure you do an azimuth check to see if the degree route is the best path for you.

Transferable Skills and Abilities

Beyond your knowledge and expertise, employers are also interested in workers with exceptional communication skills, leadership, critical thinking, problem-solving, and analytical reasoning. These are the transferable skills and qualities that transfer from one job to the next. They are portable, and chances are you possess many of them. A key to identifying these skills is to focus less on your previous job titles and more on the unique tasks you fulfilled in the execution of your duties. The skills you used throughout your career also apply to other occupations, jobs, and workplaces.

I discuss skills and abilities somewhat interchangeably throughout this chapter; however, they have distinct definitions. Skills involve manipulating data, things, or people through manual, mental, or verbal means. They are quantifiable—able to be observed and measured through testing. They refer to expertise that comes from training, practice, etc. Ability, however, refers to the capacity to presently perform physical or mental activities.

Typically, abilities represent functions completed on the job. The fundamental difference is that ability means the capacity to perform, whereas skills are the actual performance.[8] It is a subtle distinction, and I may fog the lines between them throughout this book. Once you identify your skills or abilities, you can compare them to the requirements needed for other positions you consider. You can also evaluate if your skills help make you the best candidate for a job. Doing so will help you determine your suitability for the position and whether additional development is needed—either before you apply or after you get hired.

Now, take a few minutes to review the skills listed in Table 3 - Transferable SkillsTable 3 and consider which of these best apply to you. As you find skills that apply, highlight, or write them down. Next, look over your created list and annotate your proficiency level with each skill as moderate or very proficient. Afterward, take another color highlighter or a second page and make another list. You will identify the skills you lack or need to improve on this list.

Table 3 - Transferable Skills

List of Transferable Skills	
Adapt to change	Interpret and speak languages
Administer Programs	Interpret new laws
Advise people/ peers/job seekers	Interpret schematics/codes
Assemble apparatus/equipment	Interview people/new employees
Audit financial records/ accounts payable	Investigate problems/ violations/fraud
Coach team members	Lead others
Communicate with others/groups	Maintain aircraft avionics
Compile statistics/survey data	Maintain diesel engines
Confront people/difficult issues	Maintain transportation fleet/aircraft
Construct buildings Control costs	Make organizational decisions
Coordinate meetings/ events/training	Make Sales
Counsel subordinates	Manage a mailroom/supply closet
Create and produce videos/music	Manage a retail store
Create new programs/ data system	Manage an organization
Create Websites	Manage production
Delegate authority	Market products/services/programs
Develop or revise instructional materials	Negotiate contracts/disputes
Direct administrative staff/ projects	Operate vehicles or equipment
Dispense medication/ information	Persuade others/customers

Establish objectives/ guidelines/policies	Plan agendas/conferences
Evaluate instructors/ peers/students	Prepare and deliver presentations
Evaluate programs/solutions	Prepare reports
Illustrate storyboards/ concepts/ print	Program computers
Implement new programs	Protect property/people
Improve maintenance schedule/systems	Purchase equipment/ supplies/ services
Improvise action	Repair equipment / mechanical devices
Initiate changes/improvements	Teach technical subjects
Install electrical systems/parts	Train others
Install plumbing	Write or edit proposals/ technical papers
Install software	Write or edit publications

Exercise 4.1

	Transferable Skills (Strengths)	Proficiency
1		
2		
3		
4		
5		
6		
7		
8		
9		
10		

Exercise 4.2

	Transferable Skills (Weaknesses)	Proficiency
1		
2		
3		
4		
5		
6		
7		
8		
9		
10		

Alright, having you think about your transferable skills (strengths and weaknesses) was not an exercise in futility. You will need them to better scope your resume and sell yourself to your potential employers. They will form the foundation of the bullets you place in your resume and the responses you give during interviews. As for picking skills requiring further development, these will help prepare you for that inevitable interview question when someone asks, "describe a time when you failed or had to adapt to a challenge for which you were not prepared?"

As you look over the skills you listed, ask yourself, "Why do I feel I am competent (not competent) at these skills?" Hopefully, some specific experiences and situations come to mind. For each **situation**, try to identify the **task** you were trying to accomplish at the time and the **action** you took to complete it. Finally, try to remember the **results** of your actions. This follows a technique called the STAR method, and I will discuss this later. Perhaps you even have some bullets from your evaluation reports that capture these points. If so, that is great; they will help you with our next task!

Now it is time to use this information to compose a few short and concise bullet statements that capture the situation, task, action, and result for each of your identified skills. To ensure your statements are easily read and understood by potential employers, you must eliminate or substitute the military jargon, titles, ranks, and acronyms for their civilian equivalents. The problem you now face then is just what are those civilian equivalents.

Fortunately, there are several online translators out there that can help you overcome this challenge. We will discuss some of these in later sections, but to get you started, consider the following title translations:

- NCOIC, Watch Captain: Supervisor, Manager, Coordinator
- Petty Officer of the Watch: Coordinator, Supervisor, Manager
- Commander, Chief: Division Head, Director, Senior Manager
- Executive Officer (XO): Assistant Manager, Deputy Director
- Action Officer (AO): Analyst (or Senior Analyst)
- TDY/TAD: business travel
- OER/NCOER: performance evaluation
- MOS/MOC: career field
- Commanded: supervised, directed
- Battalion, Unit, Platoon: organization, agency, department, section
- Mission: responsibility, task, objective, job
- Combat, War: hazardous environment, conditions, conflict
- Headquarters: headquarters, corporate office
- Subordinates: employees, co-workers, contractors, team members
- Service members: employees, co-workers, colleagues, personnel, individuals
- Military Personnel Office (MILPO): personnel office or human resources
- Personal Action Center (PAC): personnel office or human resources
- Regulations: guidance, policy, instructions, standard operating procedure

- Reconnaissance: data collection, survey, analysis
- TDA/MTOE: organizational structure, material resources, workforce

Exercise 4.3 STAR Statements for Skills.

1. ______________________________

   ____

2. ______________________________

   ____

3. ______________________________

   ____

4. ______________________________

   ____

5. ______________________________

   ____

Welcome to the De-Militarization Zone

While the skills you developed in the military are valuable, and in high demand, some translation is required. Even more important than identifying your skills is knowing how to express them in a way that resonates with the hiring decision-makers who read your resume, interview you, and ultimately decide if you are the right fit for their company. You should assume most hiring managers will not know much about the military. Their unfamiliarity can make it challenging for a potential employer who lacks your military experience to understand your skills' significance. This is especially so if your skill descriptions are chock-full of military jargon. Your goal is to curb the military vernacular and help potential employers bridge the gap between their understanding of your military background and their organization's needs.

Curbing the military jargon should be a key focus of your cover letter, resume, network profile, elevator pitch, interview comments, and other communications related to your career search. Fortunately, there are some steps you can use to translate your military experience into terms that civilian employers will better understand.[9] For instance, while you and your military colleagues may understand every acronym that appears on your evaluation reports and job description, many hiring managers may not. Even if these hiring managers have a military background, they may come from different service branches whose military jargon does not mirror yours. So, some translation may still be required to ensure a greater audience understands the content in your applications and resumes.

The first step in communicating your value to potential employers is taking all your skills and experiences and de-militarizing them. In previous sections, you identified your skills and experiences. Whether you were a scout for the Army or a cyber planner for the Navy, you developed marketable skills in your career that apply to the civilian workplace. Beyond your job's specific functions, you also brought one or more core values, skills, or expertise to the position. For instance, a scout leader would have led small teams to carry out high-priority tasks with minimal room for failure in high-pressure situations. Some core values, skills, or expertise someone in the above position would display include leadership, ability to carry out work with minimal supervision, attention to detail, and ability to work under strict deadlines. These elements carry a universal appeal with many hiring managers.

The next step is to paint a full description of your experiences, which will probably include the following types of skills:

1. ***Technical skills*** are gained through military occupations like cyber operators, aircraft maintainers, or health care specialists, having relevance to the civilian workforce. Include these in your resume.
2. ***Interpersonal skills*** are the skills you developed while working with various personalities, from high-ranking officers to unit

commanders, peers, contractors, and subordinates. Employers need employees who can work with many kinds of colleagues and customers to get the job done. That makes these skills highly valued in the civilian workplace and ones to be detailed in your resume.

3. ***Leadership Skills*** include the leadership experience or training you developed while overseeing subcontractors and other military personnel. It is also highly valued by civilian employers.

The third step is to take advantage of the veteran transition resources available to you. Consider CareerOneStop,[10] an online resource that allows veterans to explore careers, find training, search for jobs, and find local help. Using this resource, you can match your military skills and experience to civilian occupations using CareerOnestop's Veterans Job Matcher, which serves as a military to civilian occupation translator. The Veterans Job Matcher can also help you find civilian careers that are suitable matches for your military skills. Once you enter your information, you will get results on matching occupations, including wages, education, outlook, and a link to current local job postings. Just enter your military job to find related civilian careers. You will find career information and links to job postings in your local area.[11]

As a fourth step, look at the online profiles of some of your old colleagues, friends, and supervisors who have already departed military service. Ideally, these people will be senior supervisors, colleagues, or mentors from the same occupational specialty as you. Make notes on how they express their skill sets. This step was beneficial and an eye-opening experience for me.

Skill Classification

As you move into expressing your skills, keep the following examples in mind. You may even want to break your skills down into categories:

Communication Skills: those skills that allow you to express your knowledge and ideas effectively.

- Describing feelings
- Editing
- Expressing ideas
- Facilitating group discussion
- Interviewing
- Listening attentively
- Negotiating
- Perceiving nonverbal messages
- Persuading
- Providing appropriate feedback
- Reporting information
- Speaking effectively
- Writing concisely

Research and Planning Skills: those skills that allow you to identify, conceptualize, and solve the future needs of your organization.

- Analyzing
- Creating ideas
- Defining needs
- Developing evaluation strategies
- Extracting important information
- Forecasting and predicting
- Gathering information
- Identifying problems
- Identifying resources
- Imagining alternatives
- Setting goals
- Solving problems

Human Relations Skills: those interpersonal skills you employ to resolve conflict, build teams, and help others.

- Asserting
- Being Sensitive
- Conveying feelings
- Cooperating
- Counseling
- Delegating with respect
- Developing rapport
- Listening
- Motivating
- Perceiving feelings situations
- Providing support for others
- Representing others
- Sharing credit

Organizational Leadership and Management Skills: the skills used to direct, supervise, and guide individuals and teams toward completing tasks and objectives.

- Coaching
- Coordinating tasks
- Counseling
- Decision making with others
- Delegating responsibility
- Handling details
- Initiating new ideas
- Managing conflict
- Managing groups
- Promoting change
- Selling ideas or products
- Teaching

Work Survival Skills: those skills used daily to address sudden changes, promote positive work environments, and improve organizational effectiveness.

- Accepting responsibility
- Attending to detail
- Being punctual
- Cooperating
- Enforcing policies
- Enlisting help
- Implementing decisions
- Making decisions
- Managing time
- Meeting goals
- Organizing
- Setting and meeting deadlines

Work Ethic Traits: those traits that make you a reliable and trusted team member.

- ambition
- diligence
- drive
- effort
- initiative
- reliability
- self-motivation
- stamina

STAR Method

The STAR Method is so important and familiar to interviews and resumes that it gets a subsection of its very own. This four-step method offers a structured way of answering resume-based interview questions that provide interviewers with clear, factual, and concise statements about your relevant skills and experience. The structure of these statements follows a **S**ituation, **T**ask, **A**ction, and **R**esult (STAR) sequence to explain your experiences. By putting your statements in this format, you can better explain to hiring managers how you have successfully used your skills to achieve results. This section will cover how to develop STAR statements. But, before doing so, let us consider each section of the STAR method in greater detail.

S–Situation: Provide context for a skill you want to describe. Think of a situation, challenge, or opportunity that you or your employer faced? It can be from a previous job, volunteer experience, or any other relevant event. Specifically, describe the problem you were in or the task you needed to accomplish. Your previous counseling or evaluation reports can serve as an excellent source for identifying these situations.

T—Task: Explain what tasks were involved in completing your assigned mission, objective, or project, or the great idea for which you took the initiative. What was the goal you worked to achieve?

A—Action: Identify the approach or steps you took to complete said tasks. Describe the actions in detail and keep the focus on **YOU**. What were your specific contributions? Do not just describe what the team or group did. Your words should be "I," not "We."

R—Results: What happened because of those actions? Describe the outcome of your efforts, and do not avoid taking credit for your behavior. How did the event end, and what did you accomplish? Explain what you learned. Did you make an impact in terms of generated benefits, reduced costs, saved time, improved efficiency, or extra revenue? Put it in terms of a before-and-after you implemented changes. Also include quantitative and measurable results. Finally, focus on the positive results you achieved.

The key to success with the STAR method is to be specific and avoid rambling. Too much information (TMI) is a thing, and you need to prevent it. However, make sure you articulate the results of your actions. Job seekers often cannot convey how their efforts resulted in a successful venture for their organization. This leaves hiring managers guessing. Do not do that—tell them! Keep in mind, even some examples that have a negative outcome (e.g., "lost a game," "completed over budget," etc.) can still highlight your strengths when faced with adversity. However, eliminate examples that do not portray you positively.

Also, keep in mind that the skills and experiences discussed in this section are all about you. So, as you develop your STAR statements, keep the focus on "I," not "We." Remember, your potential employers want to know what you will do for them. What your team did for its previous organization or company won't carry as much weight, if any. Therefore, explaining your skills and experiences using the STAR format is oh-so valuable. It forces you to keep "I" in the forefront as you give hiring managers a precise set of facts that they can attribute to your capabilities. This approach may also eliminate the series of awkward follow-up questions an interviewer may ask to get to the points they wanted to learn from you all along.

Using the STAR method can also grant you an advantage over other candidates if you have strong career experiences. You probably do. For instance, suppose you are competing with another candidate for the same position, and you both have experiences with increasing generated revenues. One horrible statement that you both might put on your resume is:

We generated an increase in sales of $2.5 million in net profit last year.

On the surface, you may think, 'well, what company wouldn't want to sell an additional $2.5 million in product.' But let us break down the above statement a little further. First, who are we? 'We' is a red flag for many hiring managers since it allows candidates to indirectly claim credit for a significant achievement to which they only marginally contributed. For instance, when pressed about a particular contribution to this net sales increase, your rival candidate may have to admit that, while he was part of a team that increased sales by $2.5 million in a year, he was the guy who recorded everyone's progress.

On the other hand, let us say you were part of a similar team, and you took the initiative to secure three additional contracts that generated 50% of that $2.5 million in extra sales. You may have had a team to help demonstrate your company's products and handle scheduling and other sales-related tasks, but you can take credit for securing those contracts, and you can speak directly to how you did so. Those kinds of statements will help you stand out as the best candidate.

What is also useful about the STAR method is it will help keep you honest. It is hard to fake or exaggerate your accomplishments using the STAR method. If you do, hiring managers will probably pick up on it and share that knowledge with others. That said, always attempt to paint your experiences in a positive and favorable light, but do not allow yourself to stretch your statements beyond the facts. Consider the following STAR statement and subsequent bullet statement.

STAR Statement: My unit received a new portable generator model, and my supervisor tasked me to ensure my team members maintained them. I consulted technical manuals, developed training materials, and implemented instruction for my team members on maintenance procedures. As a result, my team maintained a 98% operational readiness rate for the generators throughout the year.

The above STAR statement is great for conversation, but in a resume, you want to condense it further into a bullet statement, such as follows.

Bullet Statement: Designed and delivered technical training for portable generators resulting in 98% operational readiness over 365 days.

We will revisit the STAR method in Chapter 5 when we discuss resume writing. For now, I recommend you perform a quick Internet search using "transferable skills inventory and STAR statements" as your search criteria. This search should generate a plethora of academic, government, and industry resources that will help you expand your identified skills. With your expanded list, you can create even better STAR statements to help hiring managers understand the value you will bring to their organization.

Another great resource you should get and use to develop your STAR statements is the Department of Labor Employment Workshop (DOLEW) Participant Guide, which is available for free at https://www.dol.gov/sites/dolgov/files/VETS/files/DOLEW-Participant-Guide.pdf. Section 4.8 of the DOLEW offers a helpful activity for creating skill statements that we can use later in this book.

5

SELL YOURSELF & DON'T SELL YOURSELF SHORT

> *One of our greatest obstacles to success in life is selling ourselves short.*

We discussed your skills, experiences, and many other marketable aspects unique to you throughout the preceding chapters. Now, it is time to generate the products you will need to gain your entrance to that coveted interview. These include your resume, your cover letter, your online profile, and your elevator pitch. In the previous chapters, we garnered some information about your experience—hopefully, you have been taking notes. And you have downloaded copies of your past officer evaluation reports (OERs), non-commissioned officer evaluation reports (NCOERs), fitness reports, awards, certifications, and any other applicable documents. You will use them to help paint a full picture of you in two or fewer pages. Likewise, this chapter will help teach you to tell someone exactly what you do and what assets you bring to a team in 45 seconds or less! Yes, it can be done! Many people have even mastered their 30-second elevator pitch, and you can too!

It is All About Marketing

Before moving forward in this chapter, let me ask you these questions. What is the reason for creating products, like a resume, a cover letter, or an elevator pitch? Why should job seekers develop an online presence? Can you guess what it is? Think about it. You are standing in front of your fellow service members to give them the bottom-line up-front reason for building a resume. What do you tell them? The answer is this—you do these things to gain the interview.

These products become your marketing tools for drawing hiring managers to you—making them think, "Hey, this person could be a valuable asset to our organization." If you do these things and do them well, you will move from a job *seeker* to a job *selector*. In the latter category, the distinction is this: you have potential employers reaching out to you regularly and offering you opportunities to select a job even after you are employed. In the former, you are still hustling to find the next interview. Job selectors also have a much stronger bargaining position when negotiating salaries and benefits. So, let's secure that first interview. Once you have that mastered, you can start letting hiring managers figure out how they can secure you.

Your goal throughout your transition process is to move from job seeker to job selector.

Your Resume(s)

Concise words are the best words!

Your resume summarizes your work history, skills, and experience. It offers a glimpse into your employment potential, and it will probably be the first document about you that an employer will see. As a result, your resume needs to stand out.

As my retirement date approached, I started visiting job fairs and attending conferences to build my network and meet others with similar interests as myself. On one occasion, I found myself standing in line to speak with a recruiter who represented a local company specializing in technical and educational services for the government. In front of me, another transitioning service member approached the recruiter, shook hands, offered a preliminary greeting, and began some small talk. Then I heard the recruiter ask the service member if he had a resume.

Unfortunately, this is where the conversation took a turn for the worse. As the service member reached into his folder to retrieve his resume, I heard him say, “Now this resume reflects 20 years of service.”

That immediately drew my attention, and I focused on the stack of documents he handed to the recruiter—it was quite thick! I then watched the recruiter take the resume and sigh as he thumbed through the pages. Fortunately, for this service member, the recruiter was a retired veteran himself, and he offered some candid advice. The recruiter explained that good resumes are concise and clearly express your value to a potential employer. The recruiter then directed the would-be applicant to another organization at the job fair that specialized in assisting

> ***“Easy reading is damn hard writing.”***
>
> ***—Nathaniel Hawthorne***

veterans with their resumes. While the service member received some valuable advice that day, he also missed a potential opportunity.

Instead of continuing his job hunt and landing some potential interviews, this service member found himself referred to some counselors for tutoring. The sad truth is too many people do not craft resumes tailored for getting them hired. Let us make sure you are not one of them. You should also keep in mind that only 1% of the American population is currently serving in the military. According to the Census Bureau, only 7% of Americans have ever served in the military.[1] That means your resume needs to be easily understandable by the other 93%.

Admittedly, writing an effective resume can be challenging. This is especially so when you consider that the average recruiter may only spend a measly 5-7 seconds reviewing your resume.[2] During one discussion, I learned that many hiring managers seldom read past the point where they placed their thumb when they first picked up a resume. Those are your seasoned reviewers.

Still, I have heard senior managers instruct their resume reviewers to spend no more than one minute on each resume unless they sensed they had a strong candidate. The reason for this is simple. Reviewers are overwhelmed with the volume of resumes they receive. Often, they must review resumes in addition to their regular workload; however, telling the boss they did not get their work done because they were reviewing resumes is a non-starter. The limited time a reviewer gives a resume can serve as a significant challenge for job hunters. This also means you must concisely convey a substantial amount of information upfront in a way that identifies who you are as a potential employee.

Much like journalists, you must "never bury the lead," and the lead must be strong enough to hook the reader. To avoid doing so, pay attention to your summary statement, experience, and the bullets you choose. In each of these areas, ensure you establish your brand with unique comments that are quantifiable and interesting enough to hook your reviewer. This will not happen if you fill the critical space of your resume—think the top left—with an abundance of adjectives that describe both you and your competition.

Taking all of this into consideration, let's look at an approach to developing an effective resume that will get you noticed. In this section, you will need copies of your previous performance evaluations, awards, and recommendations. We will use these materials to develop statements and articulate your accomplishments in a way that resonates with most employers. To do so, we will craft statements that follow a STAR (Situation, Task, Action, & Results) format, and we will put some effort into translating all that military jargon that riddles your performance statements into something more understandable for the masses. As discussed previously, in chapter four, STAR statements start with action verbs and quantify accomplishments with numbers, dollars, and percentages.

Here are some items you should gather:

1. Copies of NCOER/OERs
2. Copies of NCOER/OER support forms
3. Copies of awards and award write-ups
4. Any impact counseling statements
5. Recommendation Letters

Okay, moving on. Some human resource managers have noted that veterans spend excessive time focused on their resumes' superficial terminology, limiting the reviewers' understanding of things these veterans are qualified to do. Instead, it would be best if you thought of your military occupation as a college major. Suppose your military career directly applies to a civilian job, and it is one you want (e.g., medical technician, pilot, or electrician). In that case, use it to show your fit and qualification. If not, then your experience can still illustrate intangible characteristics rather than specific job skills. For example, former Army Rangers should have no trouble communicating that they are tough, team-oriented, and doggedly determined to accomplish their quota in a sales job or production line.

Your Employment History

Besides all the skills you have previously identified, you also want to maintain a comprehensive list of every job you ever worked. This does not mean they will appear on your resume; however, most of them, especially those you have held over the last 10-20 years, will form the foundation for your master resume. You can almost think of your employment history in terms of an outline. This is what the DOL Workshop Guide calls an Employment History Outline. Examples of employment history can also be found in the 2017 and 2019 DOL workshop participation guides, which, as stated previously, are free to download.

Speaking of outlines, that is how you want to begin your resume. Hopefully, that brings back some memories from preparing to write your first paper. Hey! It works. Doing so will help you organize your thoughts and keep your work focused. Outlines also allow you to group your ideas so that your work seamlessly flows together from one topic to the next, allowing you to make the most persuasive case for your employment. Even in developing this book, I generated a simple outline to better group my research, observations, and experiences and ultimately merged them into the book you are reading today. Granted, the content of that outline expanded, moved around, got cut, and received continual tweaks. The same applies to your resume.

To prepare for building your resume, we will begin by creating your employment history outline. From this outline, you can create your master resume and your targeted resume. From those, you can start marketing your work history and developed skills to potential employers. Fortunately, completing this process is not complicated. All you need are:

- List of Employers
- Dates (by month and year) Employed
- Titles or Jobs You Held

Multiple formats exist for capturing your employment history, but for now, we will consider something like this (notice how military titles are left out):

- Assistant Professor/Researcher, United States Military Academy, May 20xx-20xx
- Director, US Army, June 20xx-20xx
- Senior Manager, U.S. Army, May 20xx-20xx
- Aircraft Electrical System Repairer, U.S. Army, 20xx-20xx, March 20xx–July 20xx

When you develop your resume, we will discuss some other methods for listing your work history, along with the resume types. Keep in mind that we are focusing on creating a general resume. If you apply to a specific company position, focus on their priorities with a targeted resume. For instance, if you are considering Northrop Grumman, then according to their transitioning military page,[3] there are fundamental elements you should include in your resume. These fundamental components include:

1. Specific dates of employment
2. Correct job titles
3. Summary of qualifications
4. Clearance information
5. Statements describing your most recent job and prior jobs (include as many as appropriate)
6. Specific results and benefits that support your activities and accomplishments
7. Never go below 11pt font
8. No more than three pages long (I think you are stretching your luck with a 3rd page)
9. Use bullet points

10. If you are willing to relocate, indicate so near the bottom of the page
11. The average recruiter/manager will, on average, take only 20 seconds to read a resume. Put all your unique information near the top.

Their website also points out that non-military professionals with tech/business/logistics backgrounds will first review your resume. As a result, you need to answer the following questions in your resume:

1. What tools have you used?
2. How many people have you supervised?
3. Have you led a team, and how many?
4. If you have led any teams, what were the ranks (or positions) of people you led? What were the team's objectives, and what success statistics can you share?
5. How much money have you saved or generated for your organization?

Resumes often include an objective statement or summary statement. Northrop Grumman's site suggests that you mention that you are a veteran, avoid mentioning your targeted company's name, and avoid naming one specific job interest. They recommend not specifically listing your job interest because they may have opportunities for your skills on multiple projects. But you may get overlooked if your specified job interest does not match their available options. They also ask that you show your current/most recent cumulative grade point average (GPA) if you are an active student/recent graduate.

Skills Summary

Most resumes will also include a summary of the skills section. For this section, Northrop Grumman's hiring managers recommend the following.

- Use bullet points (Yes, I listed it again!)
- Brag about yourself
- Indicate quantitative and qualitative data
- If you find the civilian equivalent to your job, list it next to your job title.
    - Example: Tool Shop Supervisor (Logistics Branch Manager)
    - Example: VAW-123, Aviation Maintenance/ Production Chief - (Tool Shop Supervisor /Logistics Branch Manager)

Also, do not just say "Automation" or "Operations." Instead, describe your experience in automation or operations. For operations, say that you tracked, maintained, repaired, and were accountable for property valued at $X million dollars. For automation, state how you guided, trained, and assisted over X personnel to use various systems to track aircraft maintenance duties and flight schedules.

These are all great points and ones you should address if you have Northrop Grumman in your sites. Northrop Grumman is a well-known and respected organization with strong veteran preference and lots of opportunities for prior Officers and NCOs who served in leadership positions within the technology arena. However, remember that other employers may have slightly different preferences.

For instance, some resume writing experts and reviewers say that you should not include your GPA. Others would prefer that you not mention military rank since they may not have the familiarity with the military rank system that folks at Northrop Grumman do. For these reasons, tailor your resume to the company you are targeting. Also, keep in mind that Northrop Grumman's policies may change, and the above points are offered as an example only. If you truly have Northrop Grumman in your sights, then definitely target your resume based on the company's current published guidance.

Finally, Northrop Grumman recommends you never pay to have a resume created. If my vote counts, I second that statement. Instead, write it yourself and have a friend in a similar field you are interested in review it. Northrop Grumman also offers some resources on its page, like resume templates and automated resume reviewers.[4] We will cover other resources throughout this chapter as well.

Resume Types

As you can imagine, there is no one-size-fits-all resume. Hence, one resume type may better characterize your work history and skills over another. As you outline your resume, there are essentially three types of resumes you should consider: chronological, functional, and hybrid or combinational.

The Three Types of Resumes are Chronological, Functional, and Hybrid or Combinational.

Chronological resume - In a chronological resume, your employment history becomes the focus starting with your most recent position and then backdating previous employment from there. Each of these positions includes your responsibilities and accomplishments under each job.

Functional Resume - If you have had multiple duty stations performing similar duties, consider a functional resume that breaks down your work experience groups by specialty vs. location. This style deemphasizes your work history and highlights your skills. For example, you may express the experience and skills you gained as an Aviation Mechanic. You could annotate how many people you supervised, what you did, what tools you worked with, how you improved efficiencies, and how you saved money.

Combination resume. The combination resume focuses on the skills you have earned from various jobs but uses a job history format. Your specific skills will form the main body of the resume, followed by a concise employment history.

Build Your Resume

Okay! Let's do this already. We have discussed resumes, and we have even hinted at what should go in one. However, if you have never created one on your own, it helps to have a guide or template—just do not cave and let someone else make one for you. I promise that this is an exercise you can fully complete with the resources that are out there. It will also better prepare you for your interview. It is not unusual for an interviewer to ask a question, like, "I see on your resume that you listed X. How do you think X could benefit our company?" Everything on your resume should be something you put there and are comfortable explaining.

Fortunately, many organizations are seeking to help you build your resume. Start with them to develop your first draft and then keep improving upon it. Ask colleagues and mentors to review it and offer you feedback. If you do that, by the time you start day-1 of your TAP course, you will already have a polished resume ready for the final buff and polish.

Hiring Our Heroes

One resume source you can turn to is Hiring Our Heroes (HOH). The aid this organization offers includes support with writing resumes and finding employment. It can also help you tailor your resumes to appeal to civilian employers if you feel you are struggling in that department. This site also has a resume engine, https://www.resumeengine.org. Just follow their instructions, and you will start cranking out resumes in no time. HOH also offers a skill translation resource, which can be useful when explaining a skill you picked up in the military in civilian terms.

As a bonus, HOH also works with over 5,000 employers who might pick up your resume. For military spouses, HOH also provides a link to *CareerSpark* to help ignite their careers.

Google

Even Google, one of the most popular search engines, has a resume builder. With Google Drive, you can quickly build a professional-looking resume that summarizes your experience, education, and skills. You may even already have an account, and you can find the resume builder at https://vetsresumebuilder.appspot.com/#null. When you visit, sign in and fill in the form with your professional information. Most fields are optional, so include the information you consider necessary. Then just pick a template, and your resume will build automatically.

SimplyHired

The SimplyHired Resume Builder is another resource that can help you build your resume in minutes. They also make it easy to switch between resume templates with over 30 professional resumes from which to choose. Better yet, SimplyHired allows you to download, print, or share your resume on professional networks with no sign-up required. You can visit this resource at https://www.simplyhired.com/resumebuilder.

Other Sources

There are many other sites where you can get assistance building your resume, so please explore some of the resume builder links and templates below if you need further assistance. Many other sites are offering similar resources as well, so visit your favorite search engine and search for "free online resume builders."

- www.resume-now.com
- https://accelerate.withgoogle.com/veterans

Resume Templates

As I researched resumes and best practices during my transition, I discovered many template choices for building my resume. I also ran into many advertisements that plague such searches, offering to build my resume for me. Mostly, I passed them over. There are just too many services, including friends and mentors, who are happy to help you get your resume into fighting shape and for free. I even had a few colleagues who departed the military before I did share their resumes with me. Their generosity allowed me to compare their resumes' structure and expression of similar work experiences to my own. In turn, I have repeated that kindness for multiple other colleagues over the years since my transition.

So, unless you are desperate, having procrastinated to the last hour, do not pay to have someone create your resume. Your general resume writer does not know you as you do, and they probably will not learn more about your target company than you will either. Still, if you want to get a feel for what other resumes look like, it does not hurt to check out some templates. Below are other links where you can obtain resume templates.

1. https://money.com/best-free-resume-template/
    - Money.com offers an annual article with guidance for resumes and a free template.
2. https://www.jobscan.co/resume-templates
    - This site provides a few places to find quality resume templates already in Word or Google Docs formats.
3. https://www.instantresumetemplates.com/

With a little help from your friends and colleagues and some attention to detail on basic resume writing guidelines, you will put something together that will significantly surpass anything someone who hardly knows you can offer. Also, keep in mind that content matters. If a hiring manager sees something on your resume that they need, they will probably call you back, even if you have a shotty resume. Still, put your best effort into this document. We can almost end this chapter right there—almost!

Resume Success Verbs

Did you know that there is a category of verbs reserved for your resume to indicate success? Those are called success verbs. Your sole purpose in using these verbs in your resume is to show potential employers how you have succeeded. In short, they are used to show how you have increased, decreased, improved, reduced, or otherwise impacted some facet of business relevant to your potential employer.

Below, I provide a list of action verbs you may look for in your bullet statements or consider adding. Note that these do not have to be ten-dollar words. Simple is good, and simple is understandable.

Achieved	Exceeded	Maximized
Added	Expanded	Minimized
Awarded	Gained	Optimized
Changed	Generated	Produced
Contributed	Grew	Reduced
Decreased	Improved	Saved
Delivered	Increased	Sold
Eliminated	Introduced	

The way you use these verbs should follow formats, like the ones shown below.

- Improved/reduced x by $
- Increase/decreased x by %
- Added # to x
- Implemented x to achieve # more of something

While '$,' '%,' and '#' are self-explanatory, 'x' can be clients, costs, energy, materials, profits, time, training, etc. The list is extensive, but the format is standard.

Example Resumes

The figures in this section are adaptations of resumes presented by successful job seekers. You will notice that they vary significantly, but they still communicate the applicant's suitability for the position. If you listen to many "resume experts," you will undoubtedly notice multiple discrepancies between these resumes and the advice you receive. I am not telling you to discount the expert's advice. Just keep in mind that resume writing rules can be bent and broken most times as needed.

In the first resume, notice that this applicant is a senior leader with over 20-years of experience in the Army, covering a large variety of positions and locations. Also, see that their resume is still only two-pages long. You may break this rule, but even I advise against it. If you want to provide your resume's reviewer with more information, include a link to your LinkedIn.com profile. If your resume gets their attention, they may opt to do a little more research on you; however, if you initially put too much information in your resume, you risk them not reading it.

The second resume is for an entry-level software engineer. This applicant does not have a wealth of experience, so they capitalize on their education, grades, and accomplishments while in school. They also list their internship work and their achievements while participating in clubs that align with their career ambitions. Also, they list their relevant skills and proficiencies. While their resume is only one page long, it is easy to see all the relevant information applicable to a software engineer. If a hiring manager is looking for someone with C++ and RobotC programming skills, they will probably want to follow up with this person.

First M. Last

Degree ECE, [CERT], [CERT]

(123) 456-7890 www.linkedin.com/in/firstmlast firstmlast@gmail.com

OBJECTIVE: Retiring Army Lieutenant Colonel (LTC) seeking an influential position leading cybersecurity teams and initiatives. Available as early as July 2020.

SUMMARY OF QUALIFICATIONS

Accomplished cybersecurity innovator with a twenty-two-year track record of success with building teams, leading change, and solving challenges. High-energy and approachable leader with a documented history of accomplishing "firsts" in a wide range of positions and disciplines.

CORE COMPETENCIES

- *CISSP, CEH, & CHFI certified*
- *Cybersecurity*
- *Risk Mitigation*
- *Project Management*
- *Schedule Planning*
- *Coaching & Team Building*
- *Problem Solving*
- *Strategic Planning*
- *Communications (Oral & Written)*

SECURITY CLEARANCE: Active Secret

PROFESSIONAL EXPERIENCE

Strategic Planning and Project Management

- Led the [unit]'s strategic engagements with Federally Funded Research and Development Centers (FFRDC), University Affiliated Research Centers (UARC), federal agencies, and academia.
- Spearheaded a joint initiative with the [unit], [organization], and [organization]to introduce [product] dependency modeling into [type of] operations in the [organization].
- Orchestrated several regional engineering projects, including the installation and integration of the [organization]'s [technology] infrastructure, [capability] synchronization solution, and Information Technology Service Manager (ITSM) for enterprise ticketing.
- Developed statement of work and led efforts to add cybersecurity and trusted autonomy to [organization]'s [system] architecture.
- Received award-winning recognition as the project lead for the stand-up and migration of enterprise services to a multi-million-dollar main communication facility—completed ahead of schedule.
- Currently leading the development of the [organization]'s college recruiting program, leveraging recruiting mechanisms such as the [name of] programs to bolster the civilian workforce. Built partnerships with several trusted Centers of Academic Excellence (CAE) to recruit recent college graduates with cutting-edge highly technical coursework.

Technical Expertise

- Established one of [organization's most successful incident response teams, and led more incident responses/ vulnerability assessments over a two-year period than any other team in the Department of the Army.
- Directed two large-scale, multi-agency incident response missions in highly sensitive DoD networks, clearing the networks of adversary presence and overseeing subsequent recovery efforts.
- Program Manager for the [organization]'s [type of] program; developed the [type of] capability from the ground up, partnering with renowned [profession] experts from agencies such as [organizations] and private industry.
- Served as an invited panelist for the [national organization] on Cybersecurity Initiatives—reviewed and prioritized multiple proposals for funding with awards ranging from $1M to $4M.
- Collaborated across multiple agencies to inform military requirements for the [project] tool supporting the Army's [programs].
- Recognized as a subject matter expert in [area] and network security, authoring [#] refereed technical publications plus one book chapter, and serving as a technical reviewer for many refereed conferences.

Figure 29 - Front Page of a Senior Leader applying for a Project Lead Position

First M. Last • *Page 2* • firstmlast@gmail.com

Leadership, Coaching, and Team Building

- Cultivated strong partnerships with [organization], [other organizations] to integrate data science capabilities into the [organizations's advanced capabilities portfolio.
- Skillfully led a 130+ multi-disciplinary technology team supporting 24x7 enterprise operations across [area], maintained >99% availability while introducing new VPLS and MPLS services and host-based security. Enterprise VPLS project allowed for a new contracting venue, saving the Army $14M over a three-year period.
- Hosted the 2019 [name] workshop to develop lessons learned and capture gaps and research opportunities within the converging fields of EW (electronic warfare) and cyberspace. Recognized by [senior leader], [title and organization] for efforts.
- Received the [title] Leadership Award for performance as a Signal Company Commander and contributions to the Signal Corps.

EMPLOYMENT HISTORY

U.S. Army Unit, Post, State	
- Director of [something] (Cyber)	year – Present
- Program Manager, [Program] Cybersecurity	year-year
- Director, [department] ([type] Chief)	year-year
Operations Manager (Enterprise Services), Organization, Location	year-year
Program Manager (Logistics Automation), Unit, Fort, State	year-year
Supply Chain Manager, Unit, Fort, State	year-year
[Type of] Manager, Various Army Units/Organizations	year-year

EDUCATION

M.S.	Degree	University, City, State, Year
M.S.	Degree	University, City, State, Year
B.S.	Degree	University, City, State, Year (Cum Laude, Distinguished Military Graduate)

MILITARY / INDUSTRY COURSEWORK

Telecommunications Engineer Course (**FA24 Course**) | Joint Advanced Cyber Warfare Course (**JACWC**)
Army Cyberspace Operations Planner's Course (**ACOPC**) | Command and General Staff College (**CGSC**)

PROFESSIONAL CERTIFICATIONS / AWARDS / TECHNICAL SKILLS

Certified Information Systems Security Professional (**CISSP**) | Certified Ethical Hacker (**CEH**) | Certified Hacking Forensics Investigator (**CHFI**) | [CERT (CERT)] | Programming (C++, Java, Python) | [other]

Award [Award]

https://www.linkedin.com/in/firstmlast

2 of 2

Figure 30 - Back Page of a Senior Leader applying for a Project Lead Position

First Last

CONTACT INFORMATION	## Address City, State, Zip	(123) 456-7800 firstmlast@gmail.com
EDUCATION	**University**, City, State MS Computer Science, Year – Year • #.## GPA • First place in computer science competition during [event] **University**, City, State BS Computer Science, Year – Year • #.## GPA, Dean's List • Computer Science academic awards in junior and senior years • Business Minor	
JOB EXPERIENCE AND INTERNSHIPS	**University** Undergraduate Teaching Assistant • Helped professor with grading; answered student questions	Year – Year
	Company Software Engineering Intern • Created CleverSoftware tool to do [something cool] using Python and Java	Year – Year
	Company Consultant • Developed a software interface allowing company's x-software to query various national databases	Year – Year
CLUBS AND PROJECTS	**Club** Founding Member and Team Captain • Award • Award	Year – Year
	Club Member • Held open hours for other CS students • Participated in community events	Year – Year
	Club Participant • Created an application to display pet care centers using JavaScript and MySQL database	Year – Year
PROGRAMMING LANGUAGES	**Proficient:** Python, C, RobotC **Moderately Proficient:** C++, MATLAB, Java, SQL **Familiar:** JavaScript, PHP	

Figure 31 - Entry Level Software Engineer Application

TTP for Improving Your Resume

The military has Techniques, Tactics, and Procedures (TTP) for everything. It should probably have one for improving your resume writing. Alas, it does not—I checked. Perhaps we will see something like this make its way into your transition assistance programs (TAPs) soon. In the meantime, let's see how your resume is developing.

Now that you have constructed your resume, it is time to improve it. I know—I know. You have already added all the essential elements. You have your work history neatly tied in, along with your education and skills. You even added a summary that perfectly explains your brand. All this is great, and it may even get you noticed on its own. But think of your initial resume as you might a foxhole. You may have begun by creating a hasty prone position to provide yourself some initial cover from fire back during basic training. As time passed, you were expected to improve your position, converting it to a standing position and then adding overhead cover. While an imperfect solution, that hasty prone position was only ever met to offer you an initial product with minimal cover. Your initial resume is much the same, a minimum viable product, and it is one that needs continued development.

> ***"Imperfect action is better than perfect inaction."***
>
> ***—Harry S. Truman***

So, what can you do to improve your resume? First, realize that your target audience—hiring managers—are busy people, and we want their job reviewing your resume to be as easy as possible. Remember, they are the gatekeepers to the interview, and your resume must convince them to grant you entrance. With that awareness in mind, consider following these steps to improve your resume. Doing so will help your resume be all that it can be.

1. Modernize your resume. Hey! It is no surprise that we live in a

digital age where information is often just a click away. To a certain extent, we expect it, and we rarely appreciate how much we enjoy these features until we no longer have them. So, how can you modernize your resume to make your hiring manager's job easier? Include hyperlinks in your resume, specifically your email address. You may also include a link to your LinkedIn profile. If your resume captures a reviewer's attention, then temptation may lead them to click on your offered link to follow up with or learn more about you. While I include these features in my resume, it is far from original thinking. This advice pops up in many resources, so you are not alone if you exercise this option.[5]

2. Reconsider that objective statement. To ditch or not to ditch? Some resume experts recommend ditching it and make excellent points for why this may be for the best. Do you really know if your objective statement will align with a hiring manager's objectives? Hiring managers are not as concerned with what you are looking for as they are with finding the right hire. If you plan to tell your potential employer what you are looking for, this statement needs to check all the "right hire" boxes. Instead of an objective statement, you could use a summary statement to capture the hiring manager's attention. It, too, is placed at the start of your resume. However, this statement's key attributes include a short professional synopsis that states your years of experience, job history, and significant career achievements. Notice in the above templates that this statement is not labeled.
3. Let bold be your guide. The Internet has changed the way we review material. Many readers have grown used to perusing websites and skipping chunks of material that causes them to miss key points in your resume. As a result, it may be necessary to help guide your reader's eye with a little bold print sprinkled judiciously throughout your resume to make sure your achievements

stand out. Go easy, though. Too much, and you might as well not do it at all.

4. Beat the robots. Have you ever heard of the applicant tracking system (ATS)? If so, you may be among the few. The applicant tracking system[6] and others like it serve as virtualized gatekeepers between you and your target opportunities. These systems, which use algorithms that take contextual keywords and phrases from your resume to create relevance scores, are usually used by medium- to large-sized companies to filter out candidates from the ocean of applicants. As a result, if your resume lacks critical keywords, it may not be ranked high enough to be seen by a hiring manager. One way to beat these robots is to make sure your resume includes the exact phrasing in the job posting you are applying for. Also, changing terms like customer service to client relations can get your resume rejected, so try to use the exact words found on the job posting.
5. Use the robots. While technology can weed out your application, other applications can help you slide it past the goalie. I know that one person who passes his resume and job description through word cloud sites, like tagcrowd.com. He then compares the outcomes to ensure his resume emphasizes the right words. Quite clever.
6. Expand your real estate. A one-page resume may be appropriate if you are a recent graduate or if your experience is limited to one specific area. However, if you are someone with over 20 years of experience in multiple fields, then a two-page resume may be appropriate. Still, you need to use your space judiciously. Use bullet points and active verbs to conserve space. Also, some statements, like references are available upon request, are apparent. Do not use them. Most of all, remember you do not want to be that guy or gal with the twenty-page resume. A "resume is as long as it needs to be to convey value. And not one word more."[7]

7. Rethink your skills section. Some resume experts say you should forgo a skills section stating that potential employers may prefer to see how you have applied your skills. However, in my resume, I completely ignore this advice since the jobs I apply to are usually looking for specific technical skill sets. Sometimes, I believe it is useful to see C/C++ on a resume over an elaborate narrative. If you are applying for a skills-based job, hold on to this section.
8. Add some artistic flare. Tread carefully here. I have many talents, but very few include artistic promise. Attempting to make your resume "pop" could go good or bad. Unfortunately, it is hard to know which, so keep your industry in mind as you spruce your resume. You might find that graphic designers enjoy much more appreciation and leeway with their design efforts than, let's say, an engineer or accountant. To be honest, artistic license is so far outside my depth that I recommend you search the Internet yourself to see if any ideas resonate with your personality and the job you are seeking.

Your Cover Letter

While your resume looks back at your history, your cover looks to your future employment.

A cover letter is an essential aspect of your targeted job search, and it should complement your resume. It is your sales letter, a personal introduction, and your first impression. Some advisors out there even claim, "a brilliantly worded cover letter is the easiest way to assure your resume is the one, amongst a stack of resumes, that gets read."[8]

The chances are that most of your competition will simply "throw" something together from an old cover letter just to have something they can attach to their resume. As a result, these cover letters do nothing to land the job interview beyond checking the proverbial block. As with your resume, be careful not to create a cover letter that is too long. It is easy to stumble into the common mistake of writing a lengthy letter that reads like your resume, just in essay form. Here are some tips that can help to make your cover letter stand out.

First, do not repeat your resume. Since you are already sending your resume, it is redundant to repeat your resume's contents in your cover letter. Hiring managers will already have access to your resume. Instead, use your cover letter to describe additional details that you could not squeeze into that short and concise resume. It is an opportunity to convey your personality, passion, and drive to hiring managers. After reading it, they should have a better idea of who you are.

Second, as with your resume, keep your cover letter short. Ensure it does not exceed one page and keep in mind that less is best—half a page is ideal. Much more, and you risk the hiring manager not reading it. Short and to the point should be your mantra. It should also quickly and precisely summarize your experience and how you are the right person for the position. Finally, finish on a high note. Try to leave the hiring manager with something that will leave them thinking, "Now, this is a strong candidate!"

On the following page, you will find an example template for a cover letter you might use. Keep in mind that you need to tailor this cover letter to meet your needs. Moreover, ensure you consult your targeted company's website to determine if they have any additional guidance for your cover letter. For instance, they may have an online application that allows you to upload your resume but provides fields for you to paste your cover letter or summary. Different companies have different approaches to working with applicants, so take the time to figure out what is required to maximize your chances for success. As with your resume, let some trusted family, friends, or colleagues read your cover letter and offer you their feedback.

Dear <Name>,

I am writing regarding your job opening for <Target Role>. As a candidate with extensive experience in <job title>, I am highly skilled in <Hard Skills in Job Description (JD)>. My solid background in <People Skills> has allowed me to manage teams with exceptional performance.

The opportunity to join <Organization> greatly interests me because <Reasons>. As a holder of <Degrees, Certs>, I can competently execute <JD Responsibilities>.

I believe that I would make a valuable asset to your team, and I offer my resume for your review. As per my professional summary, my qualities and experience make me highly suitable for the role of <Target Role>, which you advertised at <Where Found>.

I am highly regarded for <Transferable Skills>. I am also proficient in <Systems>.

Throughout my career, I have demonstrated the highest levels of service and commitment to the mission of all organizations where I have worked. <List 3-4 achievements relevant to the JD>.

If you are looking for an organized <What or Who >, you are welcome to contact me to arrange an interview. I am eager to discuss how I can contribute to your organization.

I thank you for your time and consideration, and I look forward to your response.

Regards,

<Signature>

Figure 32 - Example Cover Letter

Your Online Presence (Uh-Hum—Your Resume)

Your online presence can lead employers to you, or it can chase them away!

I am going to let you in on a little secret—getting hired is more and more often about your connections, and you are more connected than you think. Technology has reshaped the way we connect and network with people. It also plays a massive role in linking us to opportunities. Beyond staying in touch with friends and family, social media is just as important as your resume. Some may even argue that Google has become your resume.[9]

If someone were to search your name on the internet, what might they find? Many human resource articles will tell you not to think of this as an "if" employers will search you out online, but as a "trust me, they will"! These articles also point out that an employer may, very well, offer a person a job because they like what they found out about the candidate from their social media.

So, instead of networking from the country club or other social event, you can now capitalize on multiple platforms that are all available via the Internet. That said, a little effort online can pay big dividends. Using various networking sites, you can grow your contacts and create a professional network that will help you research and land your next job. Even after you find your next job, your network can continue to keep you aware of current and emerging opportunities. When that happens, you are well on your way to being a job selector.

As of this writing, the three leading social media platforms used by job seekers and employers are, in no particular order, Facebook, LinkedIn, and Twitter. With that in mind, think of a list of characteristics about yourself that you would want a potential employer to walk away with should they ever visit one of your social media profiles. The same applies if you have other publicly assessable information about yourself on the web. For that matter, consider the possibility that your private posts could still become public knowledge. Take it a step further and do a little homework on yourself. What does your online presence say about you? Take some time to search your name on various search engines and see what kind of information is readily available for others to learn about you. Does what you find on the web reflect a picture of the person you want a potential employer to recognize? If not, you have identified some work to do. If so, you may still have some work to do, if only to continue improving your foxhole.

We will talk about your online network in Chapter 7; however, you should start a LinkedIn profile if you have not done so already. While you are there, seek out some of your colleagues and friends and check out their profiles. If they are ahead of you in the transition process, meaning they have already started working at their new job, then try analyzing their LinkedIn profile. Observing your colleagues' profiles may provide you with some great ideas and critical insights for developing your profile. This is especially so if your military buddies performed some same jobs and tasks that you did. Many of them will have some great ways to communicate a similar military experience that potential employers will understand. Modeling aspects of your colleagues' profiles may even help bring recruiters and potential employers to you. It can also start your networking with like-minded professionals, but more on networking later.

Perhaps you are reluctant to start a social profile. That is your decision. However, also consider how perceptions can influence both your and other's opinions. Like it or not, social media plays a part in how others see us, just as social media plays a role in how we perceive others and businesses. For instance, suppose you are considering employing a local company to do some work for you. Did you search for them on the Internet? Did you read any of their reviews? If they had less than four stars, did you delve a little deeper to see why they did not receive a stellar review? What if you could not find any information about them because they have no online presence? Would that raise any suspicions or concerns? It might be enough to make you look elsewhere. I have, and I still do. Frequently, I find out about reputable businesses through online resources, like NextDoor, Google, Facebook, Yelp, etc. If the company had good reviews, then I am far more likely to call them. Another valuable aspect of LinkedIn is the ability to research companies. If you identify a company you are interested in, you can use LinkedIn to determine if anyone in your network has contacts there. Then you can ask them about the company or request an introduction to the hiring manager.

Now, let us flip the script and look at yourself from the employer's perspective. They are looking for talented people, and many people are declaring their skills and experiences on social media for the world to see. It is even better if they have glowing endorsements on their page by others who have worked with them. But, if the employer cannot find anything concerning you online, it could serve as a red flag for them. At the minimum, it adds uncertainty about you. With all this in mind, you should consider whether establishing your brand and social media presence online is something you want to do.

If you create an online profile, then please consider these tips. First, keep it professional. Your profile should highlight your experiences, skills, and professional qualifications. Second, get a picture taken of you in professional attire for your headshot and try to mimic your resume within your profile. Hiring managers often use LinkedIn to search for people who have included vital skills and experience in their profile. Having a professional profile uploaded and ready to review can cause hiring managers to contact you with an opportunity you did not know existed. My experience has been that most of my recruitment contacts have come through LinkedIn. Some resume builders will also pull the contents from your LinkedIn profile and build a resume for you.

However, before you create that profile, I recommend reviewing the Social Media section in Chapter 7 of this book, which covers Networking.

In that section, I summarize various social media platforms and how they can further your career objectives. I will also cover some of the Dos and Don'ts of using social media to ensure you do not limit your career opportunities.

Your Elevator Pitch

> ***No one has any idea what you do unless you tell them. Whether anyone cares afterward depends on your delivery.***

In this game called life, we frequently meet people. We meet them all the time. They represent potential friends, colleagues, or even potential employers. Often these initial encounters are brief. A friend may introduce you to someone they know with similar interests as you, or you may meet someone attending a booth at a job fair. In either situation, you can expect a question like, "Tell me about yourself?" At that moment, you have a brief window to communicate who you are, your interests, and whether you are someone worthy of a follow-up. Welcome to the elevator pitch!

An elevator pitch is a swift description of yourself and what you offer. You can quickly share it whenever you meet someone through work, at a networking event, walking into an office, or at any social event. It is a professional introduction of you that sets the stage for gainful conversations with members of your network and prospective employers. It is also a great answer to keep on standby for interviews when an interviewer asks you to tell them about yourself. Consider it a 30-second commercial that is all about you.

Like any commercial, your elevator pitch needs to tempt potential employers to see you as something they want or need for their business. This makes your pitch an incredibly important part of your job search toolkit. Just like a conversation during an actual elevator ride, your elevator speech needs to be short, 45 seconds at most, but preferably 30 seconds. The real power of a thoughtfully prepared elevator speech is that it markets you by offering a quick summary of your qualifications and skills in such a way as to say who you are, what you are interested in doing, and what makes you valuable to whoever is listening.

With practice, your elevator pitch can become easy to adapt to multiple audiences. Of course, this requires you to know your audience and the job you are aiming to get. Hence, you want to target your speech to an employer's or industry's needs. Likewise, you should be able to explain to an old colleague, or a new connection, in 30-45 seconds just what you are seeking.

Jot down a few bullets for your speech. For instance, what do you offer, and what do you want others to know about you? What are your key strengths, and what problems can you apply your skill sets to solve? Why would you be an asset to a potential employer? Having answered these questions, you can now take each bullet and expand it into a sentence. Now build a paragraph using these sentences and make transitions from one sentence to the next. Once you have completed it, read your elevator pitch aloud and make sure it flows. Feel it out and see if it is what you want to say to potential employers.

Of course, the first few lines of your speech may feel artificial. That is why you need to read it out loud and time it. You may even want to read it to your spouse or a couple of friends once you get the timing down. However, that awkwardness should fade away as you become more comfortable and practiced with your delivery. Remember, your goal is to offer your name, what you are looking for, your most recent position, significant responsibilities, and a brief description of your accomplishments or what you offer. Just make sure you have rehearsed enough to deliver it in a conversational tone and within a 30-second to 45-second window. Afterward, just smile and be yourself!

Chances are, you do not have an elevator pitch prepared at this point. So that is what we are going to work on next. After all, it is an excellent investment that will positively influence your networking effectiveness and overall confidence.

Developing Your Elevator Pitch

The challenge of creating an elevator pitch is making it concise, informative, and capable of telling a story while introducing you. Of course, you may wonder why your elevator pitch must be so short? It comes down to attention span, something for which I am guilty. Maybe you are too? But people can often mentally vacate a conversation in the first 30 seconds of it beginning, sometimes, in just the first few words. Therefore, you need to catch their attention and hold it long enough to communicate a meaningful picture of yourself that they can take with them when they walk away.

That may seem a daunting challenge. Admittedly, it takes practice. But as John Platt puts it in his article, "How to Craft A Winning Elevator Pitch," employers are not looking for a "Director of Whatnot" or a "VP of Whatever." They are looking for an experienced professional who can solve their company's specific challenges. Thus, you must show potential employers, in 30 seconds or less, what you can do for them.

Vague or general statements are the enemies of a good elevator pitch. Hence, merely telling someone you are a salesman or software developer does not, by itself, communicate what it is you do, since titles often fail to concisely tell listeners who you are, how they can help you, how you can help them, or what it is you need from them. Conversely, precise and clear descriptions are your allies in communicating who you are, what you have done, and what you are now looking to do.

Instead of telling hiring managers that you are a salesman, you might try something like the following.

> ***"I'm a sales professional who helps small businesses win big contracts with large corporate and government customers."***

Similarly, instead of telling someone you are a software developer, you might try something like this.

> ***"I'm a team-focused Software Developer specializing in customized software for financial institutions using C/C++, Java, MySQL, and other web technologies to develop highly mobile platforms offering improved user experiences."***

Likewise, instead of introducing yourself as a logistics soldier, you might use the below statement instead.

> ***"I'm a logistic supervisor who specializes in improving efficiency through training to reduce annual, company, production costs while improving lead times for delivering goods to customers."***

These statements much better communicate who you are and what you can do for a prospective employer. What's more is these examples highlight the importance of precisely and concisely describing your goals, so a new contact, potential boss, or recruiter can quickly form an opinion of just where you might fit in their business and begin contributing. Likewise, this is an opportune time to clarify what kind of job you are targeting, precisely, so avoid the urge to state that you are considering anything. By doing so, you let your contact know how they can help you and how you can help them. Okay. We have highlighted the importance of the elevator pitch, and we have explained what it is. You should now start crafting one.

To do so, begin by setting the stage. For instance, consider introducing yourself using some of these statements.

- I recently completed my enlistment in the Army…
- My service obligation in the Marine Corps is nearly complete…

- I am a Signal officer about to retire after 23 years of military service…
- I am an Air Force pilot with over 12 years of experience and looking for new challenges…

You can then move on to highlighting some things that made you exceptional at your position without appearing a braggart.

- It became essential that I become good at…
- My interest in… led me to study extensively…
- I had opportunities to acquire several skills, including…
- I recognized the importance of…
- My position allowed me to develop some valuable insights into…
- I was fortunate to work with remarkable leaders/supervisors who made sure I acquired a wide range of skills, including…
- That position helped me to learn the value of…
- My boss provided me with opportunities to…
- Thanks to several challenging experiences, I learned and became good at…

You also want to address your skills or contributions you offer. These should align with the skills listed on your master resume. We've previously covered skills, but examples may include the following.

- Strategic Thinking
- Operational Planning
- Leadership
- Project Management
- Mechanical Repair

You want to convey your goal to your audience. For instance, you may include statements like what follows.

- I am looking to apply the skills and knowledge I developed over the years toward…
- I hope to work as a [your targeted occupation or position]
- I am seeking a position with a local business where my [particular skills] can make the greatest impact
- I am seeking to explore career opportunities in [targeted career field]

Regardless of the position you are pursuing, be sure to clarify how you provide value in your occupation since not everyone you speak with will be interested in all the technical things you do. According to Savannah Peterson, the founder of Savvy Millennial, your elevator pitch should boil down to answering three things about you.

- What are some unique things about you?
- What need can you [or your company] solve for the prospective employer [or client]?
- Why should you be hired?

Peterson also states that your elevator pitch should fit into the 140-character limit of a tweet—at least before Twitter increased the count to 280 characters a few years ago. If you can get there, then congratulations. I will not claim to have reached this feat myself! However, if Twitter is a part of your stomping grounds, then it might be worth the effort.

Another technique you may find useful in developing your elevator pitch is considering what other colleagues, clients, and supervisors would say about you when asked. Some candid discussions with your friends, family, and colleagues may render some insightful perspectives that you are not considering. Finally, keep in mind, once you have completed your first elevator pitch, you may need to complete this process again to develop others that are customized for different audiences. For instance, you may cultivate one elevator pitch for obtaining potential sources of information from a company's employees by emphasizing your desire to work there. That might lead to you asking about their employer, the work culture, and so on. However, suppose you are speaking with a hiring manager. In that case, you should consider focusing on your most relevant skills that could affect their company, and then seek an informational interview.

My Elevator Pitch

What follows represents one of my first attempts at an elevator pitch. Honestly, the one I show below was already tweaked and rewritten several times. Unfortunately, I did not hold on to all the versions leading to this one. Before attending the U.S. Department of Labor (DOL) employment workshop during Fort Gordon's Soldier for Life—Transition Assistance Program (SFL-TAP), I had never created an elevator pitch. However, once I did, I found many opportunities to use it. The chances are you will too!

> ***I am a transitioning military officer with a Ph.D. in electrical and computer engineering and over 20 years of experience as a program manager, researcher, and educator. I am comfortable performing research, leading teams, and integrating and managing IT infrastructure. My strengths include strategic planning, collaboration, and the ability to manage multi-functional teams. I'm currently looking for opportunities to lead research and development professionals to create solutions, add value, and enhance relationships for stakeholders and teams to create value for program managers in an information technology (or cybersecurity) organization—hopefully with ties to the military or national defense. Likewise, I love the challenge and being part of a team, so I find technical leadership roles the most fulfilling.***

So, what did you think? Did it seem kind of forced? In hindsight, I would say so. Also, did I provide an opening to continue this conversation? Not so much. Fortunately, I read this elevator pitch to someone else while attending the SFL-TAP course. Because of the feedback I received, I updated my elevator pitch to read as follows.

> ***I've recently completed a Ph.D. in electrical and computer engineering specializing in software-defined networks and network security, which I really enjoyed. I'm also finishing over 21 years of military service as an Army Cyber officer, and I'm looking forward to new challenges. Because of my service, I feel I have grown competent as a researcher, integrator, and manager of IT solutions, and I feel comfortable managing cross-functional teams of professionals. These areas have also presented me with opportunities to develop strategic plans, enhance team collaboration, and manage diverse groups. I am currently looking for opportunities to lead research and development professionals to create solutions, add value, and enhance stakeholders' relationships. I would love to chat with you sometime about your ongoing projects. If they involve military ties, all the better.***

Now, what do you think? Undoubtedly, it could be better, but it is an improvement over my original pitch. It flows better, and it opens the door to continue the discussion. Ideally, I could even pass off one of my business cards while mentioning how much I would love to chat again. Just remember, you need to describe what you do if you want someone to be your customer.

Practice, Revise, Hone, Repeat

Once you have your elevator pitch—or at least think you do—it is time to put it to work. No, that probably does not mean you are ready to wade into a crowd of strangers yet. But it is time to sit down with a friend or colleague and practice.

One of the most valuable exercises I experienced at the SFL-TAP class involved group breakout sessions where we practiced delivering our elevator pitch to our group's members. Over half an hour, we each delivered our 45-second pitch with a timer keeping us honest. After each pitch, we gave each other feedback, made changes, and tried it again.

Another option might include doing the same thing but with a speed-date approach where the line shifts to give new faces. This approach can allow you to practice adapting your pitch to new people. By the end of the event, you should feel like your elevator pitch has matured into something you comfortably share with almost anyone. Of course, you do not have to go to that extreme, I probably wouldn't, but you should practice with a friend, colleague, mentor, or coach. It can only help. This not only enables you to grow used to your message, but it also allows you to adapt your conversation. As you see your audience's visual cues, such as drifting off or losing interest, you can respond by modifying your delivery.

Practicing with different people having different backgrounds and careers can also help you learn to tailor your elevator pitch to new people. After all, it is a safe bet that most people you encounter will not have the same response to your pitch. Once you have refined your elevator pitch and practiced it with others, keep practicing on your own. Do so in the mirror and whenever you have some downtime. This will help you grow more comfortable with its delivery, making it more natural. Remember, the goal is realistic and conversational, not overly rehearsed, stiff, and devoid of passion.

6

JOB HUNTING

> *When it comes to getting hired, being the best candidate only matters if you can convince the hiring manager it is so.*

So far, you have taken inventory of your current skill sets; perhaps you are even developing some new ones. You also identified potential career options that align with the considerations you identified in chapter two. Hopefully, you have a solid resume ready to share with potential employers, and you have run through your elevator pitch a few times with one or more people. As an old brigade commander once told me, "if it is worth doing, it is worth rehearsing." Now, with those tools in hand, it is time to start the hunt!

Of course, if you are going hunting, it helps to identify the terrain where your hunt is most likely to succeed. For instance, it's challenging to hunt down a mountain goat when hunting in a swamp. Likewise, if you are fishing for opportunities, then we want those opportunities packed in a barrel. With that analogy in mind, I will spend this chapter introducing you to the terrain and tactics best employed for your job hunt.

As mentioned earlier, there are many sites dedicated to linking job hunters with potential employers. Some are even designated strictly for military members. When you begin your search, you will soon see, as I did, that there are several paths to employment. For instance, many hiring managers have different preferences for how they go about finding talent. Taking these methods into account will assist you in developing a successful job search strategy. Case in point, some employers may choose to formally advertise a vacant position and then go through the laborious process of screening the deluge of resumes until a potential candidate pool emerges. From that pool, the hiring manager then schedules interviews to screen the candidates. Through that process, the right employee is, hopefully, found. This process can be challenging, but nearly all federal and state governments and large corporations hire this way—advertising vacancies online or on paper. In other cases, employers may reach out to colleagues for recommendations to fill their vacant positions, which is one reason to always maintain your connections—especially with those who remember you as a team player.

Three hiring methods include Formal Hiring, Informal Hiring, Talent Hiring

In other cases, these employers may notice talented folks and ask them to consider joining their team. This process is more informal; however, the interview process that follows may still be formal. Many smaller businesses prefer to hire this way, and many career specialists say the informal hiring process encompasses 60% to 75% of new hires. Additionally, 70% to 80% of jobs may never get advertised.[1] These conditions leave 25% to 40% of job seekers competing for only 20% to 30% of advertised jobs. See how terrain can affect your hunt?

Of course, when you have a unique skill set, employers are more likely to consider hiring you as a talent hire, provided they realize your skills and availability. In such cases, the employer may not even have a position open, but they are forward-thinking enough to see how hiring you could affect their company and bring you on, anyway. Hence, you must keep your elevator pitch ready, but keep in mind that talent hires only account for 3% to 5% of all hires. So, here too, the terrain is not ideal, but there is always a chance for that rare encounter that will bring your hunt to an end.

Formal Hiring Process

While you still want to invest some time with formal job searches, especially if you desire a government position, keep the following information in mind. According to the 2017 US Department of Labor (DOL) Workshop Participant Guide, there are five drawbacks to the formal hiring process.

The first drawback is that the total number of advertised positions is much smaller than the actual number of jobs. Advertised positions represent roughly 25% to 40% of the total available. So, if the company you are targeting has 100 jobs open nationwide, the chances are that only 25 to 40 of those positions are advertised. The government, in contrast, tends to announce all its jobs. Of course, you need to be looking for a job when they post it.

The second dilemma you can run into while pursuing advertised positions is the substantial competition they create. Consider for a moment that the hiring manager advertises a job to cast an extensive net. Depending on how the job is advertised and how attractive potential employees see it, you may find yourself swimming in a bottomless pool of candidates. Some candidates may have resumes that more closely mirror the position's requirements. Other candidates may be more gifted at communicating their abilities through their resumes and cover letters. While others still may be extremely polished in their interviewing skills.

Regrettably, these applications must be taken at face value in a process that can be highly subjective. You may be the best candidate; however, your qualities may not immediately stand out in a crowd of candidates with similar qualifications.

For this reason, in his book, “What Color is Your Parachute?” the late Richard Bolles recommends going after the company you are interested in before they advertise a position. This will lead us to some informal approaches to job hunting a little later.

A third issue facing the formal job seeker is simple probability. What do you think the chances are that a job you are interested in will be advertised in a location (let’s say within commuting range) that you desire and matches your specific skill set at the same time you happen to be looking for a job? When you put it that way, your chances might be better than winning the lottery, but still not all that great.

The fourth drawback you must consider when drafting your resume is the dreaded Applicant Tracking System (ATS).[2] As mentioned in chapter five, this system quickly screens out most resumes. That is right. The resume you submit to that advertised position may never even get seen by human eyes. Many application systems scan your resume for keywords or buzzwords that show whether you possess the right skills for the job. If your resume does not contain said buzzwords, say hello to the black hole of tossed resumes. Avoiding the ATS’ scrutiny is one reason you want to carefully read the job’s advertisement and research the company you are targeting. If they are looking for a network operator with a background in Cisco devices, then the words Cisco and certifications, like CCNA, CCNP, etc., should appear on your resume, if you have them. If not, take a Bootcamp course and get one.

An applicant tracking system can toss your resume before human eyes ever see it—build your resume to beat it!

Finally, some employers will automatically eliminate you as an applicant if they observe that you have been unemployed for over six months. So, keep that in mind if you find yourself in this situation. Use some of that time to improve your knowledge base or gain some new skills. Likewise, as the late Stephen Covey, author of "The 7 Habits of Highly Effective People," encouraged, spend some time working on yourself and seeking continuous improvement and renewal. By the way, if you have not done so already, I highly recommend you pick up a copy of Dr. Covey's book. Mastering its habits will make you a more employable person.

As I previously mentioned, the formal hiring process can be complicated. Still, you should not discount it, especially if you are pursuing government employment, have limited connections, or are seeking entry-level positions at large companies. As you are preparing to exit the military, revisit those personal considerations we discussed in chapter two, and with those considerations firmly in mind, start the process.

Formal Job Search

When conducting a formal job search, you want to begin by focusing on the areas where you are willing to relocate or locations where you are ready to commute. Having done this, you next want to identify the employers within those areas. Below are some ways you might do that.

- Visit *usajobs.gov* and perform searches by city and zip code
- Search the National Labor Exchange (NLx) at us.jobs/index.asp for information from corporate job sites, government jobs, and state job banks
- Search job boards like the American Job Center and Veteran Employment Center
- If you are targeting a specific company, visit their website and click on their career tab

- Note any help wanted or hiring now signs as you pass through these areas
- Use LinkedIn.com—it is a powerful tool for finding jobs in various locations and meeting people who are already working in that area
- Use GlassDoor.com—another site to search for jobs by area and much more.

Once you identify potential opportunities, you need to make a strong case for why employers should want you to fill that gap for their organization. Part of doing that will involve more homework. For this task, I found some additional recommendations in the 2017 DOL I referenced earlier.

First, educate yourself on the company and its vacant position. Try to identify the challenges the company is facing and how that relates to the job you are seeking. Second, develop a packet that says, "hire me!" That means make sure you customize your cover letter and resume to the organization's requirements. Use this packet to bring attention to your abilities, knowledge, certifications, and character attributes, so they see you are the candidate they have been seeking. Provide your Situation-Task-Action-Result (STAR) statements so hiring managers can quickly determine your strengths and ability to achieve results. We mentioned the STAR statements in chapter four, but it is worth revisiting. If you knew what a STAR statement was before reading this book, you are already ahead of me when I started this journey. Thankfully, I had some mentors to call my attention to it as I developed my resume. Also, provide statements that focus the reader on what you will do for the organization. Focus on your future contributions and less on what you have done in the past. You can rest on your laurels when you permanently retire. Until then, it's what have you done lately.

Next, be sure to follow the company's instructions for submitting your resume and cover letter. This will often be online through a company web portal with specific format requirements (i.e., Microsoft Word, PDF, etc.). In some cases, you may have to email your resume. In others, you may have to copy and paste portions of it into an online resume builder. Just be sure not to deviate from the instructions or show a lack of attention to detail, or you could find your application heading for that black hole of application rejections. Furthermore, account for the buzzwords the Application Tracking System will undoubtedly seek on your application and resume.

Finally, prepare for the interview. Make sure you have prepared yourself to answer some common interview questions. Know that some non-standard questions may come your way too. Prepare your answers to follow STAR statements. Also, prepare some questions to ask the interviewer. You should design these questions to help you better understand the company's culture and opportunities for advancement. We will discuss this in greater detail later.

Informal Hiring and Unadvertised Positions

As mentioned earlier, many hiring managers, especially those belonging to small businesses, attempt to fill their vacancies through unadvertised positions. This means that these positions will not appear on the Internet, local papers, or other job posting methods. For the most part, these companies prefer to avoid the deluge of unqualified applicants that such postings generate.

Selecting the most promising candidates from such a pool and then interviewing can be a time-consuming process. Moreover, such businesses may not use Applicant Tracking System (ATS) software to screen applicants. Hence, managers or business owners may view advertising for vacant positions as pulling them from their day-to-day duties, which are required to keep their business afloat. Still, resumes and completing interviews often rely on a different skill set than what the actual job vacancy requires.

So, what does all of this mean for you? Ultimately, it means there are many opportunities out there that you and everyone else do not even know about yet. Unfortunately, these opportunities may not yet know about you either. How many times have you sat in a meeting when someone asked a question like this?

> ***"Hey, we're looking for someone to fill a position performing [X]. Does anyone have any recommendations?"***

When I was in the Army, there were many occasions when I sat in a project meeting, and precisely that kind of question came up. Sometimes, it was a contract lead asking his contractors. On other occasions, I was asked directly about specialized positions and vacancies in the government. In my current role, I hear these questions almost weekly. That said, there is just something about a referral that adds weight to a resume when it finally lands on a hiring manager's desk. As a result, hiring managers may reach out to their professional, business, personal, and social networks to find candidates that come with a highly recommended referral.

For you, there are several advantages to pursuing an unadvertised vacancy. For one, there is less competition—people just are not applying to jobs they don't know are available. Second, if your resume enters through this process, then there is a greater likelihood that the hiring manager will see and consider it. Your resume has the added weight of someone's endorsement that the hiring manager knows. This leads us to our third advantage, which is a greater chance of securing an interview and an opportunity to sell yourself.

I am sure you think this is all great, but how do you find out about these positions if they are not advertised? That is a great question. One way is through your work, social, and professional networks. Anyone you know who tells you about a vacancy can potentially put you in touch with a hiring manager. Better yet, they may serve as your reference. Of course, this requires you to actively inform family, friends, colleagues, and acquaintances that you are looking for a position. You should also let them know what kind of job you are seeking.

You can also reach out to select employees at a company of interest via email or phone and schedule a visit. I emphasize scheduling a visit. Do not just show up on someone's doorstep unannounced. Keep in mind that they are busy people with a job to do, and they probably have not planned for some random stranger to just drop in on them. They may find it creepy or just inconsiderate. You have been warned.

However, suppose you can schedule a 15-minute appointment and stick to the requested timeframe. In that case, you could learn some valuable information about the company, like whether any positions are vacant and if your skills align with the opening. If you are unsure about the required skills, you can ask how employees develop those skills before assuming the position. In other cases, where jobs do not require specialized skills and turnover is high, you may find yourself with a job offer. Just pay attention to the fact that turnover is high. There is probably a good reason.

Now is an excellent time to identify some essential tasks for pursuing an unadvertised position. Here are some pointers.

1. Select from your existing personal, social, and business contacts some key folks you can reach out to. You might find your Facebook, LinkedIn, Gmail, Yahoo, Outlook, and Twitter accounts helpful for completing this task. Your list does not have to be too selective, but you want to keep your list manageable and filled with people who will advocate for you. Once your list is complete, contact these individuals, and let them know you would appreciate their help in making you aware of any opportunities you are suited to fill. Send them a copy of your resume.

2. Make some guesses about what companies might look for some new hires. Did a contract company just win a bid at the post where you are stationed? That might indicate they are looking to hire. Other signs that a company is ready to hire include signs that they are growing, busy, or suffering high turnover. Bonus if they have positions or requirements for which you are uniquely qualified.
3. Educate yourself about the vacant position once you learn about it. Be sure to ask those you contact about what else you should know about the job. You can also ask what would help make you a stronger candidate?
4. Seek to set up some informational interviews with a few company insiders. They can tell you about the company's culture, work/life balance, work challenges, and whether they like the company themselves.
5. With this information, customize your application package so that your cover letter and resume address the specific certifications, education, skills, experiences, and traits that the company seeks. Do not forget to convey this information as STAR statements and tell your potential employer what you will do for them.
6. Pinpoint who the key decision-makers are by using your social network, the company's website, some search engine, an email, or a few phone calls. Once you have identified these individuals, ensure your resume ends up in their hands by either delivering it personally (remember, don't just show up), mailing or emailing it, or asking a contact inside the company to deliver it for you.

After waiting a few days to a week, follow up with the hiring manager to ensure they received your resume and reviewed its contents. Also, ask for an informal conversation and set a reasonably short timeframe to meet. While not a formal interview, if you get this far, make sure you prepare potential answers highlighting your past accomplishments and experiences.

Identifying Talent Hire Opportunities

One of the less frequent hiring outcomes occurs when you can convince a hiring manager who is not actively looking to fill a position to hire you, anyway. In such cases, the manager sees you as someone who will significantly affect their business. When I first heard of this hire, it reminded me how some high-ranking officers seem to get picked up as soon as they retire. I would frequently listen to them say, "I got picked up because of my Rolodex"—that is a list of contacts for my millennial readers. Still, I do not envy these folks. Far more frequently, they also carry strong leadership qualities and organizational skills that make them invaluable to any organization.

A talent-hire method might be employed for other job seekers when companies cannot find a suitable advertised or unadvertised vacancy. In such cases, these companies may hire headhunters or reach out to you directly, provided they know about you. If you are trying to get a company to notice you, then here are some recommendations adapted from the 2017 DOL Guide.

First, consider offering yourself as a substitute for one of the company's key employees. For instance, the company may have a highly skilled employee who might bring greater value to the company by putting more time toward specialized work if freed up from less technical tasks. Ultimately, this could improve productivity for the company. Hence, a new administrative assistant hire can free up salespeople to focus on sales. A new operations manager hire can free up project managers to focus on completing projects.

Secondly, you could offer the company new skills and abilities to improve their operations to produce greater profits. Perhaps you have some Lean Six Sigma experience that can boost productivity, increase throughput, and reduce inventories. As a veteran, you have a track record for mitigating risks that could help a company improve its safety record. You also have a mission focus on achieving the objective that can lead to shorter lead time requirements. You might also be someone who can develop efficient training schedules that reduce the time it takes for new employees to add value to the team.

To better position yourself to receive a talent hire offer, put on your marketing hat, and consider the recommendations below. If a hiring manager is to reach out to you, they first need to know you exist.

- Grow and use your personal, social, and professional networks. Use these contacts to learn as much about your target company as possible to understand the challenges they face and their key drivers, constraints, resources, etc. Likewise, make sure you know what problems they are trying to solve along with the opportunities they are pursuing.
- Seek informational interviews and conduct online research to determine which employers can use your skills. Rather than going for the 'hard sell' of telling someone you are looking for a job and asking for introductions, an informational meeting provides a soft-sell approach. It allows you to ask for information and for your interviewee to share their story. It will enable you to gain advice for your job search and career journey. Happy employees like talking about what made them successful.

Develop a system for reaching out to people and decision-makers who are not in your network (cold contacts) and schedule some face time with them. At these meetings, be prepared to discuss your ideas for helping their company grow and make money. Great recommendations may even justify your hire.

Paths Through Volunteer Service

Do you have a generous streak? It turns out that your goodwill could be a path to employment. According to the 2017 DOL Guide, research shows that volunteers have a 27% greater chance of finding a position than non-volunteers nationally, while rural volunteers have a 55% chance of finding employment. Not to mention, this is an excellent opportunity to give back to your community and serve the causes important to you.

The benefits of volunteering include additional experience and a greater number of network contacts, leading to a more significant number of opportunities. However, not all volunteering opportunities are created equal for employment. Consider choosing volunteer opportunities based on your experience, skills, and employment objectives. Similarly, suppose you do not possess the experience required to qualify for the job you want. In that case, you can also use volunteering opportunities to develop or improve the skills you need and create connections.

Many opportunities exist for volunteering. Local churches are always in need of talented members to exercise their gifts. Local veteran groups could use your leadership skills. Needs truly abound. The 2017 DOL Guide also suggests that you seek AmeriCorps, a service organization allowing people of all ages to gain skills while solving community challenges. Some full-time members also receive a modest living allowance, health care benefits, and childcare assistance. Visit www.AmeriCorps.gov/veterans for more information.

Helpful Organizations and Advocates for Veteran Job Hunters

You may already know of many job-hunting sites, like glassdoor.com, indeed.com, simplyhired.com, and many others. You can upload your resume on these sites, and these sites can help connect you to potential jobs. There is undoubtedly value to using these sites, and I used them to upload my resume. Because of these sites, I have and continue to receive queries about potential job opportunities. However, there are also many sites dedicated to helping veterans find jobs, and they work with companies that want to hire veterans. I discuss a few you might consider below.

FedsHireVets: Veteran Employment Program Offices (VEPO)

If you are looking for Federal employment, consider the Federal agency Point of Contact (POC) list.[3] These POCs promote the recruitment, employment, training and development, and retention of veterans within their respective agencies. As a veteran, consider reaching out to these POCs for specific information on employment opportunities within their agency. It is their job to help YOU find a suitable federal job. Let them!

SACC

The Service Academy Career Conference (SACC) group is solely administered and supported by the Alumni Associations and Association of Graduates of the U.S. Military Academy, the U.S. Naval Academy, the U.S. Air Force Academy, the U.S. Coast Guard Academy, and the U.S. Merchant Marine Academy. This group is only for service academy alumni, and you must be a graduate of one of the above institutions to benefit from their service.[4] If you are, it is an excellent resource for you.

MOJO

Military Officer Job Opportunities or MOJO is another site, comparable to SACC, which attempts to pair degreed military veterans with civilian leadership opportunities. This organization coordinates career fairs and job posting opportunities. Specifically, MOJO tries to support the development of transitioning officers, senior/staff NCOs, and student veterans and prepare them for success in the job market. MOJO's career fairs are also scheduled in upscale venues, hosting 200-250 candidates and 40-50 companies at each hiring event. Their flagship DC MOJO accommodates 350-450 candidates and 70-75 employers. During these events, MOJO offers career workshops, a Women Veterans Roundtable, and a networking reception where employers and job seekers can socialize before the job fair and hopefully make a few connections.

TrackAhead

Another site is TrackAhead. This site combines self-discovery and career exploration into a simple, user-friendly web interface. Their activities are supposed to help you discover your career personality and work style, which TrackAhead uses to help match you with companies that best fit you.

Cleared Connections

Cleared Connections is an online resource for security-cleared professionals. If you have held U.S. Security Clearance within the past 24 months, you can register on their site at ClearedConnections.com. You can network your skills and achievements on the site by creating a free Public or Confidential resume profile. Many top employers are continually looking for security-cleared professionals. However, many of the U.S. Government Contractors and Agencies that use ClearedConnections.com are often prohibited from posting their job ads publicly because of security restrictions. ClearedConnections.com lets you create a free Job Seeker Account on their website. Hiring representatives recruiting for these classified positions can then view your resume and then contact you directly! Check out Cleared Jobs at https://clearedjobs.net/seeker-home.

Career Fairs

Career fairs are an excellent way to experience many different types of companies, and you should consider attending them early in your job search to get a "lay of the land" without the expectation of landing a job. They also present an excellent opportunity to connect with potential employers. However, arrive at these events with a plan. By doing a bit of reconnaissance beforehand, you can save time and focus your efforts on the recruiters you want to meet. While this prep has an upfront time commitment, arriving at the fair with a plan can help you make the most of an opportunity.

As a part of your preparation, consider these steps. First, identify the top five or six companies of most interest to you. Second, go to each of their websites, identify what positions are available, and identify those of interest to you. Third, create a profile on those sites and apply for the listed jobs (apply to at least one opening). Finally, develop some discussion points for when you meet the recruiter at the career fair and mention that you recently applied to their company.

On the day of the career fair, try to arrive a couple of hours before the event starts. This will allow you to identify recruiters' locations. However, depending on the venue's size, keep in mind that recruiting teams may be hesitant to schedule on-site interviews with candidates they initially meet. Still, you do not want to wait too long either since recruiters can grow tired after standing for hours, and their fatigue can make it difficult for them to give you the attention you deserve.

One recommendation is to reach out to the recruiters about one to two hours after the event begins when they hit their stride. When you do, have a plan for your discussion. Let them know about your passions, skills, and desire. Aim the conversation toward your ideal position. Furthermore, before visiting your targeted companies, you may want first to visit a few companies you are less interested in to help you "warm-up" or "rehearse" your elevator pitch and approach. When you feel more confident, engage the companies you are targeting—this is a technique one of my mentors recommended.

You should also review your resume and make sure you are carrying multiple paper copies with you. You should also have an electronic copy on your smartphone, so you can directly email a copy to any recruiters or managers who ask for it. Doing so also allows recruiters access to links you provide on your resume, like an email or LinkedIn profile. Many organizations are going paperless, so carrying an electronic copy will keep you from being surprised if a recruiter asks for that instead of your paper copy.

What about your attire? Even if the job you are applying for does not require their employees to wear a shirt and tie, still do so. Remember, this is an opportunity to communicate to a potential employer your interest in their company, so dress for success! Also, do not forget to bring breath mints. If things go well, you will talk a lot. Likewise, do not forget to bring a handkerchief. With the "shirt and tie" and nerves kicking in, you may need to dab your brow a few times.

Finally, be positive and smile! Let the recruiters know that you will contribute to the company's personality and work environment. Avoid speaking poorly about your current or previous employer. That is a dead giveaway you will do the same to them when the chance arises. Instead, invest the opportunity to convince them you are the right person for their company. They do not just want your competence; they want a teammate and someone who fits into the companies' culture. Be genuine and show them you are the right fit!

Recruiters/HeadHunters

When looking for a job, reach out and let recruiters know you are available. Recruiters, headhunters, or search consultants are hired or contracted by companies to find candidates for them, and they often know about unadvertised jobs. Since they usually only get paid if you get hired, they can be great allies in the job-hunting process.

It is important to note that recruiters rarely charge the job seeker. Instead, hiring companies pay the fee, typically after a candidate is hired. When contacting a recruiter, confirm they are working to fill the positions you are seeking. You will usually find that many headhunters are open about salary ranges, locations, start dates, and other unique characteristics about the jobs they are filling. Once you have the information you need, you can send a resume and cover letter just as though you were applying for a job. If a recruiter calls you, call them back—even if you are not currently job hunting. You never know when circumstances might change, and you might gain a valuable ally in your job search later.

Military Employment Readiness Programs

The Employment Readiness Program (ERP) helps families meet the challenges associated with career planning and job search by providing expert help and resources through a cohesive and standardized employment support program. What is convenient for you is almost every military base across the U.S. has one. Also, military personnel transitioning out of the service and their spouses coming into a new area looking for work can take full advantage of their services.

ERPs offer many services for service members and spouses. For instance, Military retirees and eligible dependents can register at their local ERP at no cost to receive notices about new career opportunities with local companies (or other locations). Often, ERPs know of career opportunities before the news gets publicized. When visiting an ERP, you might find typical resources at an ERP include online job search tools, a resource library, a computer lab, free WI-FI, and fax services.

Other services available at ERPs include expert resume assistance and help with job applications, interview preparation, education training, volunteer opportunities, and career counseling. You may even find support for local job market research, home business opportunities, on-and-off post job listings, career counseling, job notification referral lists, and an employment and education resource library. Spouses who plan to register for the Priority Placement Program (PPP) should also contact the local ERP. If you are curious, PPP is an automated placement program used to match eligible, well-qualified employees facing displacement with vacant positions.

ERPs also work with industry, allowing local and national companies to submit job postings. If you file your resume with your ERP, they will forward your resume to companies whose job postings match your skill sets. It's a win-win for everyone! ERPs work with industry to support job fairs, company presentations, and other events that you can take part in so long as you contact them.

Finding Nearby Employment Readiness Programs (ERPs)

To find an ERP near you, conduct an Internet search on "military bases in (your area)" or "Military Employment Readiness Program in (your area)" or look up the ERP for a specific base. For example, you could search Quantico, Andrews AFB, NAS Patuxent River, Fort Meade, Aberdeen Proving Ground, FT Bliss, Indian Head, and so on.

Other Army Family Employment Programs

Soldier for Life Transition Assistance Program (SFL-TAP)

The Soldier for Life Transition Assistance Program (formerly known as ACAP) is the primary employment liaison for transitioning service members. Their Job Searching Strategies Workshop assists job seekers in getting a jump start with their job search. They provide information on contract opportunities, local job search engines, on and off post-employment, the Military Spouse Employment Partnership Program, and much, much more.

Boots2Business

Of course, the military also offers other transition programs. Consider the Small Business Association's Boot to Business Program. Boots to Business (B2B) is an entrepreneurial education and training program offered by the U.S. Small Business Administration (SBA) as part of the Department of Defense Transition Assistance Program (TAP). Their site includes a short video introducing veterans and leaders to the B2B program, one of three individual training tracks available to veterans before transitioning. You should contact your Transition Service Manager for this and other transition-related programs. See https://sbavets.force.com for more information.

Spouse Education and Career Opportunities (SECO)

The Spouse Education and Career Opportunities (SECO) is one program offered by Military OneSource for military spouses.[5] This program provides education and career guidance to military spouses worldwide. SECO's services include employment assistance, education, training, financial aid, and state occupational license/credential requirements. It also offers comprehensive resources and tools to support career readiness with interview skills, resume building, and links to employment sources, for example, Military Spouse Employment Partnership (MSEP) and USA jobs.

Military Spouse Career Advancement Account (MyCAA)

A Military Spouse Career Advancement Account (MyCAA) is offered to eligible military spouses by the OSD, the Spouse Education, and

Career Opportunities (SECO) program is restricted to active duty E1-E5 spouses W1-W2, and O1-O2 serving on Title 10 orders. Financial assistance is limited to $4,000. Recipients of this assistance must also repay the amount within three years of the first start date of the first class. Recipients can only use financial aid to support an associate degree, occupational license, or credential. For more information, visit Military OneSource.

Military Spouse Employment Partnership (MSEP)

Military Spouse Employment Partnership (MSEP) is an expanding partnership between military spouses seeking employment and corporate businesses committed to providing meaningful and portable careers. At the MSEP website, military spouses are encouraged to search for employment opportunities and post resumes. Military Spouses interested in this program should search for MSEP Partners.

The Virtual Career Library

The Virtual Career Library offers access to over 6,000 digital pages of career guidance information. You will find hundreds of resources like career advice videos, virtual job data cards, job bank resources, digital career books and directories, and occupational videos to help you achieve career and life success.

Passport Career

Passport Career helps individuals with their international job search by providing detailed, country-specific resources on all aspects of the job search and alternative opportunities. Content includes detailed guidance on local styles and expectations for resumes and CVs, interviews, salaries, work permits, business culture, best employers, and more. First-time users should go to Passport Career, click "Have a Registration Key?" at the upper right corner of the page, and enter army5678 as your key. Complete and submit the brief registration form. You will receive a passport by email. Visit https://www.passportcareer.com/.

7

NETWORKING

> *If you want to go fast, go alone. If you want to go far, go with others. —African Proverb*

Did you know some statistics show that only 5-7% of non-technical jobs are found on the Internet, while only 15-30% of jobs get advertised at all? That really must make you wonder, where are the other 70-85% of jobs found?

Okay. I know I have already emphasized that networking is a critical aspect of finding those unadvertised positions we spoke of in chapter five. However, let me clarify and reemphasize this. Even as an introvert, I cannot stress enough just how powerful a tool networking is in your job-hunting endeavors. Networking is the game-changer that can move you from being a job *seeker* to a job *selector*.

Networking gives you unprecedented access to resources that will allow you to discover, research, and connect with a more significant number of employment opportunities. In my own experience, networking was my single greatest ally in uncovering potential jobs. Networking is not the same as asking for a job. All it means is connecting and talking to others—either formally or informally—about your job search and career goals.

> ***Networking is the game-changer that can move you from being a job seeker to a job selector.***

More times than not, your networking contacts will not even be potential employers, or they may be an employer who is not looking to hire today. However, growing your network can give you access to inside information about newly created jobs. Employers who are not hiring today may look to hire someone like you later. As a result, networking can help you tap into the "hidden network" of jobs that never get advertised or are hard to find.

As you build your network, make sure you develop clear goals for your job search. Identify what you want others to know about you and what you want to know about them. With that in mind, make sure you are ready to answer some basic questions. For instance, a common question you might get is what kind(s) of a job(s) are you looking for?

While there are many correct answers to this question, one you should steer away from is "I'm looking for anything" or "I'll do anything" or anything else that is not specific.

Hopefully, you have already covered most of these in your elevator pitch but prepare other questions. Consider these:

- What experience or skills qualify you for these jobs?
- What industry are you considering?
- Are you set on working for a company?
- To which areas/locations would you consider relocating?

Something else you may not think of is that people in your network often get rewarded for providing their assistance to you. For instance, many organizations offer their employees bonuses for recommending someone they end up hiring. With that in mind, check with some of your contacts and see if that is the case. Regardless, if they seem amenable to it, ask if they might shop your resume around their company to see if it draws any interest. This may cause HR to reach out to you about a job offer if your contact passes your resume to the right person. Of course, you can consider it a bonus if your efforts result in your meeting with the hiring manager.

Finally, if you are still actively serving, do what you can to maintain your relationships with your friends and colleagues after they transition. For them, you could prove a tie that keeps them connected to the life they once knew. For you, it means you have scouts going out into the civilian sector ahead of you. All of them can provide you with useful information as you begin your transition. For me, I remember being disappointed when I reached out to an old active-duty colleague—one I considered a friend—to be a contact for my clearance review. He turned out to be too busy to take any of my calls or return them, so I dropped the request and moved on to others. While you may have a few similar experiences, many other colleagues will be happy to provide whatever support they can. So, make sure you build your contact list and keep it updated. However, not all contacts are the same, so we will spend a page or two identifying the connections you might already possess or need to develop.

Types of Contacts

> ***Opportunities know how to find you when the people you know also know what you do.***

According to the 2017 DOL Guide, there are four types of contacts. These include sources, recommenders, hiring decision-makers, and linkers.

Sources are pretty much anyone you know who has insider

information about a company or organization. These folks can tell you about whether the company is looking at new hires, who the hiring decision-makers are, and what skills are needed. They can even tell you about pay, advancement opportunities, and the work environment and culture. Their input can help you decide if the company is right for you.

Recommenders are those special contacts who will go to bat for you. They are willing and able to set up a meeting between you and the decision authority for hiring. They might do this directly or pass along your resume with a recommendation. If they are what I like to call your champion, they may write a letter of recommendation or serve as your reference. Such people are exceptional since they work at the company, and they will put their reputation on the line to vouch for you. For such folks, never forget to show your gratitude.

Hiring Decision-makers are those business owners or senior members in an organization who can make—you guessed it—hiring decisions. If you have someone like this in your corner and have the skills they need, then life on the job hunt trail is looking up.

Linkers are people who may put you in contact with one of the other contacts listed above, Sources and Recommenders, but sometimes Hiring Decision-makers. Most of your contacts are likely linkers, and second or third-order at that, meaning they can link you to other linkers that may be better connected.

If you were to evaluate all your contacts now, the chances are you probably have a good number of Linkers and Sources and a few Recommenders. Perhaps you know some Hiring Decision-makers. Some of these contacts might also serve multiple roles, being a Source for one opportunity and a Recommender for another.

Now that we have identified some of these contacts, let's conduct a quick exercise. Pull out a sheet of paper and brainstorm about all the people you know and interact with regularly. Keep in mind, they may not precisely know what you do, but you can provide them with the details as you explore your options. Here are some people you might initially consider:

- Relatives
- Active military members (supervisors, peers, and subordinates)
- Retired military members (supervisors, peers, and subordinates)
- Local and out-of-town friends
- Current and past neighbors
- Friends of your parents and parents of your children friends
- Informal or interest groups (e.g., hobbies, sports, teams, health club, etc.)
- Teachers
- Staff at your Military Transition Office
- Former co-workers, employers, or supervisors

Social Media

As we mentioned in chapter four, the leading social networking sites, at least, as of this publication, are LinkedIn, Facebook, and Twitter. One of these even dominated the spotlight during the 2016 Presidential Elections. Many argue that President Donald Trump used Twitter masterfully to rally his voter base. It was not uncommon for various journalists to comment on how then Mr. Trump had mastered Twitter in a way that no president ever has before. He used it as a tool for political promotion, distraction, and more.

Social media can also be a powerful ally in helping you to reach your target audience: potential employers. Using these resources, job hunters can stalk (perform due diligence), seek job openings, learn about company culture, establish themselves as subject matter experts, identify hiring managers, and connect with company associates. You can often find links to a company's social media sites on its web page.

Your first step is to establish your online presence, but carefully select what you reveal about yourself. It is common for people you meet at networking events or sites to also search for you online. Your actions here will serve as your social networking foundation. LinkedIn, Facebook, and Twitter are all useful tools for this. You may also notice that Instagram—which has over one billion monthly users—has become a popular place for job seekers, along with authors, jewelry makers, artists, and other professionals. But be judicious about which profiles you make publicly available since you must keep them all updated. You want to portray a consistent message across them all. For instance, make sure they all include the jobs and titles you have held along with your dates of employment. Ideally, your online presence will affirm what people learn about you from your resume and offer a little more.

Once you have established your online presence, it is time to build your network. As we previously discussed, these connections will serve as Linkers, Sources, Recommenders, and even Hiring Decision-makers. While I hesitate to turn down many networking requests, search out your network connections placing quality over quantity. Doing so will allow you to focus your time on your most promising connections. One approach I took was seeking people I previously worked with who held jobs I found interesting. I also sought people I didn't know directly but had some common connections with and worked in my field or in locations where I sought employment.

You may gradually add hiring decision-makers to your network, either directly connecting with them or using the requisite messaging. One of your Linkers might also arrange an introduction. Just do not be creepy. Let them know you want to learn more about their company's perspective, and don't let the first contact you have with them be a "Will you hire me?" kind of situation. Remain tactful. As your network grows, so will the number of links to potential employment opportunities. These links may also connect you to those unadvertised or talent-hire positions we spoke of earlier. Of course, the key to having your network inform you of these positions is to let others know you're looking. The best way to do that is to advertise it.

In my case, I changed my job title on LinkedIn to Transitioning Officer. The benefit of doing this was I let everyone who saw my profile know I was leaving the service and looking for employment. As a result, I found a few champions who helped me search for new opportunities and even contacted companies and organizations on my behalf. As my job search continued, I started to see research scientist and instructor positions as my best options. As a result, I ensured all my previous publications made it onto my profile. I also included my skills that were related to the jobs I was seeking. As a result, I soon received connection requests and inquiries from recruiters looking to fill these types of positions.

Finally, no introduction to social media would be complete without introducing the hashtag (#), a pound sign (#) followed by a word or phrase. It serves to identify and group messages on a similar topic. When you click on a hashtag, it allows you to view all the posts on the platform using that hashtag. You can use them to group your posts under a hashtag or find desired groups. Hashtags that may interest you include #remotework, #remotejobs, #clearedjobs, and #jobs. Also, do not use commas to separate hashtags in your posts.

LinkedIn (www.linkedin.com)

LinkedIn is probably the single greatest asset for the veteran job seeker. If you have not yet joined the LinkedIn crowd, then here is a quick overview of this social networking site. LinkedIn is a fantastic resource for helping you build your professional identity and develop your professional network. For premium members, you can even use it to gain new skills through their education portal, Linked Learning. As of this writing, LinkedIn offers a free one-year subscription to its Premium Career services to all veterans. If you are in the throes of a job hunt and are looking to improve your odds, LinkedIn can help you. However, before seeking to use LinkedIn's premium features, you need to set up a basic account. Once you set up the account, you can submit a request to have it upgraded to LinkedIn's premium service.

With LinkedIn's premium subscription, you gain several benefits over their standard free subscription. First, the premium subscription helps get you noticed by recruiters. Yes, they have algorithms working behind the scenes that help push your LinkedIn profile to the forefront of recruiters' searches. It will even tell you how often searchers viewed your profile. Second, while the free service allows you to build a network and stay abreast of new jobs, a premium account will enable you to apply to new jobs and access application statistics. You can even see just how your skills stack up against other applicants. Finally, the premium service grants you access to over 6000 courses via the LinkedIn Learning portal, which covers business, marketing, technical skills, and much more. The classes are one reason I still have a premium account with LinkedIn today. You can register for LinkedIn's veteran program at https://linkedinforgood.linkedin.com/programs/veterans/premiumform.

LinkedIn also offers several tutorials that will assist you in making the most of your LinkedIn Profile. You can find complete tutorials at https://premium.linkedin.com/#li-courses.

Some resources you will find are listed below.

- How to Build Your Professional Brand
- LinkedIn Profile Checklist
- Be a Recruiter Magnet with an Optimized LinkedIn Profile
- How to Optimize Your Profile for Job Search Success
- How to Write Status Updates that Attract Opportunities
- How to Write Emails that Get Results
- Sparking a Company Courtship with LinkedIn

If you are completely new to LinkedIn, I recommend watching the one-hour tutorial that LinkedIn offers veterans. The tutorial will teach you to create and optimize your profile to ensure recruiters can find you. It also teaches you how to use LinkedIn to gain insights into building a professional network that supports your career objectives and finding jobs. See the tutorial here:

https://www.linkedin.com/learning/linkedin-for-veterans-2/welcome

LinkedIn even offers tutorials that will help you translate your military skills into readily identifiable terms. Fortunately, the folks at LinkedIn have realized that civilian employers are looking for employees who possess the skill sets of veterans. LinkedIn also recognizes that companies cannot identify potential veteran candidates because of language barriers. Hence, LinkedIn developed a course to help veterans articulate their skills so that civilian employers can identify the skills of interest to them. Visit the link below to watch the tutorial LinkedIn put together.

https://www.linkedin.com/learning/translating-your-military-skills-to-civilian-workplace

Do you think you could benefit from a mentor—someone who has been where you are and is now thriving? LinkedIn has started a Veteran Mentor Network. The network's mission is to help service members, spouses, and veterans create and achieve their life and career goals. As of this writing, this group has over 110,000 members, and this network serves to allow veteran job seekers to reach out and ask career-related questions to a community of supportive peers and advisors. Some members even share their resumes to the site and request critical feedback. You can join this group by visiting:

https://www.linkedin.com/groups/4466143/

One last note on LinkedIn. Many of your well-meaning colleagues will agree that LinkedIn is a potent tool for a job seeker; however, there is still a lot you must do and avoid doing when you start your account. Get it wrong, and you could reduce your employment opportunities. Unfortunately, too many transitioning veterans make serious mistakes with their profiles.[1] For instance, starting an account and not using it could cause potential employers to stereotype you as technologically inept. A small number of connections may also indicate you are not savvy enough to capitalize on LinkedIn's capabilities. It is also not a good idea to use LinkedIn like you would a Facebook account. For instance, LinkedIn is not where you want to share your pets' images, nor is it a place to spread personal, political, or religious posts. I usually include my religious affiliations on my profile, but I do not want to work at a place that cannot accept that about me either. Still, treat every post you make on LinkedIn as though you are sending it to your future supervisor or employer.

Here are some additional recommendations to help you improve your LinkedIn profile.

1. Use a career-appropriate photo. Your military uniform is probably fine while you are on active duty; however, as soon as you add Transitioning Veteran to the headline of your LinkedIn page, it's time to show a photo that reflects your career interests.
2. Use military and civilian work experience relevant to your career objectives and the types of positions you seek.
3. Locate the companies you are interested in on LinkedIn and routinely visit their profiles to stay abreast of their announcements, news, and signs they are hiring.
4. Join LinkedIn groups connected to your desired profession or career. Follow these groups and contribute as you are able. Doing so will help to establish your brand and competence in your chosen

career field. Likewise, become familiar with the subject matter experts and thought leaders within these groups.

5. Reach out to others you are connected with or have access to through your network. Ideally, they will have similar occupations to you or work at companies of interest to you. You don't always have to join their network; you can message them, but long-term connections are helpful.
6. Add an appropriate short text summary to your profile. This summarized profile will reflect your current job title unless you amend it. When a recruiter sees yours, they could see "Army Officer, Warrant Officer, Noncommissioned Officer," or they could see "Transitioning Cybersecurity Professional Seeking Opportunities in Florida and Georgia."
7. Make your skills list relevant. LinkedIn allows you to select skills that other LinkedIn members can validate.
8. Obtain recommendations that lend weight to your profile. They show that someone thinks enough of you to spend their time writing an endorsement for you. That said, do not be stingy with your endorsements either. If you know folks who do splendid work, let the world know!
9. Customize your URL. LinkedIn provides a URL to your page that you can include on your resume or send to potential employers; however, it may not be a URL that is easily associated with you. What you can do is update your LinkedIn URL to something personalized, like https://www.linkedin.com/in/yourname/.
10. Demilitarize your LinkedIn profile. As with your resume, tailor your profile to a non-military audience. Visitors to your profile still need to understand your positions, responsibilities, and accomplishments without having personal knowledge of military vernacular.

Facebook (www.facebook.com)

While China and India remain the most populous countries globally, they were surpassed by Facebook in 2014 in terms of sheer numbers. A recent article by Salman Aslam, titled "Facebook by the Numbers: Stats, Demographics & Fun Facts," observes that Facebook now boasts over 2 billion active users each month. Additionally, 71% of online American adults use Facebook, so the chances are you (or several people you know) are already active participants on Facebook. According to the Pew Research Center, half of all adult Facebook users have over 200 friends in their networks. Facebook, themselves, has calculated that the degrees of separation from you to pretty much any other person on Facebook through your connections is 3.57. Hence, Facebook is also a powerful networking tool for helping you land that next job.

Of course, you may just be using Facebook to keep up with your friends and family. However, with what we have learned about networking, each of your connections on Facebook—along with their contacts—are people who may possess information on employment opportunities or details about companies you are targeting. So do not keep your job search and transition plans a secret. Your friends and family cannot help you if they do not know you plan to leave the military and are actively searching for employment opportunities. Instead, let your contacts know about the work you are looking for, along with the skill and experience you can offer an employer.

If you use your Facebook presence to aid your job search, we must address a few other items. First, ensure that your Facebook profile information—specifically the about section—is accurate and up to date. Make sure it is professional. Second, make sure the pictures and posts that you make publicly accessible will not cause an employer to become concerned about your professionalism, risk aversion, or ability to fit in and succeed at their company. Assume everything you post is publicly available while you are at it. Third, while you may opt for the highest privacy restrictions on your Facebook profile, consider making your education and employment history publicly accessible. This will help employers fill in gaps about you beyond what they find when reviewing your resume or job application. Finally, you can also seek company profiles on Facebook and "Like" the company, explore its content, and stay abreast of its activities.

Twitter *(www.twitter.com)*

Twitter is an online news and social networking service where users post and respond to brief messages, known as "tweets." Anyone can read tweets; however, only registered users can post tweets. Compared to other social media platforms, like LinkedIn, Twitter may get overlooked as a job search tool. Yet, in 280 characters or less, this platform can also aid your job search efforts.

Twitter users can send tweets to large audiences, which has several advantages. For instance, you can use it to find hidden job leads, network with industry leaders, build your brand, and research companies and interviewers. However, it is helpful to approach Twitter with a strategy for achieving your employment goals.

For one, make sure your Twitter handle is something professional. Make sure your profile highlights your relevant experiences. Since you already began identifying potential companies and hiring managers earlier, you can use Twitter to find them and follow their tweets. By following these tweets, you can quickly learn about company expansions, hiring trends, new directions, and new opportunities. Often, you can learn about these new opportunities well before the company posts them. As with LinkedIn, you can also follow the employees of the companies you are targeting. They can be a great source of insider information about potential new hiring opportunities.

As far as your tweets go, you can show your professional knowledge and interests by periodically tweeting about relevant articles that align with your background and career track. Similarly, you can reply to tweets that others post, re-tweet (yes, that is a thing) sage advice, or use Twitter's direct-messaging tool to strengthen your connections. Other options include taking part in Twitter chats or online forums of professional interest to offer words of wisdom about your own experience.

Another aspect of Twitter I mentioned earlier is the hashtag (#), and Twitter also uses them to identify keywords and topics. In fact, Twitter is the birthplace of the hashtag. Chris Messina, a social technology expert at Twitter, was credited with the first hashtag in August 2007. Just search for "#barcamp" on the Internet.

If you are going to a networking event, job fair, or conference, you can use Twitter and its hashtags to seek others attending the event. Once you identify other attendees, you can arrange face-to-face meetings or get additional information about the event. Note that hashtags are used in Facebook social media as well. Other popular hashtags you may wish to consider are shown below.

#nowhiring
#veterancareers
#verteranjobs
#freelance

#<event_name>
#jobposting
#hr
#postgrad

#itjobs
#techjobs
#sales
#govjobs

Many other online references exist to help you make the most of your Twitter account. Just search online for topics like "Twitter jobs," "Twitter resume," and "Twitter job search." Doing so will reveal many articles that you can use in your Twitter brand development. Sites like TweetMyJobs.com also offer specific job leads directly to your Twitter feed.

Social Media Blunders

As previously mentioned, before you apply for jobs, you owe it to yourself to do some focused research on your online profile. Do not let a few clicks of the keyboard on Google be the reason all your preparation comes undone. As many human resource personnel will tell you, hiring managers are known to conduct some online research about you if they think you are a viable candidate. Don't let what they find be the reason your resume gets tossed.

Review Your Online Presence

You should make it a point to figure out what your online presence says about you. Likewise, discover what you are revealing about your personal life that might be offensive or concerning to a potential employer. Keep in mind that what you follow, who you friend, what you post, and what you like may go into how an employer forms an impression about you.

Heeding this warning, take a moment, and consider your online profiles. Google your name—you can Google your image also—and review the results. You can also use Google hacks to search your name across various sites like Facebook, Twitter, Instagram, LinkedIn, and other social media that hold information about you. To target these specific sites, use the 'site' operator in your search as follows.

```
Site: facebook.com Joe Jobhunter
```

The 'site' operator tells Google to search the Facebook.com site for Joe Jobhunter's name. I encourage you to Google "Google Hacks"—you're welcome—for a powerful array of operators you can use to hone your searches better and find the information of interest to you.

As you review your profiles, look at them with the critical eye of an employer. Help them see a responsible and prepared person. Be mindful of your appearance in your photos, and make sure they are appropriate for the occasion, especially if these photos are on sites you intend for hiring managers to see. Remove images of you and your friends that depict questionable activities. If a potential employer sees pictures of you drinking, smoking, and engaging in illicit activities, this can cause them to question your maturity and decision-making skills. And while Marijuana may be legal in some states, it will still stop you from working in federal jobs or holding a clearance. It also raises powerful sentiment, both for and against, across the populace. Do not risk it!

As with photos, pay attention to your conversations and discussions on social media. If you argue the pros of marijuana use or bash your government, employers may not want to risk those conversations entering their workplace. In a similar vein, watch what you say and how you say it in your posts. Suppose your comments are viewed as discriminatory, racist, sexist, or otherwise inflammatory toward any specific group of people. That probably means you have a problem and should address it. That kind of situation will also cause employers to distance themselves from you quickly. Just mind the golden rule: if you cannot say anything nice, just say nothing. Likewise, do not speak negatively about your past, current, or potential employers. The same applies to past teammates, bosses, etc. Potential employers will think you just as likely to paint them in a negative light while working for them and after you leave.

Similarly, monitor the images and comments you get tagged in on social media. And pay attention to the comments that get left under your posts. If these can cause your professionalism to take a hit, remove them, and ask your friends to do the same. The groups you join and follow can also give potential employers concern. The same applies to the friends you keep. I get it. You can't always choose your friends, but you are responsible for the content they post to your profile. And, if a hiring manager finds inappropriate content on your profile, it may cause them to question your judgment, allegiance, or maturity. So, if you have a knucklehead friend or family member, it might be prudent to mute their crazy or inappropriate posts to your profile. I don't let anyone post to my page unless I approve it. Why? Well, we all have a knucklehead or two we love and cherish, even if we don't love everything about them.

By cleaning up your profile, you can better control what others can learn about you and ensure you communicate an appropriate message to anyone stumbling across your profile.

Yes, I am hirable.

No, I do not want to cause a public relations nightmare for you.

Yes, I am dependable, and I can get along with almost anyone.

No, you will not have to worry about me.

Yes, I can get along with people.

No, I won't be the reason everyone has to attend workplace etiquette and sexual harassment classes.

You can also ensure your personal life stays that way by configuring your account's privacy settings. Facebook, at least as of this writing, allows you to set privacy controls on your photos, albums, and posts. Of course, if you are genuine and always act as if everyone will see everything you say and post, that will go a long way toward keeping your profiles professional. As for those things you cannot control, like others' actions, you can still use privacy settings to block others from tagging you without your approval. Managing your security setting is not full proof, but it can limit others' poor decisions from jeopardizing your job search.

Your Email Address

Email addresses are another area of note. I'm sure you thought long and hard about your email address. You've probably used it for years. However, before you post your email address on your resume and other social media, consider what your email address says about you professionally. For instance, if your email address has 'AOL' or 'Hotmail' after the '@' and before the '.com,' rethink your choice before seeking employment. These email providers may sabotage your efforts. Many articles across the web point out that these email services may show that you are uncomfortable working with new technologies. Of course, you could just be incredibly loyal. My wife has been with Yahoo.com for as long as I can remember, and it works for her. She is an incredibly loyal soul. It is one of the things I love about her, but she also has a love/hate relationship with technology.

Beyond avoiding ancient email addresses, at least in computer years, note that using email addresses from cable providers or other uncommon email addresses can introduce other problems. People may not pay much attention to what comes after the '@' of your email address, and less common or wordy domain names can lead to typos. So, consider using Gmail. According to Wikipedia, has over 1.5 billion users worldwide who can complete its spelling while daydreaming.

Finally, pay attention to what comes before the '@.' That 'luvesalot@aol.com' or 'Im2Sexxy24@hotmail.com' may be cute for a dating app (maybe), but hiring managers may not feel comfortable emailing names that don't fit in the business world. They also may not want to deal with a pseudonym. Similarly, shared accounts like 'todandjess@' and 'thejonesfam@' can be off-putting and awkward for professionals who communicate directly with other professionals. The ideal email address for your resume and professional online presence is your first name dot last name [a number if needed] before the '@' and a common domain name afterward. Remember what you are trying to communicate—I am a professional, and I won't cause your company problems. However, there is still more to consider.

Seeking Guidance

Perhaps you are having trouble creating the network that you need. Fortunately, there is just something about successful people that often drives them to help others who are also trying to succeed. Case in point, I often receive notices from my LinkedIn groups. One night, I read the following title in my feed: "I am looking for feedback and guidance for my transitioning." That immediately piqued my interest, so I visited this veteran's post.

In the post, this job seeker began by letting everyone reading know that she was looking for guidance on using LinkedIn and networking. She specified her ideal field of work and location. This job seeker then started giving details, like how long she had before separating from service. She also explained how she had used LinkedIn to connect with potential linkers in her field of interest, which included personalized connection requests to people in the same field. Unfortunately, she was still struggling to find reliable contacts, so she sought help from the group. She had even expanded her search. Still, she was struggling to find potential opportunities. So, she finished her post with a request to learn how she could better connect with potential linkers and hiring managers. Finally, she solicited feedback on how she could do better.

As I read the post, I thought, 'Wow, this person knows what she wants, and she has a fairly good idea of how to get there if she could just find the right contact.' I looked at her LinkedIn profile. It did a good job telling people what she could do and what she wanted, though it could have benefited from less military jargon. Still, all-in-all, it was not bad. I then looked at the comments on her post. Sure enough, as I read the comments, I noticed that hiring managers were already reaching out to her. If I may speak in a general sense, I believe people appreciate the initiative. These hiring-managers probably saw the same thing in this veteran I did, a willingness to admit what she did not know and a desire to overcome it.

Speak with Live People

LinkedIn and all the other social media platforms we just discussed are all excellent resources. The Internet is indeed a tremendous resource, so kudos to the Internet! However, you still need to be hired by a living person, smiles and all. With that in mind, make speaking to actual people a priority. Specifically, talk with people either in person or on the phone, so text, email, and other messaging avenues do not count.

At the end of each day, during your job hunt, ask the following. Did I talk to someone today? Did I even try? Sometimes we overlook many opportunities. Sometimes, it is as easy as calling your old contacts or returning a call from the human resources representative of a company you are only minutely interested in. Even now, I make it a point to return calls from recruiters to learn about the jobs they are trying to fill. When possible, I pass along the names of other contacts who might be a good fit for the position. Doing so has helped me continue growing my network while maintaining knowledge of other potential opportunities should my current circumstances change. So, call back those recruiters, even if you are not entirely interested in their current offer. They may have others.

Reaching out to former colleagues and offering to take them to lunch is another way to stay engaged. Besides bolstering old friendships, you can learn a lot about the company they are working for and whether their company would be a good fit for you. Perhaps the meeting will serve as a source of encouragement.

Stopping my local conferences or meetups is another way to get out there and meet people. Meetups often revolve around shared interests, so you can end up in the room with many people from different companies that all work in areas of interest to you. These connections can also lead to further conversations as these new contacts learn about new job openings and remember their conversation with you. I enjoy these kinds of engagements because I get to hang out with people with similar interests as my own. For instance, I try to attend meetups dealing with programming, data science, project management, and real estate investing. I almost always learn something that makes the visit worth it. There are likely many other opportunities in your local area to meet with groups of like-minded professionals too!

Hopefully, you get that connecting with people is essential. Of course, for introverts, this may be more challenging. I should know. My advice is to save some personal energy and spend it on these activities. There is a good possibility you learned to channel this reserve while in the military since we seldom get things done independently. It is easier to tap into these reserves if you keep in mind that you need to keep talking with people who can help get you hired. It is also a lot easier to do when you engage people who like to talk about the same things you do! Regardless, keep building your network. You may not find someone who will hire you immediately, but eventually, someone will!

8

WHAT ARE YOU WORTH?

> "*If you do not know your worth, do not expect your potential employer to know it either.*"

As you begin your transition, you may wonder about what salary you can expect from civilian employment. It is useful information. Most of us make choices based on what we can afford. Banks and creditors are no exception. Even getting accepted for a rental takes your salary into account. It is an important question and one you should answer before starting the interview process and evaluating opportunities.

Despite its importance, many employment coaches do not recommend you be the first to bring up salary or offer a specific number. If your number is too high, it could immediately end the application process with a potential employer. If it is too low, then you may cut yourself short. Instead, offer the salary range you will consider depending on your expected responsibilities. By establishing upper and lower limits, you leave yourself some room for further negotiation. Just make sure your lower limit allows you to honor your financial obligations.

Knowing what your talents are worth in the current market will help you establish your upper and lower limits and tighten them if pressed. To set those limits, you need to understand compensation and its relation to positions, locations, experience, and other criteria. Fortunately, many resources exist for researching salaries. We will consider a few of those resources now.

Salary Research Resources

As you consider the following resources, keep in mind that salaries can vary by experience, education, and location. Here are some key points to remember as you review the salary information in the resources that follow.

First, a "High" wage is usually reserved for very experienced or highly trained workers in an occupation. Only 10% of workers will fall into the category of employee. The next is the "Median" wage. It is the dead center of the pay scale. Half of the workers in this occupation will earn more than the median, while the other half makes less. Finally, you have the "Low" wage category. This wage represents your entry-level employees or those who have no prior experience.

Location is also a significant factor in determining wages. Higher wages are typically found in urban areas, while lower wages exist in smaller towns and rural areas. As a result, where you plan to live or work will play a part in your expected salary. However, remote workers may experience a gambit of salary ranges on a case-by-case basis.

*O*Net Military Crosswalk Tool*

One excellent resource is the O*Net Military Crosswalk tool. This site allows you to enter your military job title, military occupational classification (MOC), or military occupational specialty (MOS) and get a set of jobs related to your field of military employment. For instance, as we saw earlier in chapter three, Figure 22 - Employment Trends, you can enter a MOS like 25B, which will map to an Information Technology Specialist. The result provides you with the MOS title and a range of comparable occupations.

You will also find employment outlooks provided for listed occupations with clickable links for obtaining additional information, like employment requirements (e.g., skills, knowledge, abilities, etc.), related careers, and wages and employment trends. This site was one of my first finds when I bracketed my salary expectations.

Glassdoor

Another excellent resource for identifying potential salaries is glassdoor.com. Using this resource, you can enter locations where you want to work and the occupation you seek. Information you can find on this website includes company summaries and reviews, salaries, and interview information. You can also filter by location.

You can also obtain company-specific information, which can better inform you about a company's work culture, the potential for advancement, and the geographic locations where it is hiring. Other useful information you will find on Glassdoor are company reviews, where employees, past and present, provide pros and cons about the company. They may grant some insight into job security with the organization. If you see a significant number of reviews complaining about frequent terminations, you may not want to relocate to work there without a backup plan.

Targeted salary data is another useful bit of information you can get from glassdoor.com; however, these salaries may be dated. They also lean heavily toward entry-level rates. Hence, posted wages may be less than what a company is currently offering for the position. Still, this website provides some initial insights into employees' salaries.

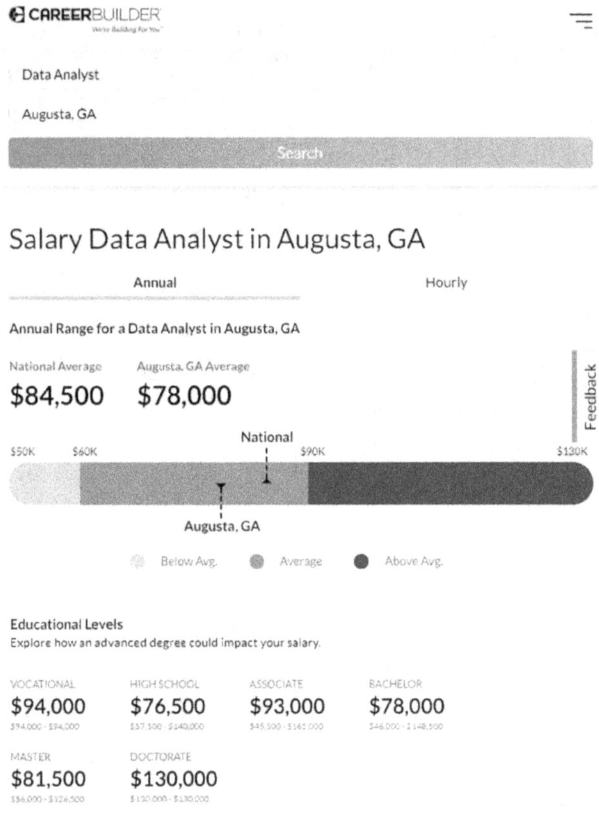

Figure 33 - Career Builder Salary Search

CareerBuilder

CareerBuilder is another website for estimating your potential employment value. Using this tool, you can see how your salary compares to others in your area. Beyond comparing salaries, you can also see what skills you must acquire to qualify for other jobs or move up in your current career.

CareerBuilder provides salary information, such as median, low, and high salary ranges, for various education levels and locations. An example of a salary search on CareerBuilder is shown in Figure 33 - Career

Builder Salary Search, and you can visit the site at https://www.careerbuilder.com/salary.

CareerOneStop

CareerOneStop offers resources for career exploration, training, and jobs. It is also packed with information, such as median wages by nation and state, career profiles, career growth and decline by area, and much more. You can also conduct self-assessments at the CareerOneStop site to help you find occupations that match your assessment, identify training needs or skills you possess, and much more. Some offered evaluations include Interest Assessments, Skills Matcher, Salary Finder, and Work Values Matcher.

However, you have a good idea of the career(s) you are interested in, so let's discuss how you can use this site for identifying your salary range. Fortunately, CareerOneStop offers wage information on over 800 different occupations, so this website can quickly help you bracket what a reasonable salary is for someone with your experience. For instance, all the following are searches you can conduct on CareerOneStop.[1]

- You can research local wages for different levels of experience.
- You can identify the highest paying careers nationally, by state, and for different levels of education.
- You can compare wages by occupation and local area to determine if wages are best in your current location or a new location.

Wages

Sometimes, it is worthwhile to peruse occupations by salary. If anything, doing so will help you realize what you are not willing to do for a salary. So, what are the top wage-earning professions today? Table 4 - Top-10

Occupations by Median Wage provides the top-10 leading careers by wage as of 2019.

Table 4 - Top-10 Occupations by Median Wage

Rank	Occupation	2019 Median wage
1	Obstetricians and Gynecologists	$208,000+
2	Orthodontists	$208,000+
3	Physicians, All Other; and Ophthalmologists, Except Pediatric	$208,000+
4	Psychiatrists	$208,000+
5	Surgeons, Except Ophthalmologists	$208,000+
6	Anesthesiologists	$200,300
7	Family Medicine Physicians	$199,900
8	Law Teachers, Postsecondary	$165,400
9	Nurse Anesthetists,	$163,800
10	Dentists, General	$162,200

Perhaps one of these careers will prove the spark to your flame. I even listed orthodontist as my career choice during my seventh-grade year of middle school since they got to drive Volvos. Of course, I did not understand what an orthodontist did or what a Volvo was, and shortly after starting my freshmen year of high school biology, I realized none of the health professions were for me. I am also more of a Chevy or Jeep guy. Fortunately, the technology and research fields also provide respectable salaries, as shown in the following figure obtained from CareerOneStop.

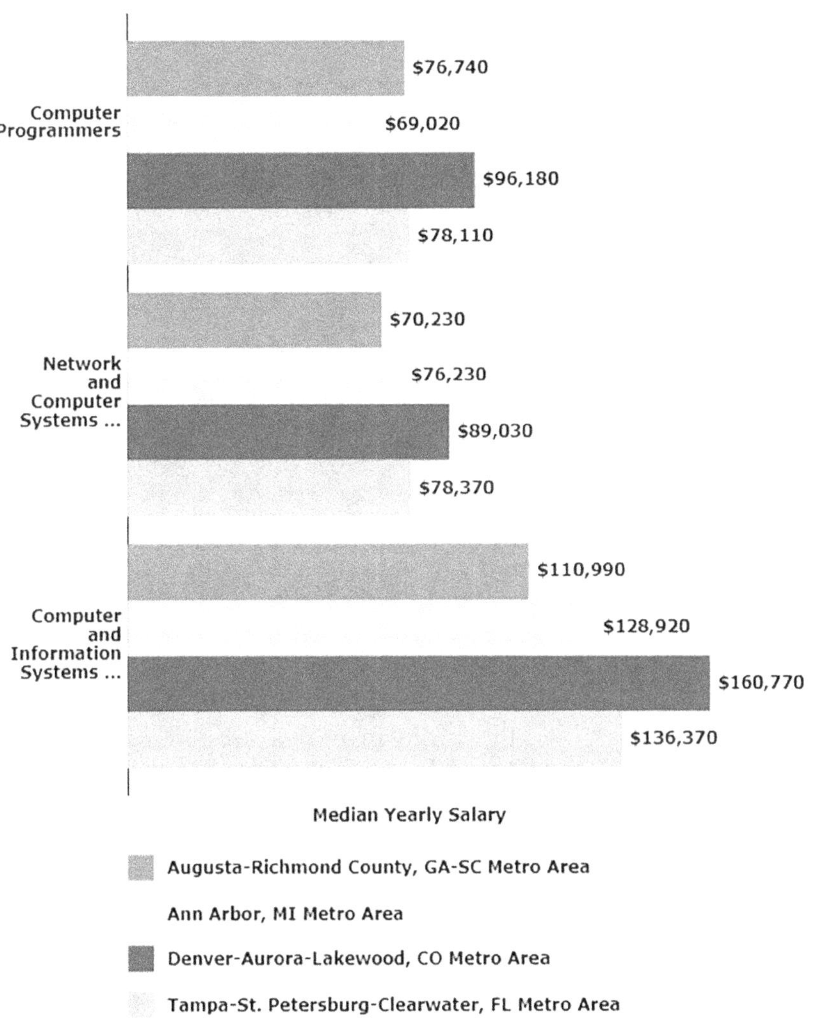

Computer Programmers
$76,740
$69,020
$96,180
$78,110
Network and Computer Systems ...
$70,230
$76,230
$89,030
$78,370
Computer and Information Systems ...
$110,990
$128,920
$160,770
$136,370
Median Yearly Salary
Augusta-Richmond County, GA-SC Metro Area
Ann Arbor, MI Metro Area
Denver-Aurora-Lakewood, CO Metro Area
Tampa-St. Petersburg-Clearwater, FL Metro Area

9

THE INTERVIEW

> *Big jobs usually go to the men [and women] who prove their ability to outgrow small ones. —Ralph Waldo Emerson*

When preparing for your interview, realize that there are impact factors that hiring managers care about deeply. Hence, we will identify some of those factors and consider some of your skills that support them. You may be surprised to learn that you already possess many of these skills, but you may need a little assistance identifying just what they are. So, while preparing for your interview, consider the skills you have already used, and then form a plan to discuss how you will continue using them.

For instance, employers need employees who can quickly solve problems or prevent them from happening again. This is an excellent opportunity to discuss how you used After Action Reviews to avoid blaming others and identify the root cause of problems. You can quickly recover from mistakes and keep them from being repeated. Improving safety, mitigating risks, and reducing accidents is something else employers care about. Of course, this has been a significant part of your training. You have handled dangerous equipment or hazardous materials. Likely, you have even run a rifle range or a live-fire exercise. Be prepared to discuss what precautions you have taken and how you applied safety guidelines to eliminate accidents or injuries.

A clear majority of companies also rely on equipment for networking, production, travel, etc. These companies value folks who can reduce equipment breakdowns, eliminate costly repairs, and improve the equipment's reliable operation and availability. Fortunately, you know the value of preventative maintenance, and you know how to inspect and maintain equipment both before, during, and after its use. Companies also value teamwork and synergy. You can highlight your experiences during your interview by discussing how you have introduced members to your team and ensured all your team members fully understood their roles and how their responsibilities affected their teammates. Helping your teammates understand they are responsible for their colleagues' success and their own allowed your team to reach more significant achievements.

Company leaders like to make informed decisions. Fortunately, your involvement in the military decision-making process has taught you to quickly generate plausible courses of action while also identifying their strengths and weaknesses. As a result, you can provide your supervisors with well-thought-out recommendations and the information they need to make informed decisions. They also need people who can create, evaluate, and choose from competing courses of action themselves. If you can do that, then you may quickly find yourself invited to a supervisor role. Of course, there are other qualities that your interview will permit you to express, and we discuss some of them next.

Personal Priorities of Hiring Managers

According to the 2017 US Department of Labor Employment Workshop Participant Guide, employers most care about four personal priorities. First, they want to know whether you will reduce their hassles, both in number and severity. Ultimately, supervisors want to see if they will sleep better at night because you're on their team, or will you be the reason they must work nights and weekends covering down on issues that should have been resolved by you?

Second, are you reliable? Will you arrive on time every day and ready to get work done? And will you let them know promptly if an emergency will make you absent from work? Basically, are you aware that your supervisors and colleagues rely on you, and are you sympathetic to the effect your absence will have on them? The third priority for many employers is whether you are a team player. They want to know that you will support and treat co-workers, customers, and the public with respect.

Similarly, they want to know that you will not be a source of friction in their organization. No organization wants an employee who will land them in a public relations nightmare or legal troubles over ethical issues, discrimination, or sexual harassment charges. They do not want someone who will hurt their relationship with customers either. Customers pro-vide money, and making money is the lifeblood of many organizations. Without it, they shutdown.

The fourth priority is to determine whether you are adaptable. Are you flexible enough to adapt and fit into an organization's culture? Even sports teams recruit people they believe will fit into their culture while also adding to their talent pool. How well do you respond to change and uncertainty? Employers also need employees who are trainable and can pick up new skills quickly. They also need people who can appropriately react when efforts don't go as planned.

Throughout your interview, you want to convey how your service has uniquely prepared you to meet these priorities. Case in point, you showed up every morning at 0-dark-thirty for physical training for the last two or twenty-plus years. So, showing up for an early shift will not be a problem for you. Undoubtedly, you have moved multiple times throughout your career. You can use these events to communicate how you have frequently adapted to new cultures and environments. You have also used counseling effectively to discuss expectations and priorities with your supervisors and subordinates to identify the latter's priorities and the former's motivations to support them better. You can do the same for your employer.

Interview Preparation

The interview presents you with your next opportunity to move forward in the employment process. If you have done your homework, this section will recap much of what we have already discussed. Still, preparing for an interview can be full of uncertainty. After all, we do not typically interview for our next position in the military. Our records, rank, and career path do our interviewing for us. As a result, this skill may need some development. Here are some pointers you should consider when preparing for your interview.

Interview Pointers

1. Slow down. Remind yourself to slow down. Get comfortable with pauses and moments of silence. Taking your time will help you articulate your responses better and help you avoid looking anxious.
2. Identify six or seven stories or experiences that you feel comfortable sharing that highlight your capabilities or highlight your personality. Bullet summaries are probably sufficient.
3. Make a list of how's. How do you lead others? How do you

perform under pressure? How do you approach problems when guidance is lacking?

4. Try to infuse a little humor into your conversation. If this suits your personality, go for it. If not, don't worry about it. This works well for some, but it can backfire with awkward moments of silence if you get it wrong. Humor is nice to have if you are hitting it off with your interviewer. Otherwise, just be you.
5. Seriously consider and write the reasons someone would want you on their team. How will you add value to their organization or bring in new business? Be prepared to explain how you are value-added.
6. Pay attention. Did your interviewers prepare for the interview? How do they treat you? Do they have a schedule, and are they on time? How did they interact with you? You want to leave knowing as much about the internal day-to-day organization as possible so you can visualize how you might fit in.
7. Write some meaningful questions of your own to ask at the end or as opportunities present. If the interviewer gives you a chance, take full advantage of it. Remember, this is part of the interview process as well. Are you interested in their company? If yes, you probably have some questions. Use them and use them well.

STAR Response

STAR is not just for resumes. You can also use it for your interview. For instance, consider the example STAR scenario below.

Situation (S): Our unit's operational readiness rate for our 18 helicopters was 86%, and our pilots struggled to get their required flight hours each month.

Task (T): My goal was to generate new ideas to address supply shortages, maintenance issues, and incentive misalignments to improve the operational readiness rate to 95% or better.

Action (A): I identified reoccurring maintenance issues and determined two commonly needed parts were often out of stock. I requested the unit to order additional inventory, and I updated our maintenance procedures to ensure we ordered extra parts anytime the quantity dropped below four. We also prioritized this maintenance ahead of other maintenance requirements.

Result (R): We achieved an operational readiness rate of 95.8% within six months of implementing these solutions. Pilots also achieved their required flight hours for the year.

Anticipate Questions

To best prepare for your interview, spend some time anticipating the kinds of questions you can expect. However, before you do that, review the following pointers to ensure you identify your talking points.

- Think about some recent situations where you showed good behaviors or actions, especially leadership, teamwork, initiative, planning, work experience, and customer service.
- Prepare brief descriptions of each situation and be ready to give details if asked.
- Ensure your story offers a beginning, middle, and an end, i.e., describe the situation, task at hand, your actions, and the outcome or result.
- Be positive. Your outcome should positively reflect on you (even if the result was not favorable).
- Do not omit or embellish any part of the story. Be honest. The interviewer will probably recognize a weak foundation.
- Be specific. Do not generalize multiple events; instead, give a detailed accounting of one event.
- Vary your examples instead of taking them all from one area of your life.

Now that we have considered how to answer questions, it is time to consider some actual problems. Those that follow are not all-inclusive. Still, answering them will help hone your skills and get you used to applying the STAR method. Here are some questions you may encounter in a job interview. As you review them, consider which ones align with the job you are pursuing, and focus on those.

- Describe a time you successfully used persuasion [presentation skills] to convince someone to see things your way.
- Describe a time you faced a stressful situation that showed your coping skills.
- Give me a specific example when you had to conform to a policy with which you disagreed.
- Describe for me an instance when something you attempted failed.
- Provide a specific example when you used good judgment and logic to solve a problem.
- Tell me of a time when your delegation led to the successful completion of a project.
- Can you give me an example of a time when you set a goal, laid out a plan, and achieved it?
- Please discuss an important written document [project or product] you were required to complete.
- Tell me about a time you went above and beyond the call of duty to get a job done?
- Describe a time when you had to decide on a moment's notice?
- Tell me about a time you worked with a team you did not like. What did you dislike about the team, and how did you cope?
- Tell me about a time that forced you to prioritize your tasks because you had too much to accomplish.
- Describe a time when you foresaw a potential problem and came up with a course of action to address it.
- How do you typically deal with conflict? Give me an example?

- Tell me about a time you successfully worked with a challenging person, even though that individual may not have liked you (or vice versa).
- Describe a time when you missed an obvious solution to a problem.
- Tell me about a hard decision you have made recently.
- Tell me of a problem that forced you to make an unpopular decision. How did that work out for you?
- Tell me about a time when you fell behind on your work. Why did that happen, and how did you catch up?
- Describe a time when you showed initiative by taking the lead.
- Tell me about a recent situation in which you had to deal with an aggravated co-worker or customer.
- Tell me about how you go about motivating others.
- Tell me about a time you had to correct a friend's poor behavior, address their subpar performance, or fire them.
- Provide an example of a time you set your sights too high (or too low).
- Tell me about a time you had to adapt to an entirely new method or system at work. How did you adapt?
- Has anyone ever been overly critical of your work? How did you handle it?

Once you search for interview questions, you will find that any of thousands could appear across a wide range of interviews—still, these questions are there to determine if you are the right person for the job. So, as you anticipate questions, consider which ones align with the job you are pursuing. Naturally, you can expect some technical questions if you apply for a technical position. Still, others will deal with who you are, how you deal with pressure, and your interpersonal skills.

Ask Questions

You may not realize this, but interviews go both ways. It is not just for them. Employers will ask you several pointed questions to determine whether you are a fit for their company. You also have every right to ensure their company is the right fit for you. Besides, asking your questions can better help you understand whether the position aligns with your skills and experience. It will also show the interviewer you are active (instead of passive) in the discussion. Asking informed questions may also leave a good impression on your interviewer, letting them know you are genuinely interested in the position.

So, while practicing for your interview questions— make sure you put together some of your own. Not only will you be prepared for when the interviewer asks, "Do you have questions for me?" but you will also be able to keep progressing the conversation forward during lulls. Here are some questions for your consideration.

1. *What do you think are essential qualities for someone to excel in this role?* This question can provide valuable information missing from the job description. It can help you learn about the organization's culture and values and determine if you are a good fit.
2. What are your expectations for this role over the first 30 days, 60 days, year? Establish upfront what defines success for this position in the near-term what they will look for by the year's end.
3. *How will this position make an impact?* Does your future position matter in the community and the world? Ask these questions to understand how you will fit in.
4. *What do you like about the company benefits?* Benefits like healthcare, retirement, and vacation can significantly affect your overall compensation and satisfaction. Ask the right questions upfront so you can make the right decision and get a more holistic picture.
5. *What are the most significant opportunities/challenges facing the*

company/department right now? This question will provide you and your interviewer the chance to discuss the company's goals, opportunities, and challenges and how you might contribute to them.

6. *What would my typical day look like in this role?* If job responsibilities such as interacting with co-workers, working at a desk, or frequent travel are essential to you, make sure they are a big part of the typical day that your interviewer describes.
7. *How would you describe the company's culture?* How else will you learn if you are a good fit for this organization?
8. *What does the career path for someone in this role look like at your organization/company?* Here you can learn if the company promotes from within and how career advancement works within the organization. It also shows you are considering your growth opportunities 'within' the company.

Ending the Interview

Throughout the interview process, you and your interviewer have hopefully established a rhythm of asking and answering questions. Your potential employer is learning about you and your skills. In return, you will learn about the position, your boss, the company, and whether the job is the right fit for you. As the interview concludes, leave yourself some time to ask just two or three more questions. These are questions you will use to identify potential weaknesses in your performance and give you an idea of when you should follow up. For instance, consider these.

1. How would you say I compare to other candidates you have interviewed for this position? This could be a risky choice, but I like it. You do not want to place the interviewer in an awkward position; however, if the interview is going well, this question can allow the interviewer to give you an honest assessment of how

you stack up for the position. It can also give you an idea of the position's competitiveness and allow the interviewer an opportunity to address something they did not mention earlier.

2. What should you expect next in the interview process? Let your interviewer know that you are interested in moving forward. You can also learn about the timeline for hiring so you can follow up appropriately.
3. If there is one thing that I can do over the next few weeks to become a better candidate for this position, what would that be? This question will help you identify noticeable gaps in your skill sets. You can also use the answer in your follow-up letter to let the interviewer know how you have progressed since you last met.

After the Interview

The period immediately following your interview may be uncomfortable. I certainly did not care for my wait. Unease can even grow as time progresses, and uncertainty grows. Regrettably, it is a sad fact that many interviewers will never follow up with you after the interview. That is one reason I recommend you ask your interviewer about the next steps in the interview process. While you do not want to harass the hiring manager, it is acceptable to follow up with your interviewer a couple of weeks later. Still, there is plenty you can do to stay active after your interview.

For one, you can send a thank-you note either immediately or soon after the interview to the hiring manager. Beyond showing them you are interested, this practice will help keep your name fresh on your interviewer's mind. When writing the thank-you letter, limit it to a few sentences, and make sure it is well written and concise. If there is a point you want to address from your interview, do so, but keep it short.

Completing one interview is also not the time to take your foot off the gas pedal. Keep the job search going until you have a signed agreement. Even if the interview went great, and you are confident of its outcome, there is still no guarantee the job is yours. There are many reasons the job may not go to you, but do not let that detour you. All it takes is one call back and an offered contract to end the interview process.

Finally, be courteous! If a company brings you in for an interview and you end up accepting an offer from another company, send a letter, email, or phone call to the hiring manager to let them know. At least consider notifying companies who either followed up with you or brought you in for an interview over the past few weeks. They very well may be working on an offer for you, and they will appreciate you saving them some work. Even if they were not planning to make you an offer, the contact might leave the door open for future opportunities.

10

THE OFFER, BENEFITS, AND NEGOTIATION

> "*When it comes to accepting offers, do not let salary be your only guide, lest you miss out on the benefits.*"

Once you complete the interviewing process, and an organization determines you are the candidate, the offer is the next step. It may come verbally or in the form of a written letter—possibly both. Congratulations! You have shown that you have the skills, characteristics, and qualities that they believe will benefit their company. Hopefully, having completed the process, you feel good about the company, and you can see yourself working there for many years.

If that is the case, then you are well on your way to an enjoyable career. Keep in mind, however, that nothing is official until you have your offer in writing. In this section, we will discuss some items the offer might include and ways to achieve better pay or benefits through negotiation.

Ideally, by the time you enter this discussion, you know what someone with your skill set typically gets paid. You may have even spoken with a few recruiters who gave you an inside scoop on what to expect. Possibly you are even sitting on one or more offers, and you need to decide which company you will select. Perhaps this is your only offer, and you are still hoping for one more. When considering your offer(s), these are essential factors: whether to accept it, reject it, or negotiate.

If you have not been through this process before, you may not know what to expect. I went through this process several times before joining the Army and twice afterward. Before I joined the military, the negotiation process was nearly identical; however, the process began changing after I left. Before the military, I just accepted offers. I was an unskilled laborer, so attempts at negotiation may have cost me the position. However, after the Army, I had more options. Still, I accepted my first offer without negotiating. It was a formal process, and I felt uncomfortable negotiating in my early career move following the Army. I was also set on the position. However, fourteen months later, I was ready to move on. During my interview for the next job, the discussion was much more casual, and it presented me with room to negotiate.

An offer letter generally begins with remarks congratulating you on your selection. You will likely next find your base-salary. For some job seekers, the salary will trigger an immediate 'yes' response since it meets their minimum criteria. It may also be their only offer. For others, there may be some hesitancy to accept for precisely the opposite reasons. In either case, the offer letter should reference the company's benefits package. If you find yourself in the hesitant category, then take some time to review the benefits. The salary may fall short of your expectations, but the benefits package could still make your offer superior to others.

Various companies will offer different benefits. If your offer does not clarify what benefits are offered, follow up and ask as the company's answers can affect your offer's value. For instance, if your company does not provide vision or dental, then the costs of future appointments will eat away at that base-pay. In other cases, benefits can be well worth a slightly lower base-pay.

Keep in mind that many companies grant their hiring managers some flexibility with pay and benefits. Make sure you explore both. They may pay you a little more in exchange for forgoing a particular benefit, or they may be willing to add one or two additional benefits to improve their offer. Before we discuss negotiating your offer, we will first explore some benefits that might come up during your negotiations.

Benefits

Employee benefits offer additional value over and above your regular salary or wage. Employers are legally required to provide some benefits, while others are optional. Regardless, benefits comprise a vital part of an employer's compensation package for potential employees.

Benefits across companies and occupations vary significantly. While some companies are known for their incredible benefits packages, others may offer nothing beyond what they are legally required. Still, knowing that these benefits exist can help you better negotiate your offer. Awareness can also be beneficial when your new company looks at employee feedback for new benefits during their annual compensation reevaluation period. Many companies annually reevaluate their compensation packages, which include benefits.

According to an Employment Confidence Survey[1] conducted by Glassdoor in 2015, nearly four in five or 79% of employees would prefer new or additional benefits to a pay increase. Table 5 - List of Employer Benefits lists many benefits your offer might include:

Table 5 - List of Employer Benefits

- Insurance
  - Health Care
  - Vision
  - Dental
  - Short-term Disability
  - Long-term Disability
  - Life
  - Pet
- Time Off
  - Personal Time Off (PTO)
  - Paid Holiday Time-Off
  - Paid parental leave (e.g., maternity leave, adoption assistance)
  - Sick Leave
  - Paid Medical Leave
- Personal Development
  - On-the-job training,
  - Paid time for self-development
  - Tuition Reimbursement
- Travel Assistance
  - Relocation Assistance
  - Commuting/travel assistance
  - Company Car
  - Company Credit Card
- Commuter Benefits
  - Company shuttle
  - Commuter checks
  - Company Car
- Healthcare Spending/ Reimbursement
  - Flexible Spending Account (FSA)
  - Health Spending Account (HSA)
  - Health Reimbursement Account (HRA)
- Retirement Benefits
  - 401K Contribution
  - 401K Matching (Vetted and Unvetted)
  - Stock Options
- Financial
  - Donation Matching
  - Performance Bonus
  - Promotion
- Memberships
  - Gym
  - Wellness Programs
  - Online Course Programs
- Workplace Perks
  - Casual Dress
  - Childcare Assistance
  - Diversity Programs
  - Employee discounts
  - Office food, snacks, and coffee
  - Recreation activities
- Work Schedule
  - Flexible Work Schedules
  - Remote Work Schedules

Explanation of Benefits

Bonuses

Many companies offer bonuses based on how much business you bring in or how well you perform. Some companies offer a one-time sign-on bonus as well. Although not guaranteed, it is worth asking about the typical bonus when talking about your compensation.

Insurance

Insurance can seriously save your bacon during times of illness or injury. Let us jump into insurance and what it means to you financially.

Health Care Insurance

Health insurance protects you from unexpected, high medical costs, often allowing you to pay less for covered in-network health care before you ever receive your deductible. It also provides free preventive care, like vaccines, screenings, and some check-ups without meeting your deductible. According to the Bureau of Labor Statistics (BLS), as of 2016, over 70% of civilian companies (and 67% of private firms) offered medical insurance to employees.

If you retired from the military, this is one of those benefits you can sometimes use to negotiate for higher pay. For instance, when I left the military, I opted for Tricare Select to cover my health care expenses. Tricare Select comes with a higher deductible than Tricare Prime, but it gives me greater freedom in which doctors I choose. I also have some military-related issues that allow me to receive benefits at the VA. Because I receive these military benefits (we will discuss these later), I do not require a company's provided insurance.

Now, according to research published by the Kaiser Family Foundation in 2019, the average cost of employer-sponsored health insurance for annual premiums was $7,188 for single coverage and $20,576 for family coverage. The premium for employees averages $1,242 for single coverage and $6,015 for family coverage. This means that companies are paying over 70% of the bill in health expenses for employees.

Your company may cover your insurance themselves or allow you to contribute to a plan. If they cover it themselves, then there is some room to negotiate with them for a higher wage that still offers them less cost than if you had taken the insurance.

Life Insurance

Many employers offer life insurance in the amount of one or two times the employee's salary at no charge to the employee. Your company's plan may also let you increase your life insurance benefit by allowing you to provide a monthly contribution.

Dental Insurance

Dental insurance is a common employee benefit, and people who have it generally receive "100-80-50" coverage. This means your dental insurance will pay 100% of the cost of routine, preventive, and diagnostic care, such as checkups and cleanings; 80% for fillings, root canals, and other basic procedures; and 50% for crowns, bridges, and major procedures. As with other plans, your company may pay for this benefit or negotiate a reduced fee for you to get dental insurance.

Vision Insurance

The most significant benefit of vision insurance is that it covers or reduces the cost of eye exams and medical eye care. Some plans also save you money on eyeglasses, contact lenses, and even vision correction surgery, like LASIK. How much that saves you depends on your company's plan, however. You may be offered vision insurance without charge or for a nominal fee pulled from your pay. If your company gives you a health account, you can often use pre-tax dollars to cover your eyeglasses and contacts—items I am blind without.

Pet Insurance

If you are a pet owner, you have undoubtedly noticed that taking care of your furry friends is expensive, especially in later years. Pet insurance can help ease some of those costly procedures your pets may require. As with other plans, this may be something your company offers, or you will have to pay a monthly fee. It is also relatively new, so do not be surprised if your company doesn't offer it at all.

Retirement

401K

The most common types of employer-offered retirement accounts are 401(k)s and 403(b)s. With these programs, you can contribute pre-tax amounts to your employer's provided 401K. Setting up contributions to come directly out of your paycheck can also help motivate reluctant savers.

401K Match

Better than just contributing to your retirement alone is having your employer also contribute to your retirement account through an employer match program. Many companies set these up differently. For instance, one company may match 100% of your contribution up to 4% of your salary. Another employer might match 100% for the first 3% of your salary and match 50% of your next 2%. Others may contribute a 100%

match up to 5% of your salary but require it to be vested. Vested means that the money your employer contributes is not entirely yours until you have been with the company for some duration of time.

Profit-Sharing

For-profit companies may also elect to only contribute to retirement through profit sharing. This form of compensation gives employees a percentage of the company's profits; however, the amount awarded is based on its earnings over a set period, usually once or twice a year.

Stock Options

A stock option is a financial instrument that gives an employee or option holder the right to buy or sell shares of a specific stock at a specified price for a specified period. This benefit allows employees to buy the company's stock and sell it when the stock climbs. The result can be a significant return on their investment.

Health Accounts

Health Savings Accounts (HSA)

HSAs are convenient but have some drawbacks. As for their advantages, these include paying for my qualified expenses (e.g., medical, dental, and mental health treatment costs), pre-tax contributions, tax-deductible after-tax contributions, tax-free withdrawals, tax-free earning, annual rollover, and portability. HSAs also never expire. You can think of them as akin to a real savings account in that money accumulates over time, and you can use it throughout your lifetime, even after you switch health plans.

The disadvantage of an HSA is its High-Deductible Requirement. A

High-Deductible Health Plan (HDHP), which you are required to have to qualify for an HSA, can create a more significant financial burden for you than other types of health insurance. With an HDHP, even though you pay less in premiums, it could be difficult—even with money in an HSA—to come up with the payment needed to meet the deductible for costly medical procedures. Contributions you make to an HSA are only tax-free while you are enrolled in an HDHP. Recordkeeping, such as maintaining receipts, is also required to prove that you use your HSA funds on qualified expenses.

Flexible spending accounts (FSAs)

A flexible spending account (FSA) is a pre-tax benefit account used to pay for eligible medical, dental, and vision care expenses that are not covered by your insurance plan or elsewhere. Comparable to health savings accounts (HSAs) in how they are used, FSAs can be used with nearly any health insurance plan. Where FSAs differ from HSAs is how they operate.

For the 2020 calendar year, an individual can contribute up to $2,750 pre-tax dollars to a health care FSA. Employers will often let you contribute to your FSA monthly. If your employer opts to contribute to your FSA, it is in addition to the amount you can elect. However, unlike HSAs, the funds you contribute to an FSA do not roll-over. As a result, your contributions are "use or lose." So, if you contribute $1500 to your FSA and only use $500 over the year, you will lose the other $1000. With FSAs, you need to consider your annual costs in medical expenses and plan accordingly.

Health Reimbursement Arrangement (HRA)

An HRA or health reimbursement arrangement is a health spending account provided and owned by an employer. Your employer entirely funds it to help make your healthcare more affordable. This benefit reimburses a portion of your eligible out-of-pocket medical expenses. And these expenses include medical deductibles, coinsurance, dental, pharmacy, and others as determined by your employer.

Time Off

Sometimes you just need some time away from work to take care of personal matters, heal, introduce new family members, or enjoy a period of renewal. Companies realize this and offer various benefits to give you some time off.

Personal Time Off (PTO)

Employers typically provided between 11 and 20 days of personal time off (PTO) per year. What is great about PTO compared to your military days is there are no required leave forms. So, no waiting on a commander to approve your leave. Likewise, no wondering if your departure is going to get approved in time for you to depart. In the civilian world, taking time off is usually as easy as notifying your supervisor that you will be absent for some range of days and updating your timecard. I cannot express how much I enjoy this benefit compared to what I had during my military days!

Additionally, unlike the military, when your time off includes weekends, those days do not count against your accrued days of PTO. So, if you take off five weekdays and include both weekends in your travels, you are only charged five days of PTO. The military would have made you claim the two weekends as well for a total of nine days.

Holiday Time Off

Coming out of the military, the first thing you should realize is that paid holidays are not guaranteed. The United States does not mandate any holidays. Additionally, the Fair Labor Standards Act (FLSA) does not require an employer to pay employees for time they do not work, including vacations or holidays. Still, many companies offer paid holidays as a part of their benefits package. The usual paid Holidays include:

- New Year's Day,
- Easter
- Memorial Day
- Independence Day (4th of July)
- Labor Day
- Thanksgiving Day
- Friday after Thanksgiving
- Christmas Day

Some organizations may also include additional days as part of their offered holiday schedule.

- Washington's Birthday or President's Day
- Good Friday
- Martin Luther King, Jr. Birthday
- Veterans' Day
- Columbus Day
- Christmas Eve or New Year's Eve.

Finally, some companies may include a float day since not all employees value certain holidays the same way. For instance, companies may offer a floating holiday that you can couple with personal time off (PTO) or another holiday, like Thanksgiving Day or Christmas, to stretch the holidays with family and friends.

Sabbatical Leave

The concept behind sabbatical leave is to allow employees to step away from their jobs for an extended period to recharge or explore other interests at the company's expense. The duration of sabbatical leave can be 30 or more days. According to various studies, only about 5% of employers offer paid sabbaticals. The ones that do are high-performance companies that use it as a reward for being with the company for a substantial number of years. For instance, some companies may offer a 30-day sabbatical every five years. Universities may offer extended sabbaticals to support a professor's independent research.

Paid Sick Leave

If a company has 50 or more full-time employees, then the Family Medical Leave Act requires they offer medical leave. This includes maternity leave, recovery leave (for surgery), and care of ailing family members. FMLA also requires companies to keep your job open for 12 weeks in cases of sickness or injury, but it does not require them to pay you for that time off.

Better than time off to deal with sickness or injury is paid time off. Depending on your financial situation, going without a check for a few weeks, let alone months, can place many people in financial jeopardy. If you are not drawing military retirement and lack any significant savings, you may try to push through an injury or sickness until you cannot.

Fortunately, a growing number of companies offer paid sick leave, which can help keep the light on while you are recovering. Maternity leave is also a significant consideration. A typical recommendation is for new mothers to take at least six weeks off after birthing their child, and many companies use this as a guide. However, not all do. If this benefit is important to you, confirm whether it is offered, and consider its impact on you if it isn't. Commonly, employers provide six weeks of paid leave and then let the employee use vacation or sick time to cover additional weeks. Others may offer the six weeks in full and then another six weeks at half-pay.

Flexible Work Location/Hours

Flexible Work Schedules

If you have children or other obligations that you must take care of during regular work hours, finding a company with flexible work hours is a huge plus. Flexible work schedules allow you to move your hours around to make your life easier while still meeting your employer's obligations. After all, if your employer has a report due this Friday, do they really care if you work on it between 8:00 am and 5 pm, or do they care that there is a report submitted on time? Some companies may also allow you to work a 10-hour day so you can take every Friday off (four-day workweek).

Remote Work

Remotely working allows for increased flexibility and autonomy for employees. According to one study, 90% of workers who work remotely intend to do so for the rest of their careers. With today's videoconferencing, collaboration, and cloud service technologies, staying connected with your supervisor, co-workers, and customers is easier than ever. This is another benefit I enjoy immensely. Not only do I get to avoid the commute to the office, but I also enjoy the amenities of home without the distractions of the conversations occurring around my open cubicle.

Remotely working is an excellent benefit for many who possess the discipline, communication skills, and technical savvy to work in somewhat isolated conditions. If you are someone who craves human interaction or cannot keep your office technology operating before meetings, remote work is probably not for you. Remote workers enjoy an exceptional level of trust from their employers. However, that trust can quickly erode if you allow family distractions, technical limitations, time management, or other personal leadership issues to affect your productivity. Seek and use this benefit wisely!

Professional Development

Since leaving the military, I have not considered any jobs that did not offer professional development opportunities. Companies use this benefit to support your professional development goals and gain commitments from you to stay with the company for some duration. Failing to honor that obligation may result in you having to reimburse the company for its expense. Ultimately, this is a win-win since it allows you professional growth while the company reaps the benefits.

Tuition Reimbursement

As the name suggests, tuition reimbursement reimburses you for college courses you complete while working at a company. You attend these courses on your own time, but your company reimburses your costs for completing the work.

Paid Time Off for Professional Development

Some companies set aside 40-80 hours every year so their employees can pursue self-development opportunities on their own. Maybe there is a new professional development course you have wanted to explore, or perhaps your certification requires some educational credits. This benefit is perfect for helping you develop new skill sets and improve your professional proficiency.

Paid Certificate Courses

Many week-long programs exist to help you quickly obtain needed certificates for advancing your career. Many companies understand the value of developing the skill sets "in-house" and support certification courses. As a result, some organizations may provide you with opportunities to attend these courses at their expense. You may still have to cover your travel and lodging, but in my humble opinion, so worth it! I like the opportunity and have, on occasion, asked for this perk instead of a pay raise.

Last Words on Benefits

As you have seen, companies can provide substantial benefits that offer the equivalent of thousands of dollars to your compensation package. These benefits range from contributions to your retirement, education, and charities to time-off for personal, health, and family matters. Hence, benefits can bring greater value to your compensation than salary alone, so don't let salary be your only consideration when evaluating job offers.

Negotiation

> ***When negotiating compensation, be true to your virtues, seek the win-win, never offer your number first, and only hold out for what matters most!***

I do not claim to be an expert negotiator. In fact, I do not think I ever considered negotiation as part of the hiring process until much later in life. However, we have all entered a negotiation at some point. Maybe an old buddy reached out to you about doing a job for them. Perhaps they even discussed a wage, but you were not interested. At that point, maybe they spiced up the offer to see if that would change your mind. Perhaps you considered it. Well, you were in a negotiation. It is that simple.

The first rule of negotiating is to remember that the process works both ways. The next is to think win-win. When you receive a job offer, the discussion that follows can determine your work-life-balance and financial security for many years. Of course, as you consider the offer, keep in mind that it accounts for many factors, like your experience, skills, and expected responsibilities, the position's market value, and their budget. Think about whether their offer is within your salary range and whether the compensation is competitive with other opportunities. There is a strong chance that they know what other companies might offer you, and it does not benefit their company to go through the hiring process, hire you, train you, and then lose you a few months later to a higher paying offer. As a result, most companies will try to find that happy medium that keeps you working with them.

Other factors play a role in your offer as well. These factors include the scarcity of your skill set, certifications, experience, etc. If what you offer is in high demand and you are the only show in town, negotiations will lean in your favor. If not, then negotiations may end as soon as you receive the offer.

That said, for negotiating job offers, some general rules can help lead to a more favorable outcome for you.

- During the formal interview process, wait until after receiving a job offer to talk about salary.
- Evaluate the offer wisely and remember to consider benefits; as previously discussed, some benefits can easily make up for a lower salary.
- Ensure you comprehend the job's description to include reporting relationships, authority, and advancement potential.
- Keep in mind that whatever number you accept is probably not your final number.
- Know the typical pay for the position you apply for; unless you have some unusual qualifications, your salary will probably be in the range you find for your location and experience.

- Know what your salary needs are for your household budget—nothing below is acceptable without changing your lifestyle.
- Consider your long-term career goals and work environment.
- Ask for time to consider the offer, so you can discuss it with a mentor and make an informed decision.
- Keep your requests reasonable and be willing to accept some compromises in place of a higher salary, such as vacation time and other benefits.
- Be firm, but polite. If the offer is less than your acceptable number, let the offeror know it; also, let them know that you are still interested if they raise the offer.
- Do not use your need for the job to negotiate.
- If you are uncertain about the job, ask for an opportunity to discuss a few items later.
- Never get emotional; instead, use your skills, experience, education, and value to negotiate.
- Do not reject an offer hoping to start a negotiation for a higher wage; when you say no, expect the negotiation to close permanently.

Surprisingly, the first offer is seldom fixed, even if the interviewer tells you it is. However, if the same figure is provided a couple of days later, you have probably reached the last offer. In that case, it is decision time. If the compensation is still an issue, you essentially have two choices. You can reject the offer and ask for consideration for future positions, or you can accept the offer and ask for a higher salary during your annual review. After a year, your company should have a good idea of your worth.

Finally, once you have an agreement, ask for it in writing and review it carefully for the items you discussed. Sometimes errors occur, or people forget specific details of a verbal agreement. Having your agreement formalized in writing ensures everyone's understanding is the same.

11

BE AN ENTREPRENEUR

> ***If you ever get tired of searching for a job, you can always create one! There is a lot to be said about being your own boss.***

Much of what we have discussed to this point has involved helping you find the right job working for someone else. However, what if you are not interested in a new employer? Perhaps you are done with punching a clock or answering to a supervisor. Maybe you just want to make your own business decisions, or you have a knack for creating business opportunities. You may not even mind the risks of business ownership, especially when you can enjoy your labor's rewards. If that is you, then perhaps you are met to be an entrepreneur. Entrepreneurs who prove successful in the face of risks and adversity while creating and running a startup are sometimes rewarded with profits, fame, and greater degrees of satisfaction.

There is a lot to be said about working for yourself and being your boss. Best of all, I hear the hiring process is incredibly simple! Many of

America's wealthiest Americans achieved their wealth by starting their own business. Of course, there are some unique challenges to running your enterprise. This chapter will help you balance some pros and cons of self-employment and provide you with some tips and resources to help you start.

In starting a business, there are four phases. Those are to plan, launch, manage, and grow your business.[1] Of course, you need to determine which venture you will undertake, whether it be a landscaping service or a consulting firm. The next is to determine how you will structure your business.

Business Structures

If you go the way of many entrepreneurs, give your business structure some thought. How will you organize to handle liability, address taxes, and manage the business? This section will cover some typical business structures that many business owners set up.

Sole Owner/Proprietorship

Sole proprietorships are the most common and simplest business structure to establish. These types of businesses are not incorporated. Instead, they are owned by one individual who makes no distinction between themselves and their business. The owner is entitled to all profits and is likewise responsible for all debts, losses, and liabilities.

Forming a Sole Proprietorship

What makes sole proprietorships so common is that the business owner requires no formal action. If you are the only business owner, then the business defaults to a sole proprietorship. If you have ever provided lawn services, house cleaning, or tutoring, you are technically a sole proprietor.

Like all businesses, however, you are still required to get licenses and permits to do certain forms of work. Since permits vary by state, locality, and industry, check with your local government agencies to determine what those are. If you choose to operate under a name other than your own, you will probably have to file as an assumed name, trade name, or DBA (doing business as) name.

Taxes for Sole Proprietorships

Because you are your business, the business is not taxed separately. This makes filing your taxes straightforward since your sole proprietor income is your own.

Advantages and Disadvantages of a Sole Proprietorship

A sole proprietorship's advantages include the ease and low cost of forming them, the control that owners have over them, and simplified tax preparation. Sole proprietorships are the simplest and least expensive business structures to manage.

Sole proprietorships do come with one major disadvantage, and that is a liability. Since there is no "legal" separation between you and your business, you may be held liable for debts and judgments your business incurs, even if it is an employee that causes the obligation to be incurred. This means that judgments against your business could also target your house and other assets, leaving you with nothing. Other disadvantages worth noting are challenges when trying to raise money outside of personal loans. You alone are responsible for your business's successes and failures, which can be a significant burden, especially if you like taking a vacation from time to time.

Partnership

A partnership business structure involves two or more people operating a business as co-owners with shared income. All partners or co-owners act on behalf of each other and benefit from the business. Like the sole proprietorship business structure, a partnership is also not separate from its owners. As a result, partnerships enjoy the same pass-through status as sole proprietorships. This means that profits and liabilities pass to the partners.

Two types of partnerships are common. The first is a general partnership. In this partnership, all the members actively take part in the day-to-day operations of the business. They are also individually responsible for a share of any debts or judgments the business incurs. Here, a member's liability is limited to the percentage of their contribution. The share of their liability is specified in the partnership agreement when the business starts. The second is a limited partnership, which may accommodate up to 20 members. In this structure, the general partner is responsible for the business's daily activities and is personally liable for all debts and judgments. Passive partners only contribute some agreed-upon capital but carry no liability for any business obligations. As a result, their liability is limited.

Forming a Partnership

Partnerships are simple to create, but they require a little more work than a sole proprietorship to administer. For instance, when forming a partnership, it is necessary to adhere to the state's legal requirements or regulations where the partnership is created.

Partners must also create a reliable "partnership agreement." This agreement will specify expectations for the business partners, and it will define how to handle disputes. It will also identify each partner's share of the business, their financial contribution, and their partnership responsibility. It will even layout mediation procedures for disputes and capture the process for dissolving the partnership. Consulting a lawyer or other business professional for a partnership agreement is highly advised.

Advantages and Disadvantages of Partnerships

Partnerships are more manageable and less expensive to set up than other business structures, save sole proprietorships. Partners can likewise perform business under a trading name or doing business as (DBA) name. Since multiple people are involved in a partnership, all their resources and expertise can be leveraged. Partnerships are also simple to administer, with profits and losses shared between partners according to their business share. Partnerships also do not have to disclose their earnings to the public, so partners enjoy greater privacy. No complex reports are required, either. Additionally, it is relatively simple to restructure the partnership into a company if the partners desire. Dissolving the association can also be relatively easy, depending on the partnership agreement.

Partnerships still maintain some of the same disadvantages of a sole proprietorship. For instance, partners are all still responsible for any debts or judgments levied against the business. For example, each partner is still liable for other partners' debts, also known as being jointly and severally liable. Partnerships also do not offer a significant tax shelter. As the business' earnings climb, so does each partner's tax bracket.

A partner also does not have the final say-so as they would in a sole proprietorship. Instead, all partners have a right to participate in the partnership's management (unless otherwise agreed). Partners can also transfer their ownership to someone outside the partnership unless stipulated in the partnership agreement. Hence, personal differences may interfere with the business' profitability. Members must use higher-level interpersonal skills such as negotiation, conflict resolution, and compromise to address these differences.

Limited Liability Company (LLC)

An LLC, or limited liability company, is a legally registered business structure limited by shares. It can have one owner or multiple owners who are called members. LLCs with multiple members are called multi-member LLCs or LLC partnerships. All shareholders in this structure are responsible for the liabilities the company incurs; however, that liability is limited to the number of shares an individual holds.

Business owners who desire LLC partnerships want liability protection from the business while still being involved in its daily management and operations. Since most businesses can form LLC partnerships, they are typically a good fit for most people. With an LLC, members have a legal shield between their assets and the business. What this business structure means for business owners is protection from lawsuits resulting in damages. Since the LLC exists as a separate entity, lawsuits must often target it instead of you and your assets. While this provides more protection than sole proprietorships and partnerships, business owners can still be found liable for the actions of another member whose negligent actions result in a lawsuit. This is especially so if you knew your partner's actions were negligent.

Forming an LLC

To form an LLC, you need to determine the business name, which denotes the business' operations. It should end with the descriptor 'LLC.' An LLC requires the filing of Articles of Organization, which regulates company directors' appointment and issuance of shares. The Articles of Organization includes essential information about the LLC, like its physical address, LLC name, all details of the filing agency, and date of incorporation.

As with partnership agreements, LLCs require an Operating Agreement. This document spells out the rights and obligations of each partner in the LLC. The contribution of each member is also recorded, along with how to split proceeds. Finally, the document includes tax considerations. You must also acquire a tax registration certificate from the authorities.

Advantages and Disadvantages of an LLC

Lacking the formal requirements of a corporation, an LLC is an exceptionally flexible business structure. In an LLC, members unanimously agree on how to run the company, and they do not require a board of directors. LLCs are suitable for small and medium-sized businesses. They need not keep sophisticated documentation or hold meetings for discussing business matters. Likewise, LLCs offer greater flexibility for taxes since LLCs can elect to change their tax classification to that of an S Corp or C Corp. Talk to your accountant before you do so.

Perhaps the most significant advantage of owning an LLC is personal liability protection. Members of an LLC can protect their assets from the business' actions and debts; however, protections offered by LLCs vary from state to state. Hence, you should consult professional services and state rules and requirements to understand their potential liability.

A significant drawback to forming an LLC partnership is that members can be held responsible for the other members' actions. LLCs are also more challenging to create than a sole proprietorship or partnership, and mistakes during the LLC's formation can cause unexpected burdens later. Fortunately, you can form an LLC online for a few hundred dollars or less. However, costs can grow much more expensive, so shop around.

Corporations

Corporations are much more complex to create and run than the previous business structures. For the most part, a transitioning veteran will do well to use one of the above business structures; however, the rest of this section is offered for completeness.

Like an LLC, this business structure is a separate legal entity, so it too is responsible for its debts and liabilities. As a result, the corporation can enter contracts, borrow money, sue, be sued, and own assets under its name. It also gets taxed under its name. As a result, corporations get taxed for any generated profits, separate from their employees. In contrast to LLCs and partnerships, a corporation is personally responsible for all its tax obligations. If you form a corporation, both the money you receive from the corporation and the money your corporation earns gets taxed.

A private corporation can also issue an Initial Public Offer or IPO to raise capital. Purchasers earn profits in the form of dividends within a stipulated period. As a result, the investor gets a market share of the corporation's assets and profits. Each shareholder also gets one vote per share to elect the board of directors, and the board has the mandate to deal with the corporation's daily operations. They must also hold meetings to deliberate on how best to achieve business strategies. The goal of this business structure is to gain profit for shareholders who pay for the subscribed shares.

Corporations can have just one shareholder or many. If a corporation goes public, it can have as many shareholders as possible. Corporations also have various formations, such as S Corp and C Corp; however, this section's intent is merely to make you aware that these business structures exist. Please consult your favorite search engine or reach out to some business professionals for more information on corporations. If a corporation is something you are interested in, remember you can still restructure your LLC into a corporation later.

Business Types

Regardless of the business you choose, you have a tremendous amount of work ahead of you as an entrepreneur. At least if you want to build something that will support you and your family. After I retired, I formed two LLCs, and I started two businesses. One was for my wife's emerging silver-smithing business, and the other was for my consulting and investment business. To date, neither business has grown to where we are willing to give up our day jobs, but they serve as additional revenue sources for us

Our businesses are slowly growing, but we need to commit much more time to see them growing substantially. Perhaps you are looking for something like that as well. Small businesses offer some tax advantages that you can't claim with a regular job. However, you may be ready to dive into a full entrepreneurial role. With that in mind, let us look at a few business opportunities you might consider. Before you jump into a business, however, check with your local laws to determine whether there are licenses, insurance, declarations, etc., you must obtain to operate legally. These are not the things you want to find out about after you have started. You also want to figure out how you are going to handle taxes for your business. A great way to approach this is to speak with other business owners and learn about those requirements.

Government contractor

Did you know that the U.S. government is the world's largest purchaser of goods and services? Okay, you may have known that, but did you know that Uncle Sam is also required by law to commit at least 3% of its contracts and subcontracts to small businesses owned by service-disabled veterans. To learn more about becoming a government contractor, I recommend visiting the 'Office of Small & Disadvantaged Business Utilization" website. Here you can get the help you need to become a verified small business and learn about the VA's unique procurement set-asides and sole sourcing opportunities for veteran-owned and socio-economic small business programs. The website is https://www.va.gov/osdbu/faqs/109461.asp.

Advisor or Consultant

As a veteran, you learned a few things over the years. They include unique skills, experiences, and education. It just so happens that some businesses need what you have, only not full-time. This provides you with great consulting opportunities in areas that include security, leadership, fitness, programming, mission systems (respecting classification, of course), and a plethora of other areas.

Franchise Owner

Thousands of veterans have joined a franchise after leaving the service. What is great about a franchise is you do not have to start from scratch. Instead, you benefit from instant recognition, and you can fall in on well-established processes offered by the franchisor, including training and support. Franchises often mirror a military structure in the way they run.

The drawback to a franchise is they come with a bar to entry. You may need tens to hundreds of thousands to start in addition to the one-time franchising fee and ongoing royalties. Still, reach out to a local Subway, Papa Johns, Waffle House, or even Gold's Gym owner and see how they like being a franchisee. I am sure most would say it was a great opportunity. However, like all endeavors, do your homework, get a feel for the market, and make sure it is the right choice for you.

You will find that many franchises also offer substantial discounts to veterans. For instance, I searched the Internet for veteran-owned franchises, and the top advertisement was from UPS. They offer a $10,000 discount from their franchise fee and a 50% discount on the initial application fee. If you're interested in more opportunities, you might consider some Internet searches of your own or visit https://bestforvets.militarytimes.com/franchises/2018/. This site offers a ranked list of 53 franchises based on their initial investment, franchise fee, military discount, royalty or similar fee, continuity and growth rates, and percentage of vet-owned businesses.

Retail

Do you excel in sales, marketing, or supply chain management? Perhaps you have a hobby you are passionate about. A year ago, I met a non-commissioned officer at our county fairgrounds selling BBQ sauce. Making BBQ was something he was passionate about, and it showed. While he had been making BBQ sauce at home for many years, he saw an opportunity to grow his love into a business. My wife and I sampled some of his BBQ sauces, and we bought a few bottles. I just knew he would go into full production as soon as he retired. As it happens, I just pulled out one of his bottles and searched for his company name online. I found the company's website, and it appears the business is in full swing.

Perhaps that is you too! If there is a market for it, then your hobby may be a great opportunity. As a veteran, you can also advertise veteran-owned on your business. That may tempt some civilians to patron your business.

Services

Do you have HVAC, plumbing, electrical, locksmithing, flooring, painting, handyman, lawn care, or other skills? It is a busy world, and many people need these services. If you can provide them, then you already have the foundation for a business. If you have some business savvy and desire, you could bring on others to work with you.

Service-oriented businesses can also be highly lucrative, with some service providers charging over $100 per hour. More impressive is that I have noticed many of these services are in such high demand that I must often wait weeks to have them address an issue for me. If you are aware of a similar high-demand field in your area and have a talent for it, that field could serve as a potential option for you.

Real Estate

Is there something about houses and land that draws you in, then becoming a real estate agent could lead you toward many potential opportunities to grow a business as a broker. As someone with access to the Multiple Listing Service (MLS), you will also be the first to know about many opportunities before they are public knowledge. Working as an agent can open substantial investment opportunities besides providing you with a source of funds. While I am not a real estate agent, I network with several real estate investors in my area who are.

As a real estate agent, you also can set your hours. Of course, if you become an agent to stand up your own brokerage, you need to work with a real estate broker for one to three years before becoming one yourself. To become a broker, one must hold a valid real estate sales agent license and work under that license for one or more years. Some states may only require one year, while others require three, so check your state regulations to see how long it will take you to become a broker.

Becoming a licensed broker may also be required to start a property management business. In Georgia, critical components of property management (renting and leasing) are regarded as real estate activities, so again, check your state laws if property management is of interest to you.

12

KNOW YOUR BENEFITS

Say what you will, the military offers some great benefits! But I will not complain if it adds a few more.

As a transitioning service member, a multitude of resources are at your disposal. These services range from medical and estate planning to educational services and career planning. However, for the sake of space, this section will provide a cursory overview of these benefits that can help you better adjust to life during and after your transition and point you to references where you can gain more information.

DD Form 214

As a veteran, many VA benefits are available after you depart the military. However, the key to accessing them is your DD Form 214. This document serves as proof of your military service, providing the nature of your discharge, record of service, and current classification code. Your retirement services office will provide you a draft of your DD Form 214 before your retirement. Given its importance, make sure you thoroughly inspect this document for accuracy as soon as you receive it.

CAUTION: NOT TO BE USED FOR IDENTIFICATION PURPOSES
THIS IS AN IMPORTANT RECORD. SAFEGUARD IT.
ANY ALTERATIONS IN SHADED AREAS RENDER FORM VOID

CERTIFICATE OF RELEASE OR DISCHARGE FROM ACTIVE DUTY

This Report Contains Information Subject to the Privacy Act of 1974, As Amended.

1. NAME *(Last, First, Middle)*
2. DEPARTMENT, COMPONENT AND BRANCH
3. SOCIAL SECURITY NUMBER

4a. GRADE, RATE OR RANK
b. PAY GRADE
5. DATE OF BIRTH *(YYYYMMDD)*
6. RESERVE OBLIGATION TERMINATION DATE *(YYYYMMDD)*

7a. PLACE OF ENTRY INTO ACTIVE DUTY
b. HOME OF RECORD AT TIME OF ENTRY *(City and state, or complete address if known)*

8a. LAST DUTY ASSIGNMENT AND MAJOR COMMAND
b. STATION WHERE SEPARATED

9. COMMAND TO WHICH TRANSFERRED
10. SGLI COVERAGE ☐ NONE AMOUNT: $

11. PRIMARY SPECIALTY *(List number, title and years and months in specialty. List additional specialty numbers and titles involving periods of one or more years.)*

12. RECORD OF SERVICE	YEAR(S)	MONTH(S)	DAY(S)
a. DATE ENTERED AD THIS PERIOD			
b. SEPARATION DATE THIS PERIOD			
c. NET ACTIVE SERVICE THIS PERIOD			
d. TOTAL PRIOR ACTIVE SERVICE			
e. TOTAL PRIOR INACTIVE SERVICE			
f. FOREIGN SERVICE			
g. SEA SERVICE			
h. INITIAL ENTRY TRAINING			
i. EFFECTIVE DATE OF PAY GRADE			

13. DECORATIONS, MEDALS, BADGES, CITATIONS AND CAMPAIGN RIBBONS AWARDED OR AUTHORIZED *(All periods of service)*
14. MILITARY EDUCATION *(Course title, number of weeks, and month and year completed)*

15a. COMMISSIONED THROUGH SERVICE ACADEMY — YES ☐ NO ☐
b. COMMISSIONED THROUGH ROTC SCHOLARSHIP *(10 USC Sec. 2107b)* — YES ☐ NO ☐
c. ENLISTED UNDER LOAN REPAYMENT PROGRAM *(10 USC Chap. 109) (If Yes, years of commitment: ______)* — YES ☐ NO ☐

16. DAYS ACCRUED LEAVE PAID
17. MEMBER WAS PROVIDED COMPLETE DENTAL EXAMINATION AND ALL APPROPRIATE DENTAL SERVICES AND TREATMENT WITHIN 90 DAYS PRIOR TO SEPARATION — YES ☐ NO ☐

18. REMARKS

The information contained herein is subject to computer matching within the Department of Defense or with any other affected Federal or non-Federal agency for verification purposes and to determine eligibility for, and/or continued compliance with, the requirements of a Federal benefit program.

19a. MAILING ADDRESS AFTER SEPARATION *(Include ZIP Code)*
b. NEAREST RELATIVE *(Name and address - include ZIP Code)*

20. MEMBER REQUESTS COPY 6 BE SENT TO *(Specify state/locality)* ______ OFFICE OF VETERANS AFFAIRS — YES ☐ NO ☐
a. MEMBER REQUESTS COPY 3 BE SENT TO THE CENTRAL OFFICE OF THE DEPARTMENT OF VETERANS AFFAIRS (WASHINGTON, DC) — YES ☐ NO ☐

21.a. MEMBER SIGNATURE
b. DATE *(YYYYMMDD)*
22.a. OFFICIAL AUTHORIZED TO SIGN *(Typed name, grade, title, signature)*
b. DATE *(YYYYMMDD)*

SPECIAL ADDITIONAL INFORMATION *(For use by authorized agencies only)*

23. TYPE OF SEPARATION
24. CHARACTER OF SERVICE *(Include upgrades)*

25. SEPARATION AUTHORITY
26. SEPARATION CODE
27. REENTRY CODE

28. NARRATIVE REASON FOR SEPARATION

29. DATES OF TIME LOST DURING THIS PERIOD *(YYYYMMDD)*
30. MEMBER REQUESTS COPY 4 *(Initials)*

DD FORM 214, AUG 2009 — PREVIOUS EDITION IS OBSOLETE. — SERVICE - 2

Figure 34 - Sample DD Form 214

Addressing errors on your DD Form 214 is much easier if you do it while you are still on active duty. Afterward, a different office will handle any issues with it, and your time to correct errors moves from days (hours sometimes) to months.

When you ETS or retire from military service, you receive two copies of your DD 214. Those are the member-1 copy and the member-4 copy. Your member-1 (short form) can validate military service, while your member-4 (long form) provides your length of service and the character of discharge you received. Your member-4 may be required to validate your eligibility for VA benefits.

You should inspect your entire DD Form 214 for accuracy, but make sure the following blocks include everything they should and know what the entries mean. Key areas to check for accuracy include:

- Block 12—provides a tally of your total years of service. Make sure it adds up to what you think it should.
- Block 13—lists service-connected conditions and awards received during service that may affect your access to VA health care (e.g., Purple Heart or Iraqi Campaign Medal).
- Block 23—provides the type of separation.
- Block 24—provides the character of separation.
- Block 26—gives one of the hundreds of codes used to categorize the reason for a veteran's separation. For example, RBD means "Sufficient Service for Retirement," while RHK means "Substandard Performance."

Once you receive your completed DD Form 214, keep it in a safe and accessible location. Also, make sure your spouse and family members know where to find it should the need arise. You probably want to digitize it as well for quick access. However, keep in mind that you also want to keep this file secure as it contains personally identifiable information that could lead to identity theft and severe headaches if the wrong person gains access to it. Therefore, consider the implications of storing your DD 214 at the county records office. If you keep your files there, they may become public record, putting you at risk for identity theft.

Education, Training, and Upskilling

The VA's Education and Career Counseling (aka Chapter 36) program provides opportunities for service members, veterans, and their spouses to get personalized counseling and support.[1] Not only can these services help guide your career path, but they can also help ensure that you are making the most effective use of your VA benefits to help you achieve your education and career goals. Services include:

- Benefits Coaching — receive guidance on the effective use of VA benefits and other resources to help you achieve your education and career goals
- Career Choice — understanding the best career options based on your interests and aptitudes
- Personalized Support — academic or adjustment counseling to help you remove any barriers to success
- Information on resources to help achieve your education and career goals
- Assistance with understanding your academic strengths and weaknesses
- One-on-one counseling with a qualified counselor who will help you evaluate your skills and strengths and compare them to your personal career goal

These programs are available to transitioning service members within six months of discharge and veterans within one year of their active-duty release. They are also available for any service member or veteran currently eligible for VA education benefits and all VA education beneficiaries. You may find this handy to remember should you decide that you need to make some modifications to your transition plans.

To connect with a VA counselor and receive this personalized assistance, get and fill out a VA Form 28-8832, Education/Vocational Counseling Application, which can be found on va.gov, and mail it to your nearest VA Regional Office. You can also write a letter requesting counseling services. After the VA receives your application or letter, they will contact you to schedule a counselor meeting.

GI Bill

Service members and veterans often equate their GI Bill® benefit to attending a four-year college or getting an advanced degree. GI Bill® programs, however, it can be used for many other types of training, such as

- Vocational and Technical Training
- On-the-Job Training and Apprenticeships[2]
- Correspondence training
- Flight training
- Licensing and national testing reimbursement
- Tutorial assistance

There are two types of GI Bill®: the Post-9/11 GI Bill® and the Montgomery GI Bill® (MGIB).

Post-9/11 GI Bill® (Chapter 33)

The Post-9/11 GI Bill®, or Chapter 33, is an education benefit program for individuals who served on active duty and received an honorable discharge. You may use this benefit for college, business, vocational or certificate programs, apprenticeships, correspondence courses, and on-the-job training. Additionally, remedial, refresher, and deficiency training are available under certain circumstances. For more information about eligibility and other benefits offered by this program, please consult the Post-9/11 website.[3]

Montgomery GI Bill®- Active Duty (Chapter 30)

The MGIB-AD, or Chapter 30, provides up to 36 months of educational benefits for college, certificate programs, on-the-job training, apprenticeships, and correspondence courses. In particular circumstances, some remedial and refresher courses and flight training may be approved. Veterans have ten years from their last date of discharge from active duty to use the MGIB-AD. Payments are made directly to the student. You can visit the MGIB-AD website[4] for more information about eligibility and other benefits of this program.

Yellow Ribbon Program

The Yellow Ribbon Program allows degree-granting institutions in the United States to voluntarily partner with the VA to fund tuition and fee expenses that exceed in-state tuition rates. So, if you plan to attend a Yellow Ribbon partnered school, costs that exceed your GI Bill benefit may be covered by additional funds that are available for program participants. This benefit can be useful if you plan to attend a private institution, graduate school, or an out-of-state (nonresident) status program.

When institutions voluntarily enter a Yellow Ribbon Program agreement with the VA, they choose the tuition and fees they will contribute, and the VA will match the university. So, benefits may vary from one institution to another. To learn more, use your favorite search engine and search for the Yellow Ribbon Program.

Great Education Resources

Beyond the information provided below, I highly recommend you download a copy of the VA Benefits I & II Briefing | Participant Guide available at eBenefits.[5] Not only will you find a more extensive explanation of the above education benefits, but other resources as well. Some of which follow.

- GI Bill® Comparison Tool: www.vets.gov/gi-bill-comparison-tool/
- Resources for Choosing a School: www.dmdc.osd.mil/tgps/
- Montgomery GI Bill®- Selected Reserve (Chapter 1606): www.benefits.va.gov/gibill/mgib_sr.asp

Employment Assistance

AMVETS

AMVETS (American Veterans) is self-reportedly the nation's most inclusive congressionally chartered veterans' service organization. They represent the interests of 20 million veterans, with over 250,000 members nationwide.[6] Their Mission statement is to enhance and safeguard the entitlements and quality of life for all American veterans who served honorably, their families, and the communities where they live through leadership, advocacy, and services.

AMVETS Career Centers provide free-of-charge career training and employment assistance for veterans and service members, Active Guard Reserve, and spouses. They are staffed by volunteers who reach out to the local community and companies to match job-seeking veterans to employers seeking to hire them.

AMVETS is also partnered with the Call of Duty Endowment (CODE), a non-profit public benefit corporation that helps service members transition to civilian careers after their military service. Some services you can get from this organization include:

- Resume, Cover Letters & Interview Tips (including resume scanners)
- Blogs
- Advocates (people who will take your resume, tweak it, and forward it to other companies)
- Education Resources
- Career Services
- Career Center Locators
- Career Assessment

American Job Centers

American Job Centers (AJC)[7] serve nearly a million veterans each year with various free services for career and employment-related needs. Almost 2,400 AJCs exist throughout the United States, and staff members are usually available to help job seekers build a resume. They can also help you with generalized career exploration and job searches. However, these services vary by location. Some services may include:

- Employment plan development, job training, and search services
- Career counseling and interview practice
- Resource rooms with phones, free internet, and resume writing tools
- Skills testing
- Access to your state's job bank or CareerOneStop's national Job Finder
- Labor market, employer information, and employment workshops
- Supportive services (including information about SNAP, financial

assistance, Medicaid, training services, childcare, emergency funds, and other benefits)
- Referrals to community resources and other agencies
- Unemployment insurance information
- Access to Worker Reemployment website for laid-off workers
- Hiring events and business service information
- Accommodations for people with disabilities

US Department of Labor: Veterans' Employment & Training Service (VETS)

Because of the VOW (Veterans Opportunity to Work) To Hire Heroes Act of 2011, service members separating from the military must attend the Transition Assistance Program (TAP). The VOW Act also requires the U.S. Department of Labor to have its employment workshop model today's job market realities. VETS offers the employment workshop at hundreds of military installations worldwide for thousands of separating service members. If you visit their website,[8] you can get various participation guides. You can also sign up for virtual training. The full, virtual TAP curriculum is also available to veterans and spouses of service members through the Joint Knowledge Online (JKO) system.

Estate Planning

An estate plan can help ensure your heirs are cared for in your absence and save you and your loved ones' time and money. They provide specific instructions and authority for others to act on your behalf in your absence. For this reason, estate plans are tailored to your family's needs. These plans can include the following documents.[9]

- **Power of attorney (POA)**: a legal document giving someone the authority to act on your behalf on legal/money matters if you become unable to handle your affairs.

- **Living will (advanced medical directive)**: In case of a severe injury or terminal illness, this legal document allows you to describe which medical treatments you want. You can also assign the person you prefer to make medical decisions for you if you cannot do so.
- **Last will and testament**: This legal document will allow you to dictate your wishes after your death. Without a will, state law governs how your property will be distributed and who should be responsible for the care of your children.
- **Testamentary/Non-Testamentary Trust**: A legal document used to manage or protect assets, provide for multiple beneficiaries, provide privacy, and provide for children or tax planning. This document can help your family avoid the delays and costs of probate court.
- **Survivor benefits**: If you die because of an injury or illness incurred or aggravated during your service, your survivors may be entitled to benefits from the Department of Defense and the Department of Veterans Affairs. Some benefits are automatic, but your family must apply to others.
- **Funeral and burial arrangements**: Including funeral and burial arrangements in your estate plan ensures your last wishes are carried out. Your family is also eligible to receive funeral and burial benefits through VA.

To put your estate plans in order, try contacting an estate planning attorney at your installation's legal assistance office. The following organizations can provide additional legal assistance:

- Armed Forces Legal Assistance Legal Services Locator[10]
- Defense Finance and Accounting Service[11]

- Military funeral honors[12]

VA Housing Benefits

VA housing assistance[13] offers service members and their surviving spouses opportunities to buy a home or refinance a loan. It also provides benefits and services to help you build, improve, or keep your current home. Services include:

- Veterans housing assistance
- VA home loan benefits

VA Health Care

For qualified veterans, VA health care can offer you regular checkups with a primary care provider and appointments with specialists, and you can get medical equipment, prosthetics, and prescriptions. To see if you qualify, visit the VA Health Care Eligibility site.[14]

Compensation

If you are determined to have any disabilities when you leave service, you may qualify for VA disability compensation (pay). This benefit offers a monthly tax-free payment to veterans who became ill or injured while serving in the military and veterans whose service made an existing condition worse. Many conditions qualify for disability, so visit the va.gov/disability website to learn more.

Retirement

If you are retiring, you really should get to know your Retirement Services personnel as early as possible. They will not only help you retire, but they will also be there for you and your spouse throughout your retirement years, no matter where you settle. They are also a huge blessing for your spouse and loved ones should anything untoward happen to you.

- Air Force Personnel Center
- Army Retirement Services Officer
- Navy Retired Activities Branch

Facilities

One benefit of staying near a military installation as a retired service member is you and your family are usually allowed to use the installation's facilities so long as space is available. Examples include the Commissary, Exchange, Fitness Centers, Golf Courses, and Campgrounds, among others. However, this benefit varies at each military installation, and the installation commander determines whether retired personnel may use said facilities. Retirees are usually accommodated, providing their use of the facilities does not adversely affect active-duty service members. Of course, access to facilities may also become reduced or suspended, as shown during the COVID-19 Pandemic, for safety reasons.

Veterans Service Organizations

Veterans Service Organizations (VSOs) are congressionally chartered organizations serving Veterans, their families, and their survivors to address their needs. Many VSOs exist across the country, and they can help you fill out VA forms and provide VA benefits information and other forms of assistance. These VSOs are also classified as "recognized" or "non-recognized." The primary difference being that a recognized organization can legally represent you before VA, while a non-recognized organization cannot. Still, both can provide you with information.

You can also appoint a recognized service organization to serve as your representative. That organization can provide you with a VA Form 21-22, Appointment of Veterans Service Organization as Claimant's Representative, which acts as a limited power of attorney (POA). This limited POA allows the VSO to represent you only for VA-related claim issues. To find a local VSO, try the following link:

https://www.va.gov/ogc/apps/accreditation/index.asp.

You can find all recognized VSOs and accredited national, state, and local VSO representatives, attorneys, and claims agents on the VA database. Leave all fields blank to see all VSOs. Your local VA Medical Center and military installations should have VSOs on location. The eBenefits portal can also help you find a nearby accredited representative. Visit www.ebenefits.va.gov/ebenefits/apply and click "Manage Your VA Representative." You can choose "Request Representative" on the following page.

Homelessness

Have you ever heard that the average American is about two missed paychecks away from homelessness? Many Americans, 63%, state they could not even deal with a $500 emergency.[15] That is concerning! It means that most people are living from paycheck to paycheck despite promotions and years of employment. Unfortunately, corporate America's sad truth is that most companies can fire their employees with no notice.

In contrast, there is high job security in the military, ensuring you will receive a monthly paycheck. Even if you are dismissed or chaptered from military service, this comes with a long, drawn-out process that helps prepare you for your transition. Once you are working in the civilian sector, however, employment can be much more erratic. Many employers maintain *at-will employment* clauses allowing them to dismiss an employee for any reason (without having to establish "just cause" for termination), and without warning,[16] so long as the reason is not illegal (e.g., firing because of the employee's race or religion or for retaliatory reasons).

Illness is another possibility that could wreck your financial balance. If you become ill enough to miss work and your company does not offer sick pay, you could find yourself quickly in arrears. Once you fall behind financially, you may find yourself on a downward slope toward homelessness.

In January 2016, communities across America identified 39,471 homeless veterans.[17] According to the VA, on a single night in January 2017, just over 40,000 veterans were enduring homelessness.[18] I highlight these numbers because homelessness is a real possibility if your debts get the best of you, and support from friends and family is unavailable. Fortunately, veteran Affairs is taking decisive action to end veteran homelessness. Their stated mission is to provide easy access to health, housing, and employment programs and services to all veterans at risk of homelessness or attempting to end their homelessness. As a result, the VA offers various resources, programs, and benefits for homeless veterans or those at risk of becoming homeless. They provide free, 24/7 access to trained counselors, who can connect you with resources for housing, health care, food, and other assistance. Hopefully, you will never need them; however, the government has provided you with a tool to help protect your financial future. Use them! Or point others to them. To contact VA counselors:

- Call: 1-877-4AID VET (1-877-424-3838)

I do not mention these resources because I believe homelessness is in your future. Quite the contrary, after all, you are a forward-thinking individual applying this book's principles. Nevertheless, I'm giving you a tool, and it is one you can share with others. Once you achieve your thriving transition, you can help others achieve theirs.

More Information

To obtain more information concerning your VA Benefits, please consult the following table.

Table 6 - VA Benefits Table

Benefit Program	VA Toll-Free Number	Website Address
Disability Compensation	1-800-827-1000	https://benefits.va.gov/compensation/
Educational Assistance	1-888-442-4551	https://benefits.va.gov/gibill/
Health Care Information	1-877-222-8387	https://www.va.gov/health/
Home Buying Assistance	1-800-827-1000	https://www.benefits.va.gov/homeloans/
Life Insurance	1-800-669-8477	https://www.benefits.va.gov/INSURANCE/
Vocational Rehabilitation	1-800-827-1000	https://www.benefits.va.gov/vocrehab/

13

BUILDING WEALTH

> *Managing debt and consumption are your greatest challenges to building wealth; but know this, plenty of people do—plenty of people just like you.*

You may wonder why I would include a chapter on wealth building in a book about transitioning from military service. However, wealth building is what sets this book apart from many others. Millions of veterans can and do demonstrate the ability to survive and succeed beyond their active-duty service. But this book is not about surviving or even just landing well. No, this book is about thriving during your post-military years. Of course, complete books are dedicated to building wealth, and I do not pretend this book will cover every wealth-building step out there. That said, what it will do is, as concisely as possible, introduce you to a systematic and disciplined approach to building wealth. Better yet, it is an approach you can start right now!

There is one other advantage you will gain from my single chapter on wealth building, no fluff! I have no room to drag on for countless pages. Moreover, I do not run seminars on wealth building, so I will not try to sell you my latest game or weekend seminar. Nope, you will get as much of it as I can scrape together in a single chapter. These are strategies that have allowed me to grow a substantial net worth of my own. Let's get started!

What's Required to Grow Wealth?

Not too long ago, my wife asked me, "do you think it takes money to make money?" It was a thought-provoking question regarding a recent rental property I purchased. Because I had money available, I made a great purchase that would ultimately lead to a substantial return on investment (ROI). After giving the question some thought, I responded, "Yes. It does, but not much."

My wife and I had very little when we were newlyweds. What we did have were a mortgage and a student loan, so making purchases like the one I just made wasn't a possibility, then. However, after starting a regular saving plan and learning to live off less than what we earned, we began accumulating the savings we needed to get started—and our wealth grew.

The coup de grâce to obstacles standing between you and a thriving transition is building wealth!

It should be no surprise that it takes money to make money. But do not let that discourage you. That is only one avenue. What may surprise you is how little is needed to accrue wealth. Sometimes, the money does not even have to be yours. However, many high-income earners never make this connection, as many wealth experts share. For instance, in their book, "The Millionaire Next Door," Dr. Tom Stanley and Dr. William D. Danko make an odd discovery.[1] While surveying their subjects, they found that most people living in expensive homes in upscale neighborhoods and driving high-end cars were not actually wealthy. Instead, they found that while these people may have substantial incomes, they were also spending it all.

What many people do not seem to realize is that wealth is not the same thing as income. Instead, the authors sagely define wealth as something you accumulate, not what you spend. If you spend everything you make, you can't grow wealthy, save some unlikely event. Stanley and Danko also say that wealth is often the result of hard work, perseverance, planning, and self-discipline. These habits applied over time provide a steady path to wealth. Those are the same traits that veterans have consistently used during missions throughout their military service. So, make financial freedom your next mission.

> ***"There is profit in all hard work, but endless talk leads only to poverty."***
>
> ***—Proverbs 14:23 (CSB)***

With a little discipline, you, too, will be well on your way to building wealth. Therefore, we will spend this chapter learning about what wealth is and what it takes to obtain it. Isn't that one of the reasons you picked up this book? After all, you are not just looking for a pension or a job you are tied to forever. Nope. You are looking for a more fulfilling future.

If you are reading this book early in your military career, then congratulations! The earlier you apply the principles I cover in this chapter, the sooner you will begin securing your financial future. You may even approach or surpass millionaire status as you approach retirement. Chris Hogan, the author of "Everyday Millionaire," another book you should read, tells readers that anyone in the United States can become a millionaire regardless of where you come from and what you do for a living. It is a bold statement, but many first-generation millionaires have proven him right.

So, if anyone can become wealthy, then why don't they? What is the big secret to growing wealth? Earlier, I wrote that wealth is what we accrue, so what do we need to accrue to grow wealthy? The answer is assets!

These are the things that make money for us, whether we are working or not. Of course, our assets must exceed our debts for us to have wealth. Let us now look at how we do that.

Play Offense

In the world of sports, strategy, and competition, our offense is how we gain points. It is what allows us to create a deficit between our opponent and us and eventually win. If we never put points on the board, then our best outcome is a tie where no one wins. So, how does one play offense? Keep reading!

Accumulate Assets

The first rule of wealth building is to acquire assets. But, before we talk about assets, let us take some time to make sure you understand exactly what an asset is. In fact, for some folks, this requires a paradigm shift. Perhaps you are one of them. A clear way to find out is through self-evaluation. What do you consider to be your assets? Take a moment and list them below. This does not have to be a lengthy process. Just name your top four or more. Once you have completed this task, we will further explain what qualifies something to be an asset.

1. ______________________________
2. ______________________________
3. ______________________________
4. ______________________________
5. ______________________________

Great! Now that you have listed your "assets," let us consider whether they qualify. To do so, we apply two simple qualification questions, which are used by many book authors, seminar hosts, and online articles. It's also Investing 101.

First question, do you own it? For some of the items you listed, there is a chance you do not actually own them outright. So also ask, do you own a portion of it? For instance, you may own a home—at least you may pay a mortgage on a house that has allowed you to accrue equity in the home. Owning something or owning the right to use something is the first criterion for establishing an item as an asset.

To grow wealth, you need your your money earning for you.

Second question, does the listed item improve your net worth? This last question is a colossal disqualifier. You may own several things, but if those things are not generating revenue, then they are not assets. What is worse, they may even be a liability. For instance, if you owned a home in 2008 when the housing bubble burst, then you may have found yourself upside down on your mortgage. This turn of events meant you could not sell your house without taking a loss. At that point, many property owners had a liability.

Did the above questions serve as an eye-opener? Chances are you own a car or are completing payments on one. Based on the two qualification questions above, would you call it an asset? While you may own the vehicle, does it generate revenue? Did your net worth improve because you bought it? If you answered no, then it is disqualified as an asset. What about your house? Ooh! That is an interesting question. For many Americans, owning a home is the American dream. However, is it an asset? If you live in it, then the answer is maybe.

Wait! What?

Yep, the item representing one of the largest payments you make each month may or may not really be an asset. I do not know that I would call it a liability, though. For instance, if the property is appreciating and increasing your net worth, it could be considered an asset. Still, appreciation rates for homes do not tend to be great compared to other investments, and some actually depreciate. However, if you are subletting a room, your home generates an income and is an asset. Homes are one of those gray areas. Nevertheless, your wealth building strategy should include more than paying off your home.

An asset is something you own and grows your networth.

Now, if you turn that property over to a property manager as a rental or manage it as a rental yourself, and the net return after paying the mortgage, insurance, taxes, etc., is in the positive, then you have an asset. Congratulations! So, maybe that house you went upside down on earlier becomes an asset after all—mine did!

So, what else might you consider an asset? Do you have money in a Thrift Savings Plan, a 401K, an IRA, a savings account, or stock? If so, these are also items that generate a return on investment (ROI) and improve your net worth. They are assets. Some of these can even help you with accruing wealth by limiting the number of dollars you have to pay to Uncle Sam's tax collection service.

Just remember assets are something you own and improve your net worth. In the sections that follow, we will discuss some assets that may warrant your attention in greater detail. Also, keep in mind that the period leading up to your transition is an ideal time to take a snapshot of your current assets and assess your goals. By putting a financial plan in place, you will begin to understand what is required to transition into your desired lifestyle. You will also develop a clear picture of whether you need to pay down debt or save and invest more during your remaining work years. The good news is that your military retirement paycheck—if you have one—can be leveraged to do just that. If not, there are other sources of leverage that I will introduce.

Military Retirement

If you are fortunate enough to retire from military service, congratulations, you are already well on your way to financial freedom. Some may argue that you are a millionaire already, given the tremendous boon your retirement or pension offers. It may even be your single greatest asset. Think about it. For the rest of your life, you have a monthly stipend that requires no additional contribution from you. And, if you use it to support your wealth-building strategy, your wealth can grow by leaps and bounds during the years following your transition. Let us assume your pension will be approximately $40,000[2] if you retire this year. What is that really worth to you?

Table 7 - Retirement Asset Value

Year (2021)	Pay $(x + (1+0.0215)^{year})$	Total
0	$40,000.00	$40,000.00
1	$40,860.00	$80,860.00
2	$41,738.49	$122,598.49
3	$42,635.86	$165,234.35
4	$43,552.54	$208,786.89
5	$44,488.92	$253,275.81
10	$49,481.59	$490,486.07
15	$55,034.57	$754,316.76
20	$61,210.70	$1,047,755.31
25	$68,079.96	$1,374,124.41
30	$75,720.09	$1,737,119.61
35	$84,217.62	$2,140,851.21
40	$93,668.77	$2,589,890.76

To calculate what your retirement is worth in today's dollars, consider Table 7 - Retirement Asset Value, which accounts for an inflation rate of 2.15% per year.[3] You will quickly notice that for every year you live, the value of your retirement grows. Just imagine retiring at 42 years and living at least another 40 years. Because of this windfall, the years immediately following your retirement could be your most lucrative. For instance, you could choose to invest your retirement while living off your new career's earnings, which will add greater financial security for your later years. Of course, many military members do not retire, so we will cover other ways to achieve financial freedom en route to your thriving transition as well.

Real Estate

Real estate investing is perhaps one of the most potent ways to accrue wealth and secure passive income. Even if you do not retire from military service, you can eventually achieve a comparable (or much better) monthly cash flow through real estate investing. This subject truly deserves a book all its own. There is just way too much information to cover. Fortunately, books and online resources are available to quickly put you on the path to financial freedom through real estate investing, and I will share them throughout this section.

For instance, an excellent source of information about real estate investing is Brandon Turner's book, "The Book on Rental Property Investing." Unlike many other books that entice you with how the author grew rich by investing in real estate, providing no actual "how-to" information, Brandon's book is both practical and informative. Many authors also spend more pages marketing their much more expensive workshops, mentoring programs, and courses instead of giving you the information you need. While Brandon encourages readers to visit and become members of BiggerPockets.com—a site where he frequently blogs and contributes podcasts and webinars—that site, at least, has free and useful resources.

The resources you will find at BiggerPockets.com include blogs, newsletters, podcasts, and financial calculators. Multiple other real estate investors and authors also credit the site, and its contributors, with their success, so it must be doing something right. If you visit the site, you can also sign up for the group's free weekly newsletter, which contains loads of real estate investing advice.

Unfortunately for me, I had already bought my third rental property and was working on my fourth when I found Brandon's book. Okay, his audiobook! As I listened to his book, I found myself lamenting over how I could have done somethings better had I only read Brandon's book sooner. Granted, I still had a positive net cash flow from my properties, and my net worth was growing. However, Brandon offers pointers that would have helped me earn a better return on investment (ROI). I have since made some adjustments, and I am now up to seven properties. Of course, I am also looking for number eight—real estate investors never stop looking for deals.

So why invest in real estate? Well, when done correctly, real estate can provide you with a substantial ROI. Not only do property values generally appreciate over time, but they offer rent too! For example, assume a property you purchased for $90,000 appreciates at a rate of 2% per year. Assume also that you can rent that property for $1000 per month. What is that investment worth to you at the end of five years? Here is a simple, high-level calculation. Note it excludes costs incurred from insurance, taxes, maintenance, and other typical expenses.

Value = $90,000 $(1.02)^5$ + $1000 * 12 [months/year] * 5 [years]
= $159,367
Total Earned = $159,367 - $90,000 = $69,367
ROI = $69,367 / $90,000 = 77%
Annual ROI = 77% / 5 = ~15%

That's not bad! Actually, a 15% ROI is outstanding compared to many investment options out there. Of course, you may not have $90,000 to purchase that property. So, financing is another option. Some even argue it is the better option.

If you are curious about what kind of ROI financed real estate can yield, then just consider Table 8 - Real Estate Investing Rate of Returns.

This table assumes you are purchasing a property for $100,000 using a conventional loan with a 4.5% interest rate and paying a 20% down payment. These values are comparable to a purchase I recently made. Typically, I get 30-year loans for lower monthly payments; however, I have provided comparisons for 15-year and 30-year repayment options.

Table 8 - Real Estate Investing Rate of Returns

Loan Type (4.5%)	Mortgage Taxes Insurance	Down Payment	Annual Cost	Rent	15-Year Profit	15-Year Equity	15-Year Net Gain	15-Year ROI
15-Year	$987	($20,000)	($11,842)	$950	($5,304)	$110,000	$84,696	423%
30-Year	$755	($20,000)	($9,060)	$950	$35,100	$54,000	$69,100	346%

For the table, we assume the property appreciates by $10,000 over the next 15 years. This gain represents a conservative appreciation rate of less than 1% per year. While some properties do worse or even depreciate, all of mine have exceeded the above numbers. Now, observe the 15-year gains for both finance options. For a 15-year loan, you pay out of pocket (roughly $37 per month). However, the accelerated payoff schedule results in the property being owned free and clear by you at the end of 15 years. So, what does that mean for your initial investment of $20,000 and $37 monthly payment? Well, after 15 years, you now own a $110,000 property, having paid $25,304. That is a 423% return on investment or 28% per year.

For the 30-year repayment plan, you begin with a cash flow of $195 per month; however, you only achieve equity of $54,000 by your 15th year. The upside is you have also earned $35,100 from cash flow. So, from your initial investment of $20,000, you earn $69,100 for an ROI of 346% over 15 years, or 23% interest per year.

Of course, the above calculations represent ideal conditions where your property stays rented, and it discounts the costs of purchase fees, management fees, repairs, vacancy rates, etc. It also doesn't account for increased revenue from rent increases. Still, as good as those numbers are, many real estate investors manage much better returns, doubling their money every five to seven years. Real estate investing is also something you can do while on active duty—I did!

For instance, your reoccurring permanent change of station or PCS puts you in a great position to build wealth through real estate investing. Say you bought an ***affordable*** property where you live today—preferably discounted. Now, say you turn that property over to a property manager when you move to your next assignment. When you arrive, you again buy a property and live in it for two or three years while receiving rent from your previous property—minus mortgage and other fees. Now, say you move again, repeating the process. You currently have two properties doing very cool things: accumulating rent, gaining value, paying down principal, providing tax incentives, and waiting for you to pay them off and retire. Consider that you keep repeating this process even after leaving service. Before long, you will increase your wealth, accumulate a substantial net worth, and ensure a future income source.

As I mentioned, I currently own seven rental properties, and I acquired them through various methods. My first two were properties I purchased and lived in after changing duty assignments. One is a cash purchase I made using my savings after departing the military. Another I acquired after doing a cash-out refinance against my first property. The next was purchased using a conventional loan with the down payment provided by the funds left over from my cash-out refinance. I acquired my sixth property from a foreclosure auction. My most recent property was a deal my property manager brought to me. I bought it with a conventional loan. So, multiple paths exist for acquiring real estate; however, my experiences only represent a handful of the possibilities that exist.

Naturally, real estate investing is not without risk. Few high-return investments are, though I feel it is less risky than other investment options. That said, I encourage you to do your homework, starting with the reading list at the end of this section. I have also summarized some of my lessons learned on real estate investing in the following list. Use them as a starting point for identifying what you need to know before jumping into real estate.

1. Use a real estate agent. As a buyer, they cost you nothing, and they can help you find great deals.
2. Visit biggerpockets.com. This site offers free podcasts, calculators, sample forms, and several other features to help you pave your way into real estate investing. They also provide a pro-plan for less than $400 a year, but that is optional. I have only ever used their free services.
3. Only buy great deals. Always remember that you make your money when you buy! That means you want to pick up equity when you buy a home. If you do, your net worth will grow with every purchase. You can also sell if necessary without real estate agent fees causing you to lose money. To find these deals, consider bank-owned and distressed properties, foreclosure auctions, and let your real estate agent know what you are looking for great deals only.
4. Only buy homes that generate positive cash flow. If properties cost you money each month, then logistics may eventually catch up to you. I seek properties that generate a monthly rent equal to at least 1% of the purchase price after closing costs and repairs. Some investors set rates of 1.5% and higher, but these rates may not be achievable in all areas.
5. Know the financing available to you.
    a. VA (Veteran Affairs Loan)–Your VA guaranteed loan, use it
    b. FHA (Federal Housing Administration)—Low down payment for a primary home
    c. Conventional—Generally requires 20% down, with bank financing the rest
    d. Cash-out refinance–If you own a home, pull out 70% to 80% of its value to buy another property

    e. Private Lending–Use with caution—these have high-interest rates and limited payoff periods, but they can be useful for short-term acquisitions
    f. Owner Financed–Flexible options and not carried on your credit report, so no hit to your credit
6. Know where to find great deals. Search these for more information.
    a. Foreclosures
    b. Bank Owned for Real Estate Owned (REO)
    c. Tax Lean Sales
    d. Wholesalers
    e. Distressed properties
    f. Motivated Sellers
7. Identify Your Core Four.
    a. Real Estate Agent–helps you find deals, has access to the MLS, and can take care of all the paperwork
    b. Lender–enables you to get your loan cleared quickly
    c. General Contractor–distressed properties often need work, and you need to turn the property quickly; a contractor can make that happen
    d. Property Manager–you have your life, career, and other opportunities to manage. Let someone else manage your property
8. Other allies:
    a. Lawyer–can help you close on your properties, offer estate planning, provide contract assistance, etc.
    b. Abstractors or title researchers–can research properties for you and determine if there are any issues with the property before you purchase
    c. CPA—puts your taxes in order, helps with depreciation schedules, reduces your tax liability, and offers business advice
9. Know the real estate investing groups in your area and network with them. Many of them have a passion for sharing knowledge.
    a. REA
    b. Meetup.com

Real Estate Reading List:

Finally, many resources can aid you in your real estate investing adventure. Below, I list some books I have found useful.

1. "The Book on Rental Property Investing: How to Create Wealth and Passive Income Through Smart Buy & Hold Real Estate Investing," by Brandon Turner
2. "The Book on Investing in Real Estate with No (and Low) Money Down: Real-Life Strategies for Investing in Real Estate Using Other People's Money," by Brandon Turner.
3. "Finding and Funding Great Deals: The Hands-On Guide to Acquiring Real Estate in Any Market," by Anson Young
4. "Bidding to Buy: A Step-by-Step Guide to Investing in Real Estate Foreclosures," by David Osborn and Aaron Amuchastegui.

Stocks, Mutual Funds, and ETFs

Wouldn't it be nice if there were things in place that could put your dollars to work, making money and multiplying the value of your savings? It just so happens that there are. For instance, several investment vehicles beyond your savings account exist for accruing wealth. These investment vehicles have also shown a much better return on investment. While your savings account might generate an interest rate of 0.85% to 1.25% annually, these other vehicles provide 8% to 25% and higher.

The risk is that you can also see a negative swing, meaning you could suffer a substantial loss. But, on average, these vehicles have shown significant growth over extended periods. These vehicles include stocks, mutual funds, and exchange-traded funds (ETFs). As far as which option is right for you, it likely depends on your tolerance for risk and preferences. These investment vehicles need time and disciplined contributions to be effective. However, with long-term investment strategies, you can significantly benefit from compounding. Compounding is when you receive interest on top of the interest you have already earned. As a result, over time, compounding can help multiply your wealth.

For example, assume you contribute $10,000 to a mutual fund that provides 10% interest per year. Now, assume you contribute nothing else to this account for the next seven years. Well, after the first year, you would have $11,000. Not bad! You earned $1,000 for your $10,000 investment. But how much would the second year bring? Not $1000, but ten percent of $11,000, which is $1100, so your new value is now $12,100. If you continue this process for seven years, then at the end-of-year seven, your initial investment of $10,000 will be worth $ 19,487.17. If you take it one year further, you will more than double your initial investment of $10,000 to $21,435.88. Welcome to the power of compounding. Of course, that is if you just made a one-time investment. Most savvy investors, including myself, invest monthly, and the gains are much better.

At this point, you may wonder how to get started. Here are some investment options to consider.

Stocks

When you invest in a stock, you are purchasing a share of a company. Stocks are a good option when you want to build a portfolio by picking stocks from companies that interest you. There are other pros to stocks. For one, they are highly liquid with no annual or ongoing fees. You also have complete control over the stocks you buy. You can invest in any company you choose and decide when to sell them.

You can also employ tax-efficient strategies to avoid capital gains taxes on the stocks you buy and sell. For all this, you typically pay a minor commission when you make a trade. The flexibility of stocks, however, is what makes this investment option highly attractive to me.

The downside of stocks is they carry more risk than mutual funds. Buyers must ensure that their stock portfolio is diversified to mitigate risk. Researching and monitoring stock performance can also be time-intensive, as investors must research and follow each stock in their portfolio for changes. Fortunately, you can download applications to your phone, tablet, or computer to track this for you.

Since investing in stocks carries substantial risk, I do not advise placing large investments in a single stock. ***You could lose it all!*** Let me repeat that. ***You could lose it all!*** For instance, when the Enron Corporation went bankrupt in 2001, many lost their entire life's savings overnight. Why? Because they only had one stock in their portfolio—Enron. The lesson here is to not tie your life savings, or even a significant portion of it, to a single stock, or even a couple. Instead, try to diversify your stock investments and track their performance regularly. Doing so will protect you when you make that eventual blunder on that surefire stock that tanks two-days after purchasing it. If you are diversified, you can weather such mistakes and still grow your portfolio. If not, the impact on your savings could be devastating.

Mutual Funds

Mutual funds (also known as equity mutual funds) are like a middleman between you and stocks. Mutual funds pool investor money and invest it in multiple different companies. A mutual fund offers more diversification by bundling many company stocks into one investment. Rather than picking individual stocks, you can build a portfolio of many stocks in a single transaction through a mutual fund. Many mutual fund investors prefer the simplicity of making monthly contributions through their broker, accruing wealth.

Mutual funds are also useful if you are looking for quick and straightforward diversification and want to invest in many stocks through a single transaction. Mutual funds are often actively managed instead of being passively tracked as an available index. Sometimes, this brings added value to a fund. However, many mutual funds require a minimum investment to open an account. The fees associated with mutual funds are also higher, including annual expenses, short-term redemption fees, transaction fees, etc.

Exchange-Traded Funds (ETFs)

Exchange-Traded Funds (ETFs) entered the trading world in 1993. Since then, they have grown in popularity, and they have many positive characteristics. For one, you can buy ETFs through virtually any online broker, whereas mutual funds do not share the same level of availability. ETFs can be a great alternative if you find it challenging to meet initial minimums for mutual funds. Starting with an ETF can also help you achieve a long-term buy-and-hold strategy that holds to mainstream indices.

As a standard index, ETFs are more tax-efficient and more liquid than mutual funds, making them a good choice for investors looking to build wealth over the long haul. Many online brokers offer commission-free ETFs, regardless of your account balance. One drawback of an ETF is that it will do what the index it is tracking does. Hence, if your ETF is tracking the S&P 500, and that index takes a 25% loss, so will your ETF. I have never owned an ETF, but it may be worth considering if your research pushes you that way.

Trading

I first started contributing to a mutual fund back in 2001 through a company that targeted military members. While that investment vehicle did not prove ideal because of its fee structure, it got me started with a healthy investment routine. Today, many financial institutions provide brokerage services, making it simple to trade with affordable fees. Given the convenience and low costs of trading, I started trading on my own. Once I realized I achieved substantially better returns managing my investment portfolio, I decided to keep doing it. Of course, I've made a few mistakes along the way, but I made it a point to stay diversified, so the mistakes have not prevented me from increasing my net worth each year.

When I finally decided to manage my portfolio, I cashed out all my mutual funds and started trading. Initially, I made a few blunders, but I soon found my niche focusing on stocks with a little more volatility than others. I also started using Charles Schwab after USAA broke away from the brokerage business and transferred my accounts. I was happy with USAA; however, Charles Schwab has proven to be a superior resource, and my portfolio continues to grow. I even accrued substantial returns over the COVID-19 Pandemic.

I feel obligated at this point to add one caveat. I am following an investment strategy that is right for me right now. I am not an expert. Wrong choices could crash my investments as quickly as they could yours. Consider this my disclaimer. You should consult other stock trading resources and professionals if you are considering trading stocks. Despite that warning, sound investing over time has proven itself a reliable means to increase one's wealth.

Retirement Accounts

Retirement accounts are a great way to accumulate assets. They offer many tax benefits, and by setting up automatic deposits, you can create an artificial economic environment of scarcity. All that means is you learn to live without the money you contribute because you never see it. It also supports the principle of paying yourself first. Before a dollar goes to anything else, some portion is already committed to your investments. Meanwhile, you are accruing wealth.

You can begin making withdrawals from your retirement accounts by age 59 ½ (55 for TSP). Earlier withdraws will probably result in you owing both federal income tax (taxed at your marginal tax rate) and a 10% penalty on the amount you draw, besides any relevant state income tax. If that sounds like a bad deal, do not forget that these are retirement accounts, and they are incentivized to ensure you use them accordingly. With that in mind, make sure you diversify your investments so you still have other assets you can liquidate should the need arise or other asset-building opportunities present.

Thrift Savings Plan (TSP)

Retirement accounts offer great, tax-deferred ways to accrue assets. The *Thrifts Savings Plan (TSP)* is one such example. It offers military members a tax-advantaged way to save for retirement. As a federal government-sponsored retirement savings and investment plan, the TSP provides service members the same savings and tax benefits that many private corporations offer their employees under "401(k)" plans. As such, the TSP represents an excellent way for service members to accrue assets before leaving the service, and one I used heavily during the last ten years of my career.

Better yet, as part of the military's new retirement plan, the government contributes 1% of your base pay to your TSP account and will match up to 5% of your contribution for a combined 11% of your base each year. It is an excellent plan for building wealth, and funds typically go into a mutual fund investing vehicle. If you are still on active duty, investing that 5% of your base pay is an easy decision, yet I fear too many will not take advantage of this opportunity.

Of course, once you leave the military, you must decide what to do with this account. You have three tax-free options to consider.

- Leave the funds in your TSP account.
- Roll your TSP into a traditional Individual Retirement Account.
- Roll your money over into your new employer's plan

As stated, all these choices are tax-free and allow for the continuation of tax-deferred compounding. As a bonus, any tax-free combat pay contributions in your TSP balance can also be rolled into a Roth IRA, so its tax-free status remains in place while continuing to accumulate tax-free earnings. Interpret that to mean Uncle Sam will not hit you with any income taxes for combat pay transferred to a Roth IRA, nor will he tax the interest you earn off of it over the hopefully many years that follow.

The third choice might be worthwhile if your employer's plan offers a quality investment selection. This choice would allow you to merge your accounts while retaining the ability to maintain borrowing power from the TSP's balance. You may even gain the opportunity to access your money at a younger age if you roll your TSP funds over to a future employer's plan.

Of course, you could cash in your TSP, but this is considered a bad move, especially if you are under the age of 55. It is also counter-intuitive to your wealth building strategy since you will undoubtedly lose money on this maneuver. First, income taxes would come due, and you may get hit by a 10% early withdrawal penalty. Most advisors recommend maintaining the account for its tax-deferred status and opportunity for continued growth.

401(k)

Once you leave the military, other options become available to aid you along your wealth-building journey. One such option is the 401(k) plan. A 401(k) is a tax-advantaged, defined contribution (DC) plan. Simply put, it is a retirement plan where the employer, employee, or both make contributions regularly using pre-tax dollars. With a 401(k), you can make contributions through an automatic payroll withholding, just as you did with your military TSP. Employers may also match some or all the contributions you make.

The 401(k), like the TSP, is a great way to grow your wealth. All contributions to a 401(k) are pre-tax dollars. Hence, your contribution is not taxed until you withdraw the money in your later years—typically, after retirement. In 2021, you can contribute up to $19,500 in pre-tax dollars to a 401(k) account, plus anything your employer contributes. For example, some employers may provide employee match options of 3%-6%. This is virtually free money, and it provides an instant return on your investment. Even if you do not max out this option, both my wife and I do, you should at least invest enough to get your employer's full match.

Consider this. To make the math easy, assume you get a job earning $100,000 per year, and you maximize your 401(k) contribution. Assume also that your employer offers a 4% match. In this case, you would contribute $19,500 ($26,000, if you are over 50) to your account, and your employer would add an additional $4,000. Your total contribution would be $23,500 for the year. Even before you consider interest (mine was 25% last year), you have a return of 20.5% from your employer's contribution alone. But, as the infomercials say, that's not all. You also get tax savings. Instead of paying a federal and state income tax on $100,000, you only have to pay taxes on the $80,500 remaining after your contribution. It's a great deal any way you slice it.

Here is another interesting tidbit. Did you know that most millionaires today did so by maxing out their employer's 401(k)? According to Chris Hogan, author of Everyday Millionaires, that is how most of them did it!

403(b)

A 403(b) is comparable to a 401(k). For instance, it is a tax-sheltered annuity (TSA) plan, and employers may offer this retirement savings option as part of an employee's benefits package. Employers may also match employees' contributions. However, this plan benefits employees of tax-exempt organizations (e.g., nonprofits, churches, hospitals, and public education institutions).

Traditional IRA

With a traditional Individual Retirement Account (IRA), you receive many of the tax-deferred benefits we discussed in the 401(k) section. You also gain access to other investment opportunities beyond the limited investment options found in your employer's 401(k) plan. However, for IRAs in 2021, your contribution is limited to $6,000 per year. If you are over age 50, you may contribute up to $7,000 annually. You will typically set up these accounts with your broker instead of your employer, so employer match options may not be available.

Now, if you take that $100,000 salary and max your IRA contribution and your 401(k) contribution, your total taxable income drops to $74,500. You will also have contributed over 25% of your annual income to your investments. One drawback to Traditional IRAs, however, is there are limits to tax-deductible contributions. Restrictions begin after your adjusted gross income exceeds a specified amount. That amount is determined by multiple factors, like whether you are single, filing jointly, enrolled in an employer retirement plan already, have a spouse enrolled in one, etc. Check with your broker or CPA to ensure you get the numbers right.

Roth IRA

A Roth IRA is an individual retirement account that offers tax-free growth and tax-free withdrawals in retirement. Unlike the Traditional IRA, Roth contributions are not tax-deferred. Instead, you pay taxes upfront on your income, and the Roth IRA will provide you with tax-free income when you withdraw from your IRA later. Roth IRAs can be a good option if you believe you will be in a higher tax bracket when you draw. If you are applying the principles offered in this book, that may be a possibility.

Roth IRA rules dictate that as long as you've owned your account for five years and you are age 59½ or older, you can withdraw your money when you want to, and you will not owe any federal taxes. You should also know that the $6,000 contribution limit applies whether you contribute to a Traditional IRA, a Roth IRA, or both. Also, like Traditional IRAs, your adjusted gross income may restrict your contributions. Check with your broker for additional guidance.

Other Saving Options

Savings Deposit Program (SDP)

One option for boosting your savings is the DoD *Savings Deposit Program (SDP). It is* available to members of the uniformed services serving in designated combat zones. If you serve in an SDP-eligible combat zone, you can start your SDP account once you have deployed for a minimum of 30 consecutive days. Your military finance office can help you establish an account and set up a convenient deposit method. Once started, you can deposit up to $10,000 during each deployment and receive 10% interest annually.

Your money will continue to draw interest for 90 days after you return home or reach your next duty station. Deposit methods include cash, check, or allotment. These allotments may be increased or decreased as your financial situation changes, and they stop when you depart the combat zone. Your account gets closed 120 days after that, and the funds transfer back to you via direct deposit. To find out more about SDP, visit the Defense Finance and Accounting Service (DFAS).[4] Just keep in mind, once you receive this money, use it to acquire assets.

Bonds

A bond is a debt security that serves as an IOU. A borrower issues a bond to raise money from investors who will lend them cash for a certain amount of time. So, when you buy a bond, you are lending to the issuer—who could be a government, corporate, or other organization. In return, the borrower agrees to return your money plus some agreed-upon interest after a period in which the bond matures. Bonds also are low yield with interest rates ranging from .15% to 1.45%. That is not great, but it is better than leaving your money under your bed mattress. Unfortunately, inflation may compete with your interest rate, essentially allowing you to break even. For instance, according to the U.S. Labor Department, the United States' annual inflation rate was 1.4% in 2020 and 1.3% in 2019. Think of how much worse it could be if you just left it under your mattress, though.

CDs

A certificate of deposit (CD) is a financial product commonly sold by banks, thrift institutions, and credit unions. They differ from savings accounts in that CDs have a specific, fixed term, from one month to five years, and a fixed interest rate. Banks expect the CD to be held until maturity, at which point, the CD can be withdrawn with interest. Interest rates for this investment vehicle vary depending on the duration the investment will be left in place. According to Investopedia, five-year CDs have the best interest rates, and those can run as high as 1.59%, with the average being 0.43%.[5] I do not own any CDs, but they represent a stable and slow means to grow wealth. These also may not keep up with inflation.

Savings Accounts

A savings account is probably something everyone reading this book is familiar with. A savings account is a great place to store your emergency fund for ready access while still earning a little more interest than you will receive from your checking account. Interest rates can be highly varied. For instance, USAA Federal Savings bank offers 0.05% interest for savings accounts holding less than $50,000,[6] whereas other banks, like Citibank and CIBC Bank, offer 1.05% as of 2020.

Play Defense

Returning to our earlier sports analogy, you can probably agree that every good offense also needs a strong defense. In wealth building, your defense is determined by how well you manage your consumption and your debts. Poor management of debts means that the points you accumulate on offense could be undone by those you lose through poor defense. Just as a good defense can give your team's offense more time on the field earning points, sound debt management can provide your income more opportunities to build wealth.

> ***"One person pretends to be rich but has nothing; another pretends to be poor but has abundant wealth."***
>
> ***—Proverbs 13:7 (CSB)***

Perspective

My wife and I enjoyed a wonderful time in our pool earlier this year. Our pool is smaller than average, but it came with the house we purchased, and it provides us with a lovely retreat and a healthier alternative to the couch. Being able to grab a drink, head down to the pool, play some music, swim a few laps, and hang out for a bit is also not a bad way to spend some time, especially during this COVID-19 Pandemic.

Still, while I enjoy these moments, I have a love-hate relationship with that pool. Mostly, it is because I am acutely aware of the financial expenditures it requires of me. When we are not swimming in it, the pool just seems to suck up money and time. This year alone, we had to replace the pool liner, repair the pump, fix the Polaris (the thing that runs across the pool's floor collecting leaves), and fill the pool with water. That is on top of the regular maintenance we already perform (e.g., balancing chemicals and emptying the skimmer and the Polaris) to ensure the pool is available when we want to use it.

However, my wife really enjoys that pool. It is her little getaway, and it adds value to her life. As a result, by proxy, it adds value to mine. Still, that pool represents one of what I am sure are many things that hamper my ability to build wealth. What would that money be worth in 10 years if I had invested it earlier this year?

Perhaps you have a similar relationship with your boat, your recreational vehicle (RV), your timeshare, your summer home, your BMW, your dream home, or something else. If these are things that add value to your life and you can afford them, then great! Do not let me dissuade you from having them. Part of thriving includes some of those occasional indulgences. With a little temperance, such extravagances are entirely manageable. That said, it is just as vital that you realize you are surrendering your time and financial growth for these indulgences. Still, if the value you receive from these things exceeds your expenditures, then more power to you.

Nevertheless, going after too many of these indulgences, or even one of them too soon, can seriously cripple your financial growth opportunities. So, if you find yourself in a position where you cannot accrue assets, then maybe you need to play better defense until you can. How you allocate your time and finances leads us into our next facet of wealth building.

In our previous discussions on building wealth, I primarily focused on leveraging your offensive tools (e.g., income, gifts, pensions, etc.) toward accruing assets. With a strong offense, you can afford much more and still accrue wealth. However, as Paul "Bear" Bryant so aptly stated, and I paraphrase here, your offense may sell tickets, but defense wins championships. Yes, a strong offense is flashy, it makes games interesting, and it is needed. However, if you lose the points you gained on offense to poor defense, your path to financial freedom will be a grueling one.

In his book, "The Next Millionaire Next Door," Thomas Stanley, Ph.D., shares that 70% of millionaires indicated that they are and have always been frugal, regardless of their career choice or income levels. What this means for Stanley's millionaires is that they rarely buy luxury vehicles, extravagant homes, or other high-end items. Furthermore, they have a sound awareness of how they allocate their finances to address their debts and other expenses. They know where they are bleeding dollars, and they address them accordingly. In other words, they practice good defense.

Debt Management

You may find this surprising, but many people find it challenging to put money aside. After paying their bills (e.g., mortgage, rent, cable, cell phone, power, water, grocery, medical, auto loan, student loan, credit card, etc.), there is just too little remaining. Even more surprising is that many of these people have six-figure incomes, yet they still cannot seem to put anything away.

Doesn't that seem odd? Is it possible these people are spending too much on things they don't need or living beyond their means?

Let us make this discussion a little more personal now. How well are you managing your spending and consumption? One of the best ways to answer that question is to look at how much you invest each month. What percentage of your annual income are you contributing to investments? Take a look at the table below. Place your initials in the box that best describes how much of your income you invest each month.

Table 9 - Percentage of Income Invested

5% or less	6% - 10%	11% -20%	21% - 30%	31% or more

In May 2020, the average American saved around 7.7% of their annual income. This percentage means that the average American saves the equivalent of one year's salary every THIRTEEN years!

Waite! What?

If you are the average investor, you may only save two years' salary after 26 years! That is not the salary you finish your career with either—unless you kept your initial salary from 26 years ago. Of course, interest may help you out, but you will need a great ROI. Unfortunately, that 7.7% average is optimistic as some investors (the outliers) contribute so much that they pull the average up. The median, which is the value separating the upper half from the lower half of contributions, is probably substantially less.

Consider this. According to a survey by GOBankingRates, over 69% of Americans have less than $1,000 in their savings account.[7] Half of their surveyed respondents reported having $0 in their savings account, and only a quarter of their respondents made retirement a priority. In another survey by the Federal Reserve, researchers found that families' median net worth trailed significantly behind the average (see Table 10 - Net Worth by Age).[8] For instance, they found that the median net worth for someone between 45-55, which was $59,800 between 2013 and 2016, significantly trailed the same group's average of $288,700. Again, the very wealthy tend to pull the average up.

Table 10 - Net Worth by Age

Age	Median Net Worth	Average Net Worth
Under 35	$11,100	$76,200
35-44	$59,800	$288,700
45-54	$124,200	$727,500
55-64	$187,300	$1,167,400
65-74	$224,100	$1,066,000
75+	$264,800	$1,067,000

The survey also broke down these statistics by education (Table 11

- Net Worth by Education). Keep in mind that these values represent all age ranges grouped by education.

Table 11 - Net Worth by Education

Education	Median Net Worth	Average Net Worth
No high school diploma	$22,800	$157,200
High school diploma	$67,100	$249,600
Some college	$66,100	$340,600
College degree	$292,100	$1,511,100

Now that you have seen the numbers, how are you doing? Are you above or below the median? How about the average? Do these numbers reflect twice your annual salary? Depending on your answers to those questions, you may need a severe course adjustment to get to where you need to be.

Did you notice something else about these statistics? Some may say that education is overrated with all those school loans. Still, on average, people who complete higher education accumulate a net worth of three to four times their non-degree counterparts. Even so, these values seem low for a household earning somewhere between $65,000 and $140,000 per year.

Speaking of income, where is your salary or expected salary sitting right now. Suppose you are an E-7 with 22 years of service. Your combined income of $92,186 (BAH and all) places you near the average for someone between 35 and 44. If you are an O-4, your estimated salary of $131,625.36, again, BAH and all, places you well above that average.

Considering these salaries and your savings, have you beat the average for net worth? If you only meet or just barely beat these averages, your financial future is still in jeopardy. Average just does not cut it. So, what does the savings rate look like for the top 1% of net worth holders? Well, brace yourself. Their average saving rate is 38%.

Table 12 - Salary by Age

Age	Median Salary	Average Salary
Under 35	$40,500	$56,400
35-44	$65,800	$97,100
45-54	$69,500	$131,400
55-64	$61,000	$141,300
65-74	$50,100	$106,600
75+	$40,000	$77,100

That is pretty significant, and admittedly, many of us would struggle to achieve that savings rate. I did not reach it until I retired from the military. At that point, I contributed my entire retirement check to investments. I can do that because I found employment after the military that allows me to cover all my expenses and even pay the tithe on my retirement.

Many of these elite savors also benefit from high incomes. After all, having a high income makes it more likely to have money left over after paying all your regular bills. When you consider that these elite savors also do not chase after extravagant purchases, it is no surprise that you end up with people who can accrue significant amounts of wealth in a relatively shorter period when compared to others.

You may never reach the point where you contribute 38% of your income to investments. Fortunately, I have good news. You don't have to! Research has shown that if you can build the financial discipline to commit just 15% of your income toward retirement, you too can reach the millionaire status and achieve financial freedom. Do that calculation right now.

____________________ * 0.15 = ____________________

[Your Annual Income] [Total Investment]

The total investment you calculated should reflect the minimum amount that you actively invest each year. At a 15% rate, you are roughly contributing the equivalent of your entire income every 6.5 years. So, if you have a household income of $100,000, you will save $400,000 over 26 years. With compounded interest over 26 years, the actual value of that contribution at 6% interest would be more like $890,000. At 8% interest, you are looking at $1,199,316, and at 10% interest, $1,637,726. Clearly, persistence and time are your most valuable players when it comes to creating wealth.

Of course, saving money for savings is a moot point if you cannot manage your debts and spending habits. Debt and consumption are your most significant threat in building wealth. It is not always easy, but plenty of people just like you do. They may not even have your financial resources. However, their defense is strong, allowing them to keep their offense on the field longer, earning more points throughout this game called life. When they hit their 50s, work is optional. The question is, will that be so for you? How about in your 60s or 70s? How about ever?

Debt management requires you to exercise self-discipline in your purchases—balancing your needs, your wants, and your savings to achieve equilibrium. Put another way, we are merely talking about managing your money. Paying down or paying off debts is a massive part of achieving financial independence. After all, it is with the money you save that you accrue wealth.

It is with the money you save that you accrue wealth!

Granted, in your early years, you will likely incur some debts. Few people can buy a car, a house, or an education outright. However, these purchases saddle you with obligations to return portions of your income to lenders at rates that ensure they profit from you. For bankers, the loan is an asset; for you, it's a liability sucking away your wealth.

As I mentioned previously, your money represents your energy and time. That is what you give up, earning it. That cup of coffee at Starbucks might set you back 20-30 minutes; however, buying that new $50,000 car could set you back 20 years from achieving financial freedom. Ultimately, you must decide if the tradeoff is worth it. If those items bring joy to your life, then spending some of your life's capital might be worth it. If not, then maybe cut back on the Starbucks or consider a used vehicle. Just know that your choices play a large role in whether you ever achieve financial freedom.

Get Tax Advice

Wow! Just wow! When you leave the Army, get ready to pay taxes as you have never paid before! When in the military, my wife and I consistently received a substantial tax return each year, even with both of us working. And then I retired! Come the next filing season, not only did I not get a refund, but I also had to pay over $12,000 back to dear old Uncle Sam. What's worse, since I did not pay enough taxes quarterly, I got penalized for that too! That is right. If you did not know already, let me enlighten you. If you do not pay enough taxes quarterly, you get charged a penalty, even after filing your taxes and paying your debt in full.

When you start your next career, you will fill out a W-4 form to let your employer know how much tax to withhold from your pay. On that form, my wife and I always forgo claiming dependents to ensure our employers take the maximum withholding. That had worked for us during my military career. However, that first year out of the Army, I landed a job making more than I earned in the military, and my wife kept her current position as a nurse practitioner. I also had a new retirement check, and our total earnings significantly increased. As a result, we found ourselves in a higher tax bracket. It turned out that our employers withheld amounts that fell far short of what we were supposed to pay in taxes. So, when we settled with Uncle Sam at the end of the year, we found him holding his hand out for payment instead of us. Then, a few

Ever wonder why mathematicians, scientists, and engineers balk at doing their taxes, me either!

months later, adding insult to injury, we received a nastygram telling us we had failed to pay our minimum quarterly taxes. I did not even know that was a thing! It is—I'm telling you now!

I soon shared this news with some of my veteran colleagues and received a "welcome to the club" response. It turns out this happens to many veterans that first year after leaving the military. Fortunately, the penalty I received was not terrible. I think it came to less than $200. Still, getting penalized for something I did not even know about was not enjoyed!

While not a terrible problem to have, it was frustrating. I should have discussed my new employment situation with a tax adviser way before filing taxes. Had I, they probably would have pointed out that I was not paying in what I should. I could have also obtained a quick estimate of how much I would owe Uncle Sam by visiting the IRS' Tax Withholding Estimator at https://apps.irs.gov/app/tax-withholding-estimator.

Fortunately, once I realized the issue, fixing it was simple. I just visited my myPay account and increased my federal withholding to ensure I was all paid up by the end of the year. The website's URL is https://mypay.dfas.mil/#/militaryretired. You can also request a higher withholding from your employer.

Beyond helping you determine your lot in life with the Internal Revenue Service (IRS), tax advisers can also help you identify deductions to help alleviate some of your tax burdens. So, let me encourage you to meet with some tax advisors as soon as you get situated and determine which one is right for you. It may take some time to find someone you connect with and trust, so start early.

Honor Contracts and Be Honest

Another sure-fire way to see your gains vacate the premises is to deal with others dishonestly. I've read some books by "professionals" who talk about "methods" for contracting with sellers that skate the truth. They talk about loopholes and contingencies that allow them to promise everything the seller could want, only to exit the contract, provide nothing, and waste the seller's time.

Now, contingencies are helpful and necessary in certain instances. They can protect you from issues that may not be disclosed or known by the seller. For example, a due diligence period of five to ten days to inspect a property before buying it is a reasonable request. Likewise, if you need a loan to purchase the property, include a loan contingency in your contract. However, I find it best to be upfront and honest with people about what you hope to achieve in your dealings with them. If you need to include a loophole in your contract, explain to the seller why it is there. Remember, people like to make informed decisions.

> ***"Wealth obtained by fraud will dwindle, but whoever earns it through labor will multiply it."***
>
> ***—Proverbs 13:11 (CSB)***

Finally, enter contracts cautiously. And, when you do, honor them. If you make an agreement with someone, follow through. Failing to do so could damage your reputation and cost you opportunities later on. Worse, it could put you in the crosshairs of a lawsuit for damages. Once that happens, who knows where it will end.

Make Paying Yourself the Priority

Nearly 100 years ago, an American author, George Clason, wrote a book that is timeless for its wealth-building principles. The story introduces Arkad, the son of a humble merchant with no hope of inheritance, who grows his wealth to become the richest man in Babylon. Because of his success, the King of Babylon, seeking to make his kingdom wealthy, asks Arkad to share his "secret" to building wealth. Akron accepts the task and begins teaching 100 men the "seven cures for a lean purse." Arkad's first lesson to this group of students was to "start thy purse to fattening."

For every ten coins they earned, they were to keep one. The result of which was a fattening purse and a satisfied soul. In essence, Arkad was telling his students to pay themselves first. He told them to set the money they had purposed to save aside before they ever paid their monthly expenses. This first cure for the lean purse has proven the catalyst for creating many fortunes throughout the centuries. It can be the catalyst for yours too! This philosophy of "pay yourself before all else" ensures you have the money you need to invest later.

Perhaps, you realize that the problem has been you all along, and you have over-committed to debts and expenditures. Do not worry; you can also be the solution! It is never too late to drop your bad habits, allowing you to get off the sidelines and into the game. The road to recovery begins with acceptance. Maybe, you already save regularly. Congratulations! You are well on your way to joining the ranks of the wealthy. The techniques we next discuss can help you start or improve your savings plan and strengthen your defense.

Find Your Leaks

If you earn an average salary or even the median salary, there is no reason you should not be saving money. If you do not have enough to pay your bills every month, excluding some tragic medical expenses or catastrophe, you have some leaks, my friend. It is time to pull out your credit card statements and your checkbook and find them.

As you comb through your expenses, identify those 'must' expenses. These include your mortgage, rent, utilities, or taxes. Next, identify items that might be considered a luxury expense. These may consist of fast food, restaurant meals, cable bill, car note, subscriptions, gym memberships, IOUs, credit card fees, and haircuts (Excuse me, hair styling). They may also include clothes, jewelry, music, apps, collectibles, games, and even the extras you buy at gas stations. How much of your budget are these items eating away each month?

If your number came up higher than expected, then you are not alone. Based on research conducted by OnePoll for Ladders, there is a strong chance that you, like many Americans, are spending substantial amounts of your potential savings on nonessential items. Now that you have identified all your expenditures, can you still say you cannot afford to save? Is it possible that you could cut back on a few non-essential expenses? What if you could shave just $400 per month to pay off your debts and invest in your financial future? You could start paying yourself first.

When you invest first, it may feel backward because you have been paying yourself last your entire life. Yet, doing so will force you to avoid massive debt positions and reduce your monthly expenses, allowing you to accrue assets. When you come up short with your bills, do not let yourself off the hook by robbing your savings to pay them. Instead, avoid the bad habits of the poor, and get creative. Keep in mind that I am not telling you to skip paying your bills. Far from it, I believe it is important to honor our commitments. But you also want to maintain a good credit rating and learn to live off of your leftover income after investing. Instead, adjust your spending or find other sources of income. Mastering this ability will allow you to boost your financial intelligence and increase your wealth-building potential. Soon enough, you will be able to afford that big house and nice car!

We just covered another one of Arkad's cures for the lean purse, "control thy expenditures." Arkad's third cure is to "make thy gold multiply." We covered that cure in our previous section, Play Offense. We also covered Arkad's sixth cure in that section, which was to "ensure future income." We will return to the rest of Arkad's remedies soon, but for now, let's look at some strategies to stop the bleeding.

Stop the Bleeding

Now that you know where you are leaking, it is time to stop the bleeding. It can be frustrating to realize that you cannot pay yourself ahead of expenses. If you are still over your head in debt after identifying your leaks, consider what else you can do to reduce your overhead beyond reducing your purchases of nonessentials.

For instance, if your mortgage or rent is hurting your ability to save, then consider taking on a roommate, downsizing your home, or finding a more affordable rental. You can also reduce your cost from dining out by cooking your meals or buying prepared meals. What about your car note? Did you know that the average American commits to paying over $500 per month for a vehicle? Did you know that the average millionaire buys their car used with a couple of years on it and pay for it outright to avoid a car note altogether? According to current depreciation rates, which may vary by make and model, the average car depreciates 20% in its first year and then 10% for every year after that. So, buying a car with a few years on it can save you almost 50% of the vehicle's original cost. For instance, if you purchased a 2020 Dodge Challenger the same year, that would have cost you roughly $44,000, but if you bought the 2017 model, you would have paid approximately $26,000. Chances are you would still pick it up with a warranty.

Some other tricks I use include making my coffee in the morning and bringing it to work. Coffee can run $2 per cup where I work, and I drink a lot of coffee. I reserve Starbucks for an occasional treat. Venti Mochas are my poison, but at $4.65 and 450 calories, this drink hits all the wrong places: my wallet and my waistline. A couple of years ago, I bought some travel mugs that keep my coffee hot for up to 6-8 hours. Now, instead of spending $30-$40 per week on coffee, I spend roughly $8-$10. It could do better by brewing my coffee instead of using the Keurig, but I prefer the convenience.

Meals are another area where many of us overspend. My wife and I both work full-time jobs and have active hobbies. Neither of us likes to cook. At one point, we found ourselves eating out far too frequently or using food apps to have the same meals delivered for $8-$12 more after delivery fee and tip. Heck! I just went to Waffle House to pick up lunch a few days ago, and that ran me $27 for two hamburgers and two orders of hash browns.

Occasionally, these are pleasant indulgences, but they add to your debt and your waistline. One thing we did to circumvent our food purchases was to pay for a meal delivery plan. Not only does it provide us with meals for a fraction of our dining bills, but we also consume far fewer calories doing so. Now, we pay to have six to ten meals delivered every week, prepare one or two ourselves, and dine out for one or two others. Granted, we could probably cook all our meals, but that is one of the value-based decisions we've made. We pay more for the freedom not to cook, but that is now. Fifteen years ago, we did a lot more cooking, and it involved a lot more cans and boxes.

Credit card debt is another wealth killer. According to the 2019 Experian Consumer Credit Review, the average American carries $6,194 in credit card debt.[9] Credit card interest rates tend to be over 18% for new offers and around 15% for existing accounts.[10] For this reason, many financial experts recommend you pay these off first. Some even suggest you not carry them at all. For instance, Dave Ramsey is outspoken on the credit card debt issue and says in many articles, "There's no good reason at all to have a credit card." He has also gone on record saying that responsible use of credit cards does not exist. Just search David Ramsey and credit cards, and you will find many, many quips and quotes that Mr. Ramsey has provided over the years. Many are quite clever, and I'd love to include them here, but copyright. That will not stop you from looking them up, though, will it? However, as my non-commissioned officers used to tell me in the Army, that is a way.

I like credit cards. I like the convenience. For instance, they make it easier to track my expenses, offer fraud protection, provide cashback and discounts on purchases, and even offer purchase insurance. I also carry multiple credit cards, which helps me separate business expenses from personal ones. That can be useful when you are doing your taxes at the end of the year.

Moreover, I really don't like carrying cash, and I get annoyed when businesses do not accept credit. So, I do not fully share Mr. Ramsey's view of credit cards; however, I have not helped over one million people escape the chains of debt either. I would also be lying if I said I have never paid interest on a credit card. I have occasionally carried a balance to the next month. Hey, surprises happen. That said, if you have a credit card, and you cannot pay it off in full each month, then you really are robbing your financial future. Use them wisely.

> ***"Honor the Lord with your possessions and with the first produce of your entire harvest."***
>
> ***—Proverbs 3:9 (CSB)***

Bad habits can also kill your financial future. I consider myself fortunate to have never taken up smoking. Did you know, according to the National Cancer Institute, that the average cost of a pack of cigarettes is $6.28? At that rate, you spend $2,292 per year at a pack a day, or $191 per month. If the health reasons for not smoking are not enough, then maybe knowing you are destroying your financial future along with your lungs will help push you to quit.

Finally, eliminate your debts. Like Dave Ramsey, various financial advisors recommend you make paying off one debt your focus while still paying the minimums for your other obligations. Once you pay off a debt, roll those payments into your next debt. As you do, the amount you pay toward each debt will grow, and eventually, you will create a snowball effect. Some advisors also recommend you begin with your smallest debt, pay it off first, and use it for motivation. That is a technique. I, however, tend to focus on my debts with the highest interest rates. Whatever you choose, you must be consistent every month. Do not stop, and do not let up until your debt is firmly in your rearview, like your last duty assignment. The sooner you clear yourself of debt, the sooner you can put your money to working for yourself instead of someone else.

Capitalize on Raises

Your goal, at least initially, is to save at least 15%. You may not be there right now, so start where you are. Try 5% this month. Keep adjusting what you allow yourself to spend on nonessentials. Push for 10% a couple of months later. Within a few years, you should achieve 15%. Once you get there, congratulate yourself! You are well on your way to living below your means.

More importantly, you will have put yourself on a trajectory with millionaire status. If your monthly salary is $4,000 ($48,000 per year), then you should first pay yourself $600 and then figure out how to live off the rest. If you can make this happen without ever seeing the money, then all the better. Doing so will help create that artificial economic environment of scarcity I covered earlier.

What if you are newly enlisted and living off the salary of an E-2 or E-3? Then the following strategy may work for you. That is where I began when I joined the Army back in 1996. Now, back then, I will admit that saving was beyond my capability. At the time, my wife had just graduated with her bachelor's degree in science education from Florida State University. However, she was not yet certified to teach in Tennessee, and she could not apply for employment until she was. As a result, we had the added expense of student loans with only my salary to cover everything. Financially, it was a challenging time for us. It made tithing difficult for us as well. Still, giving back to God is a firm tenant of my faith, and I believe I have benefited from God's blessings because of it.

To help keep up with our bills, I took a second job—with my commander's permission—as a Papa John's pizza delivery driver. My wife found occasional employment as a substitute teacher as well. We also took advantage of military benefits, like the commissary, and kept to low budget activities. When I wasn't working nights, I used the military tuition assistance program to complete a few more college courses. I am thankful for those times. That is where we learned to live off what we had and to do the little extra it takes to climb out of debt and start building wealth.

Eventually, my wife found employment as a high school teacher, and I got promoted to E-4 (Army Specialist). Those two events proved substantial windfalls as we could release our financial restraints and start looking to the future. With my promotion to E-4, I committed to putting half of my raise into an investment plan, and I started my Roth IRA with T. Rowe Price. It was a proud moment for me. Of course, the monthly difference between E-3 pay ($1,183.20) and E-4 pay ($1,280.40) was only $97.00. Thankfully, with my wife's new annual income of $22,000,[11] we began investing $100 each month, and we started paying down our loans. From that point forward, I have always committed a portion of my raises to my investment strategy. As my salary grew, so did my investment contributions.

In 2000, we started two new IRAs with another investment company. They were not our best investments, but it helped keep us focused on building wealth. Now, post-military, I am still working, but my entire retirement check goes to investments while my wife and I max our contributions to our employer-provided 401(k) accounts. This strategy follows another one of Arkad's "cures for the lean purse." That is this, increase your ability to earn. If you apply the earlier chapters in this book, you are well on your way to accomplishing this too!

So, if the thought of saving seems daunting, then start small, but get started. Keep that 15% monthly contribution at the forefront of your mind as you rise through the ranks and continue to evaluate where you can cut expenses or bring in extra income to reach your goal. Remember that time and persistence are your most valuable teammates for helping you achieve wealth—use them! Additionally, once you commit to the plan, you must be faithful to your contributions every month, or you will never establish the habit.

Give

You may find it odd to have a chapter on building wealth interrupted by a section on giving. However, this section may prove one of the most rewarding. Have you ever noticed how unselfish people make better employees, employers, friends, and spouses? They have better finances, too! There is something about giving that draws more opportunities toward us. It's as if some cosmic entity, some creator of all that is, sees generosity and rewards it.

While this section discusses biblical reasons to give, it also offers some practical reasons to do so. Hopefully, one of these reasons will encourage you to start and continue to give and allow you to grow into the best version of yourself. Here is how it works.

For every dollar that enters my checking or savings account, I give at least 10 cents of it to my church. That habit was ingrained in me during my early years in Clarksville, TN, while stationed at Fort Campbell, KY. During one Sunday worship service, I remember our pastor saying, "it's better to live off 90% with God's blessing than off 100% without it." Those words were profound. They were a game-changer. At another point in the sermon, our pastor explained that this is the only case where God encourages his followers to test Him. If you know the Bible, you also know that testing God is not encouraged—just check out Matthew 4:7. However, God says these words to His followers:

> ***"Bring the full tenth into the storehouse so that there may be food in my house. Test me in this way," says the Lord of Armies. "See if I will not open the floodgates of heaven and pour out a blessing for you without measure." Malachi 3:10 (CSB)***

> ***"Each person should do as he has decided in his heart, not reluctantly or out of compulsion since God loves a cheerful giver. And God is able to make every grace overflow to you, so that in every way, always having everything you need, you may excel in every good work."* –2 Corinthians 9:7-9 (CSB)**

That is a big blessing to miss out on, and I feel my blessings have been many. Beyond that, people who do not give just seem to come across odd and unexpected expenses that just pop up and take their money, anyway. Perhaps it is part of the promised blessing. I'll let you decide. Now, I realize not everyone reading this book will share my faith, and I know of many charitable people who are not Christians, even if I hope they one day make that leap of faith. That said, let me point out a few more reasons to give regularly.

In his blog on financial literacy, Dave Ramsey wrote that the goal of financial freedom is to use your money to do the things you genuinely want to do. Those things include retiring with dignity, spending free time with family, and giving to worthy causes.[12] When we give before doing anything else with our money, even paying ourselves first, we make giving a priority instead of an afterthought. We also prioritize our money differently. By sacrificing a portion of our income, we defeat harmful habits like selfishness and poor discipline. We move away from a scarcity mentality (thinking too little is available) to one of abundance (thinking there is enough for everyone) while becoming more aware of others' needs. As a result, we become more generous, and our money becomes just another tool we use for our daily operations.

These are all things that will contribute to your quality of life, and a better quality of life fully supports a thriving post-military career. Still, when it comes to giving, it is ultimately a personal/spiritual decision. It is also a decision tied to a bigger picture and a higher purpose. Once you see it, you realize that giving, tithing, or both is not just about managing your finances but understanding that you are blessed to be a blessing for others. Even our dear friend Arkad from the "Richest Man in Babylon" was generous.

> ***"In old Babylon there once lived a certain very rich man named Arkad. Far and wide he was famed for his great wealth. Also was be famed for his liberality. He was generous in his charities. He was generous with his family. He was liberal in his own expenses. But nevertheless each year his wealth increased more rapidly than he spent it." –Richest Man in Babylon, George S. Clason***

Manage Risk

> ***"Misfortune loves a shining mark. Gold in a man's purse must be guarded with firmness, else it be lost." –Richest Man in Babylon***

Could you imagine saving up decades of wealth to secure your financial freedom, only to lose it all overnight in a bad investment or lawsuit? Unfortunately, the world is still full of get-rich schemes and people looking for quick and fast money. Depending on where you are in your accumulation of wealth, your untimely death could also leave your family struggling after you are gone. These concerns bring us back to another one of Arkad's "cures for the lean purse… Guard thy treasures against loss."

When it comes to managing risk and guarding your treasures, there are two approaches the wealthy typically use. The first approach is to avoid overly risky ventures or investments, and the other is to use insurance to buy down risk. Let's discuss why these two approaches matter.

The first approach is straight forward. It requires us to be patient and take a long-term view of investing. As we grow older, this approach is even more critical because it is substantially more challenging to recover from the mistakes we make in our forties than in our twenties and thirties. Remember, our teammates—time and persistence—need to be a part of our investment strategy. If someone has a get rich scheme or someone else is pushing the next stock option getting ready to blow the market away, do not be fooled into placing a substantial amount of your wealth into either of these "opportunities." In fact, you should probably assume that there is a 99% chance you will lose 50% to 100% of your investment. It would be best if you stay away from business opportunities you are unfamiliar with. If you do not understand the market demand for your proposed service or product or how the financials will work, you have probably already failed well before you start.

So, exercise prudence in your investment strategies. While I regularly invest in the stock market and have achieved outstanding returns, I do so with caution. I may invest 20% of my total portfolio in stocks like Ford and other established companies. Still, I seldom invest over 1% - 5% in riskier stocks, which helps keep me diversified, minimizing risk. Hey, it has taken me a while to get here; I do not want to lose it all at once!

Moreover, I only acquire stocks with a portion of my assets. My wife and I still max our 401(k) contributions into managed accounts. In a few years, we may reevaluate that strategy, but it is working for us now.

The second approach involves using insurance to reduce the chance that one accident or another unfortunate event could rob us of our financial freedom. Project managers and other business professionals might recognize this as "transferring risk." Of course, there are many insurance types out there, so let's look at some common ones and see how they might factor into your wealth-building/keeping strategy.

Home/Renter's Insurance

Our home is likely one of our most significant expenses. If it were to burn down overnight, that could be devastating—especially if we do not have adequate coverage. A typical homeowner's insurance policy will cover the property's dwelling and structure, and it may cover personal property, personal liability, and additional living expenses. Of course, how much you pay out of pocket for these events is determined by your deductible. That is the amount you must pay out of pocket should your insurance be needed.

When choosing a deductible for my rentals, I often seek the highest permitted. My reasoning is two-fold. First, the higher my deductible, the lower my premium, or what I have to pay for the insurance. The lower my premium, the better my cash flow. Second, I only need protection from huge expenses. If I have to re-shingle my roof, I can handle that out of pocket. If my house burns down, however, well, that's not a loss I'm prepared to absorb. Ultimately, I need insurance to cover the big-ticket items, like a complete loss of my house, severe damage, or a substantial liability suit. Other things I can handle on my own. Do your math here and see what works for you and your budget. If you can't afford a $10,000 expense, then you should seek a lower deductible. Also, keep in mind that insurance companies track your insurance claims. What that means for you is if you file an insurance claim for a minor issue, your insurance premiums may still take a hit. As a result, so will your cash flow.

Vehicle Insurance

While the concept seems crazy to me, where you live may not require liability insurance. If that is the case, I believe it is a great idea to carry it anyway. Some experts even recommend that you have as much as $500,000 in liability coverage for property damage and bodily injury.[13] As with home insurance, I carry a high deductible to receive a lower premium. Again, I only really care about the things that can financially hurt me, so I am willing to pay more in deductibles with the understanding I will pay for less costly issues out of pocket. The larger claims will hopefully only come due on a rare occasion.

Umbrella Insurance

Umbrella insurance is extra liability coverage. This insurance protects you from large claims or lawsuits that go above your other insurance policies, such as homeowners or auto policies. If you have assets, then understand that a lawsuit can target everything you have. Hence, your umbrella coverage needs to go beyond your other insurance coverages to ensure one unfortunate event does not erase decades of disciplined investing.

Health Insurance

Health insurance helps pay the costs connected to a medical event, like surgery or illness. Some of these bills can reach hundreds of thousands of dollars, which can quickly devastate your savings and living expenses. If you retired from service, then your Tri-Care benefits represent a substantial boon to your financial future. However, if you left service before retiring, try to secure health insurance. As you grow older, stuff happens, and there is no reason a health emergency should straddle you with untold amounts of debt.

Life Insurance

Two types of life insurance typically permeate the market: whole life insurance and term life insurance. My wife and I both have multiple term life insurance policies. For instance, I have a Veterans Group Life Insurance (VGLI) policy and another through my current employer. My wife carries one through her employer. However, we have never considered a whole life policy.

Whole life insurance is marketed as permanent life insurance, meaning it is in place your whole life, with a fixed premium. Initially, you decide with your insurance provider what the policy amount or death benefit will be. That amount gets paid to your beneficiaries if you die.

For that, you will pay a premium to maintain the coverage. Your policy's cash value will take a portion from that premium, as will your policy's overhead. At the policy's initiation, a more significant percentage of your premiums go toward your policy's cash value. In contrast, in the later years, more of your premiums go toward your policy's overhead since insurance costs increase as you age.

Meanwhile, that cash value will grow at a very modest interest rate, and once the policy matures and you survive to the maturity date, you can receive that cash value back. However, many whole life insurance policies consider maturity to be when your age reaches 100 or 120! Of course, you can surrender, which sounds like giving up, your policy and take out a percentage of your cash value, but this will not yield you a favorable return.

Term life makes no pretense at offering you a savings plan. Its sole function is to replace your income in the event of your death. Typically, term life insurance will last 15-20 years, and you can expect higher premiums as you age. However, since term life offers no cash value, your premiums usually are much cheaper than whole life policies. More affordable premiums also mean you can contribute more of your savings to an actual investment plan with much higher return rates. Better yet, you can access your investment dollars before you turn 60, let alone 100 or 120.

Long-Term and Short-Term Disability Insurance

Both long-term and short-term disability insurance can provide you with a percentage of your income should you become disabled. Typically, that amount can be 40% to 70% of your income. The critical difference between short-term and long-term disability insurance—of course—is the time an individual has coverage. For short-term disability, coverage is usually for 9-52 weeks; however, the actual coverage period is determined by your policy. This coverage also starts 1-14 days after you cannot work. For long-term disability, coverage may last for 5-10 years or, if you are permanently disabled, until the age of 65. This coverage also depends on your policy.

Long-term disability insurance temporarily replaces between 50% and 70% of your income should you lose your ability to work. My wife and I currently get this coverage from our employers. For me, my company covers 100% of the premium for this insurance, while my wife's company requires a small fee. Dave Ramsey, the author of "Total Money Makeover," suggests that you get long-term disability insurance and maintain it your whole life.[14] He also recommends you carry all you can get and don't purchase your long-term disability insurance with pre-tax dollars. Otherwise, you will pay taxes on the disability income you receive from your insurance. Instead, pay post-tax.

Short-term insurance, however, covers the time taken off work for things like pregnancy, back problems, arthritis, cancer, and other problems requiring short periods away from work. However, you may forgo short-term disability if you maintain an appropriate amount of savings to cover a "bridge period" or the time it takes from when your doctor declares you disabled until the insurance company starts paying. The average time is around 90 days, so look at your long-term policy and see if your finances will support your bridge period to ensure this strategy works for you.

Other Risk Management Options

Of course, you should consider other risk reduction strategies, like long-term care insurance, identity theft protection, credit fraud, and many others. In this section, I only attempted to cover some of the more common options to consider. For more recommendations on protecting your financial future, I recommend putting your favorite search engine to work. After a few hours, you will have a reasonably good idea of the options available to you. If you visit daveramsey.com, I believe you will find lots of prudent advice to protect you against that massive leak that may just pop up.

Wealth Building Resources

I know I have mentioned Arkad's "Cures for the Lean Purse" multiple times. Perhaps you are wondering what the rest of them are. Well, let me put your curiosity to rest. I have listed Arkad's seven cures in Table 13 - Cures for the lean purse - The Richest Man in Babylon. Of the seven listed, we have already discussed cures one, two, and four in our previous section, Play Defense. And, while I did not explicitly mention it in Play Offense, that section addressed Arkad's third and sixth rules, covering how to "make thy gold multiply" and how to "ensure a future income."

As far as Arkad's seventh rule is concerned, well, that was the purpose of all the previous chapters of this book. I hope you have your next career targeted, your resume ready, your certifications and education in progress or complete, and your network growing. If so, you are well on your way to increasing your ability to earn.

Table 13 - Cures for the lean purse - The Richest Man in Babylon

The Richest Man in Babylon: Cures for a Lean Purse

1. Start thy purse to fattening
2. Control thy expenditures
3. Make thy gold multiply
4. Guard thy treasures against loss
5. Make of thy dwelling a profitable investment
6. Ensure a future income
7. Increase thy ability to earn

The one cure we have not talked about just yet regards your home. Our dear friend Arkad says, "make of thy dwelling a profitable investment." We spoke briefly about whether you should consider your home as an asset earlier. Technically, your home may not be an asset until you own it, but your equity is, and your continued payments cause it to grow. However, some homeownership critics point out that renting can be cheaper than sometimes buying, which means you can afford to invest the difference. Leasing also lets you off the hook for unexpected repairs and makes it easier to pick up stakes and move when the time is right.

Throughout my military career, my wife and I have chosen to buy on some occasions and rent on others. For us, it came down to what we could afford at the time and the risk we were willing to accept. During my two assignments in New York, we rented. Prices were high, and a mortgage may have proven too expensive for us after changing stations if the property went unrented. For example, there were times when our careers forced us to live apart for six or more months. During those times, funds got tight. Where I have purchased, such as in Georgia and North Carolina, those proved excellent investments. That said, do your math and weigh your risks before deciding to rent or buy.

As I mentioned at the beginning of this chapter, complete books exist to help everyday people achieve great wealth. These are also books written by authors who have spent years, even decades, researching the wealthy's characteristics, traits, and habits. You can find some of these characteristics in Table 14 - Characteristics of the wealthy. I genuinely hope you do not let this chapter become the end of your wealth-building journey.

For instance, if you find the characteristics in Table 14 - Characteristics of the wealthy interesting, you may enjoy reading "The Millionaire Next Door" by Thomas J. Stanley and William D. Dank, "The Next Millionaire Next Door" by Dr. Thomas J. Stanley and Dr. Sarah Stanley Fallaw, and "Everyday Millionaires" by Chris Hogan. These books are incredibly informative and chalked full of characteristics you can develop to secure your future wealth. One of the fundamental things you will no-tice as you read these books and research the wealthy is that nearly all of them, regardless of how they achieve wealth, take responsibility for their financial future.

Table 14 - Characteristics of the wealthy

Millionaire Characteristics

- Represent roughly 3%-9% of the U.S. Population
- Represent nearly 40% of the Global Population
- Roughly 80% of millionaires are first-generation or self-made
- The average age of a millionaire is over 60
- Just 1% of millionaires are under the age of 35
- Work in the finance and investment industry, fashion and retail industry, real estate, and tech industry
- Typical occupations include accountants, engineers, and teachers
- Create multiple streams of income
- Read at least 30 minutes every day
- Save 15% or more of their income
- Over 80% put in 50 hours or more each week at their career
- Over 70% see gambling as a waste of time
- Most, over 90%, have college degrees; over 70% attended public universities
- Invest in themselves

As you review these qualities, self-assess where your attributes overlap. What I found is I model some of these qualities, and I could stand to model a few more. The chances are you see that some of these characteristics mirror your own and can identify a few more that you could stand to emulate yourself.

Make a Mark

We have spent this chapter discussing how you can accrue wealth. Say you achieve it. What will that wealth mean for you? A pastor of mine, when I lived in Marietta, GA, once stated that work is a gift of God, and wealth is to be shared. Here is the thing about wealth; you cannot take it with you! Beyond taxes, there is another unavoidable event coming. That is when we leave this earth behind. And, like it or not, there is no U-Haul truck carrying your stuff behind you when you go. Nope. It all stays here.

Instead, at that point, a date is added to a dash. It is a dash that proceeds your date of birth, and this date-date will get added to your obituary or memorial, tombstone, or earn. Of course, the dates are only bookends to the dash. It's a small thing, a dash, but it carries in it everything you did in this world when you depart. So, here's the question I hope you will ask yourself. What will your dash say about you?

Having found your way, maybe you will help someone else find their way too. They could be family members, friends, or even strangers. Fortunately, your wealth will give you opportunities to impact the lives of others. Will you do it? If so, these people will become a part of your legacy. If you manage your wealth appropriately, you will gain the opportunity to extend your legacy even further through scholarships, trusts, and other worthy causes. That sounds like a worthwhile way to finish your race and close that dash, having lived a life worth living.

14

TIME TO THRIVE

> *Sometimes we need to reach the end, so we can start again anew.*

In the preceding chapters, I focused on providing you with the tools you need to navigate your transition. These tools can help you land your next job and build wealth. Other habits we discussed will help keep you moving forward long after your military journey ends. Incorporating these tools and habits into your transition preparations will help you start building momentum well before your first job gets offered or your wealth starts growing. Just you reaching this last chapter tells me you already possess some of those qualities.

> ***Successful people find opportunities in all conditions, which leads them in an iterative process of moving into better situations with new opportunities.***

Throughout my career, I made it a point to study the habits of successful people. In doing so, I sought to identify what it is they do regularly to succeed. Naturally, this book represents my discoveries and the culmination of my choices and lessons learned. Of course, I have learned much over my 21 years of service and now, three years living as a civilian. Perhaps one of my better discoveries is this. There is something that stands out about successful people. Successful people find opportunities in all conditions, which leads them in an iterative process of moving into better situations with new opportunities. Eventually, this process becomes their steps to success wherever they are in life. Successful people also keep improving their metaphorical foxhole.

If you have ever read Stephen Covey's book, "The Seven Habits of Highly Effective People," you are already familiar with the concept of improving your position. If you have not read it, then I highly recommend you do. Besides being an excellent book on personal leadership, Dr. Covey advocates for continued personal growth. In his book, he makes an analogy of sharpening a saw to preparation and renewal.

A short story of an old woodcutter demonstrates Dr. Covey's concept perfectly. In the story, an old woodcutter explains how he would go about chopping down the most massive tree in the Northwest within five minutes if his life were on the line. He says, "I would spend the first two minutes sharpening my ax." It's all about preparing for what's coming.

The military has a similar concept—*improve your foxhole*. It represents a consistent and never-ending process—a habit, if you will—of building and growing. I mention this because where you are now is not where you must be ten, five, or even one year from now.

Opportunities abound, and recruiters are always looking for new talent. If you are not prepared for your dream job when you leave military service, that is okay! Nothing is stopping you from accepting the next best opportunity and committing some extra hours to get the certifications, diplomas, or experience you need. Even if you find that job you have always wanted, you owe it to yourself and your employer to maintain your relevance. There is still uncertainty in any career, and the better you prepare yourself, the better prepared you will be for some of life's more difficult storms. Companies frequently lay off employees or go under themselves. As a result, you should always be prepared to adapt, improvise, and overcome. Make it a way of life. Continuing to improve your foxhole will help you do exactly that.

So, as we close this book, let me first say congratulations on ending one career (whenever that occurs) and laying down the foundation to start another. More importantly, thank you for your service! Your specific combination of patriotism, selfless-service, warrior spirit, and sacrifice has ensured this country's freedom for yet another generation.

Hopefully, as you approach your path to a successful transition, you now realize that your kit bag is a little fuller, and you are better prepared to use the tools it contains. I hope you have gained greater confidence in what you want to do after your military service and how you will get there. Still, keep in mind that it is up to you to put those tools to work. You may even make some mistakes along the way, and that is okay, too. We all do. The good news is none of us are alone in this. The most successful people in the world still fail regularly.

Fortunately, I have made some good choices too. Better yet—occasionally—I have made some great ones. For instance, I accepted Jesus Christ as my Savior many years ago, and that decision has comforted me beyond measure. I give God praise for my every success and teachable moment. I decided to tithe and learned to treat my money as a tool. There always seems to be enough. I asked an awesome woman to be my wife, and over 24 years later, she still challenges me to be a better person, and I love her even more for it. I invested in my future: financially, educationally, and professionally, and those decisions led to financial stability, a love of learning, and a career I enjoy. I mostly followed the principles I discussed in this book, even if I came to some of them later than others.

Now it is your turn. I hope your departure from service and transition will reach a similar outcome to my own or ultimately exceed it.

I have already mentioned some of my mistakes, so you do not have to make them. Of course, it is not me you should compete with — it is the guy or gal you were yesterday! So, get out there. Transition time is coming, and it's time to thrive!

ABOUT THE AUTHOR

Jacob Cox lives with the love of his life and wife, Laura Cox, and his two cats, Epic and Saga. In 2018, Jacob retired from the U.S. Army, having risen from the rank of Private First Class, E-3, to the rank of Major, O-4. As a Soldier, Jacob served as an armament and electrical system repairer for the Apache Helicopter before earning his commission through Officer Candidate School. Over the years that followed, he served as a Chemical Officer, Signal Officer, Telecommunications Engineer, and finished his 22-year career as a Cyberspace Operations Officer.

During Jacob's service, he earned a Bachelor of Science degree in electrical engineering from Clemson University, a Master's degree in electrical and computer engineering from Duke University, and a Ph.D. in electrical and computer engineering from the Georgia Institute of Technology. His certifications include the Certified Information Systems Security Professional (CISSP) and Project Management Professional (PMP). He has published in scientific and military journals, conference proceedings, and magazines. As a lifelong learner, Jacob is obsessed with audiobooks and online courses. His reading interests include fantasy, wealth building, self-development, programming, and spiritual sanctification.

Jacob works as a Data Scientist for the government. When he is not writing, working, completing an independent research project, or spending time with his wife, Jacob is an active real estate investor and stock trader. Jacob's favorite bible verse is, "Whatever you do, do it from the heart, as something done for the Lord and not for people, knowing that you will receive the reward of an inheritance from the Lord. You serve the Lord Christ." –Colossians 3:23-24 (CSB).

Follow Jacob at https://www.facebook.com/jcoxbooks.

Join the Transition Time Group at

https://www.facebook.com/groups/422585885850869.

RESOURCES

Resources for veterans are updated continuously, with links being changed or removed. The resources here are not all-inclusive; however, they reflect some resources I used to pursue my transition. For the most up-to-date list of resources, visit our website at themilpost.com and like us on facebook.com/themilpost.

Books

- United States Department of Labor; Veterans' Employment and Training Service. "2017 US Department of Labor Employment Workshop Participant Guide: Transition from Military to Civilian Workforce." United States Department of Labor. Kindle Edition.
- US Department of Veterans Affairs, "VA Benefits I & II Briefing | PARTICIPANT GUIDE." May 2017. Available at https://www. benefits.va.gov/TAP/docs/CUR_BBI_II_PG_201706_508_FINAL.pdf

Military Resources

- Soldier For Life: https://soldierforlife.army.mil/retirement/
- Military One Source: https://www.militaryonesource.mil/separation-transition-resources
- MyArmyBenefits: http://myarmybenefits.us.army.mil/
- Retirement Services Officer (RSO): https://soldierforlife.army.mil/retirement/rso
- Reserve Army Reserve Regional Support Command RSO: https://soldierforlife.army.mil/retirement/reservecomponent

- Army National Guard RSO: http://myarmybenefits.us.army.mil/Home/Benefit Library/Resource_Locator.html

Company Research

- Hire Purpose Employers List: https://hirepurpose.com/employer/list/A

VA Resources

VA representatives are your primary resources for accessing benefits, and you must understand the differences between the various VA facilities to take full advantage. Knowing this can better prepare you to know where to go to find the right assistance. For example, a VA outpatient clinic or medical center is where you want to go for medical issues; however, visit your VA Regional Office or benefits office to file a claim for disability compensation. Sometimes, if you are lucky, the VA facilities are co-located. Below are some resources that can help you navigate these waters.

- **Federal Benefits for Veterans, Dependents, and Survivors** is a comprehensive guide to VA benefits and is available online. (www.va.gov/opa/publications/benefits_book.asp)
- **VA Benefits I & II Briefing Participant Guide** provides detailed information about the benefits discussed during the briefings, links to online resources, and activities conducted during the briefings.
- **eBenefits** is a joint DoD/VA web portal with resources and self-service capabilities that enable service members, veterans, and their families to apply for research, access, and manage their VA and military benefits.
- **vets.gov** is a joint web portal that allows service members,

veterans, and their families to research, apply, access, and manage their VA benefits. It also provides employment tools to support all stages of the job search process. (www.vets.gov/)

- **va.gov** offers current resources, tools, and contact information for all VA benefits. The Inquiry Routing and Information System (IRIS) is VA's secure email messaging system. IRIS is a secure way to send queries that contain your personally identifiable information (PII) via the internet. (iris.custhelp.com/)
- **My Healthe*e*Vet** is VA's online personal health record designed for active-duty service members, veterans, and their dependents and caregivers. It makes it easy for you to partner with your health care team and provides tools to help you make informed decisions to manage your health care. (www.myhealth.va.gov/)

NOTES

CHAPTER 1

1 https://www.pewresearch.org/fact-tank/2017/11/10/the-changing-face-of-americas-veteran-population/.

2 https://www.pewresearch.org/fact-tank/2019/09/10/the-changing-profil e-of-the-u-s-military/.

CHAPTER 2

1 Veteran Job Retention Survey Summary. 2014. https://ivmf.syracuse.edu/wp-content/uploads/2016/10/VetAdvisor-ReportFINAL-Single-pages.pdf.

2 Citroen, L., "5 Reasons Veterans Leave Civilian Jobs." April 2018.

3 Members who entered the service after July 31, 1986 are given a choice of two retirement plans when they reach their 15th year of active service: (1) High-3 Year Average, (2) Career Status Bonus (CSB)/REDUX. https://www.dfas.mil/retiredmilitary/plan/estimate/csbredux.html.

4 If you entered active or reserve military service after September 7, 1980, your retired pay base is the average of the highest 36 months of basic pay. If you served less than three years, your base will be the average monthly active duty basic pay during your period of service. https://www.dfas.mil/retiredmilitary/plan/estimate.html.

5 https://www.faa.gov/other_visit/aviation_industry/designees_delegation s/designee_types/ame/fasmb/media/201203.pdf. 2012.

6 U.S. Department of Labor Workshop Participant Guide. 2017.

7 "Military Occupational Codes Crosswalk-Translating Your Training and Experiences." Participant Guide. 2018.

CHAPTER 4

1 Rosalinda Maury, R., Stone, B., and Roseman, J., "Veteran Job Retention Survey." Institute for Veterans and Military Families and VetAdvisor. December 16, 2013 to February 11, 2014.

2 Davis, Richard H. (January 1, 2018). "Henry David Thoreau, Yogi". Duke University Press. Retrieved March 7, 2019.

3 DISA 8570 IAWIP Frequently Asked Questions: http://iase.disa.mil/eta/iawip/iaetafaq.html#G6.

4 Burning Glass Company. "Majors That Matter: Ensuring College Graduates Avoid Underemployment". https://www.burning-glass.com/wp-content/uploads/underemployment_majors_that_matter_final.pdf.

5 10 Benefits of Having a College Degree | Bachelor's Degree .... https://www.northeastern.edu/bachelors-completion/news/is-a-bachelors-degree-worth-it/.

6 Check out the following link for a larger list of degrees: https://en.wikipedia.org/wiki/List_of_tagged_degrees.

7 The name of the SAT exam was actually changed to drop the meaning in 1997—but, who uses an acronym for a name and doesn't expect people to ask what it means.

8 https://www.fedcareerinfo.com/ksa.htm.

9 Many of these same resources also provide transitioning services to help aid your transition.

10 CareerOneStop. https://www.careeronestop.org/.

11 Veteran's Job Matcher. https://www.careeronestop.org/Toolkit/Jobs/match-veteran-jobs.aspx.

CHAPTER 5

1 "Veterans." United States Census Bureau. https://www.census.gov/topics/population/veterans.html.

2 "Eye-Tracking Study." Ladders. https://cdn.theladders.net/static/images/basicSite/pdfs/TheLadders-EyeTracking-StudyC2.pdf. 2018.

3 Northrop Grumman. "Transitioning Military." https://www.northropgrumman.com/careers-old/resume-tips-for-veterans-transitioning-to-civilian-careers/.

4 https://www.theladders.com/resume-reviewer/.

5 Enelow. W. and Kursmark, L. "Modernize Your Resume: Get Noticed." Emerald Career Publishing. March 2016.

6 Understanding Applicant Tracking System Basics. https://resources.careerbuilder.com/recruiting-solutions/master-the-basics-applicant-tracking-system. 2017.

7 Baniel Bortz. "What Your Resume Should Look Like in 2016." Money. May 15, 2016.

8 Staff Writer. "Use this to craft the perfect cover letter." The Career News. Los Angeles, CA.

9 Bolles, R.

CHAPTER 6

1 https://www.businessinsider.com/at-least-70-of-jobs-are-not-even-listed-heres-how-to-up-your-chances-of-getting-a-great-new-gig-2017.

2 A Resume That Gets Past the ATS. https://www.ivyexec.com/career-advice/2019/write-a-resume-that-gets-past-the-ats. 2019.

3 http://www.fedshirevets.gov/AgencyDirectory/index.aspx.

4 For the rest of us, we have our own university alumni programs that are worth tapping into.

5 Employment Readiness Program | Army Family Web Portal. https://www.armyfamilywebportal.com/content/employment-readiness-program.

CHAPTER 7

1 "6 Mistakes Veterans Make on LinkedIn. How Many Are You Making?" Military.Com. 2019. [Online] https://www.military.com/veteran-jobs/career-advice/job-hunting/6-mistakes-veterans-make-linkedin-how-many-are-you-making.html.

CHAPTER 8

1 https://www.careeronestop.org/Toolkit/Wages/find-salary.aspx.

CHAPTER 10

1 Glassdoor. "Q3 2015 U.S. Employment Confidence Survey." 2015. https://media.glassdoor.com/pr/press/pdf/ECS-Q32015-Supplement.pdf.

CHAPTER 11

1 U.S. Small Business Administration (SBA). https://www.sba.gov/business-guide.

CHAPTER 12

1 https://www.va.gov/careers-employment/education-and-career-counseling/.

2 www.dol.gov/featured/apprenticeship.

3 www.benefits.va.gov/gibill/post911_gibill.asp.

4 www.benefits.va.gov/gibill/mgib_ad.asp.

5 https://www.benefits.va.gov/TAP/docs/CUR_BBI_II_PG_201706_508_FINAL.pdf.

6 https://amvets.org/prepare-for-employment/.

7 American Job Center Finder | CareerOneStop. https://www.careeronestop.org/localhelp/americanjobcenters/american-job-centers.aspx.

8 https://www.dol.gov/agencies/vets/programs/tap.

9 The Importance of Estate Planning in ... - Military OneSource. https://www.militaryonesource.mil/financial-legal/legal/estate-planning/estate-planning.

10 https://legalassistance.law.af.mil/.

11 https://www.dfas.mil/retiredmilitary/provide/sbp.html.

12 https://www.militaryonesource.mil/military-life-cycle/veterans-military-funeral-honors.

13 https://www.va.gov/housing-assistance/.

14 https://www.va.gov/health-care/eligibility/.

15 https://www.marketwatch.com/story/most-americans-are-one-paycheck-away-from-the-street-2016-01-06.

16 Jay Shepherd, Firing at Will: A Manager's Guide (Apress Media, 2011).

17 https://endhomelessness.org/resource/veteran-homelessness/.

18 https://www.va.gov/HOMELESS/pit_count.asp.

CHAPTER 13

1 Stanley, T. J., & Danko, W. D. (2010). The millionaire next door: The surprising secrets of America's wealthy (1st Taylor Trade Pub. ed.). Lanham, Md.: Taylor Trade Pub.

2 In 2020, retirement for an E-8 (with over 26 years of service) would be roughly $38,000 before taxes, while an O-4 (with over 20 years of service) and a CW-4 (with over 24 years of service) would both receive close to $49,000 before taxes.

3 Inflation rates may vary, so pay and totals may not follow the trend indicated.

4 https://www.dfas.mil/militarymembers/payentitlements/sdp.html.

5 https://www.investopedia.com/best-cd-rates-4770214.

6 https://www.usaa.com/inet/wc/bank-savings?wa_ref=lf_product_bank _savings.

7 "Survey: 69% of Americans Have Less Than $1,000 in Savings." https://www.gobankingrates.com/saving-money/savings-advice/americans-have-less-than-1000-in-savings/.

8 "Changes in U.S. Family Finances from 2013 to 2016: Evidence from the Survey of Consumer Finances" Federal Reserve." 2017. https://www.federalreserve.gov/publications/files/scf17.pdf.

9 https://www.experian.com/blogs/ask-experian/consumer-credit-review/.

10 https://wallethub.com/edu/cc/average-credit-card-interest-rate.

11 https://nces.ed.gov/programs/digest/d99/d99t080.asp.

12 https://www.daveramsey.com/blog/what-is-financial-literacy.

13 https://www.daveramsey.com/blog/how-much-car-insurance#.

14 https://www.daveramsey.com/askdave/insurance/6114.

www.ingramcontent.com/pod-product-compliance
Lightning Source LLC
Chambersburg PA
CBHW072145100526
44589CB00015B/2096

9781735988900